Open
HOUSE

I0896326

OTHER SYRACUSE UNIVERSITY PRESS BOOKS BY CHUCK D'IMPERIO

Graves of Upstate New York: A Guide to 100 Notable Resting Places

Monumental New York! A Guide to 30 Iconic Memorials in Upstate New York

A Taste of Upstate New York: The People and the Stories behind 40 Food Favorites

Unknown Museums of Upstate New York: A Guide to 50 Treasures

Open House

35 Historic Upstate New York Homes

Chuck D'Imperio

With a Foreword by Bob Beatty

Syracuse University Press

First Edition 2020

22 23 24 25 26 6 5 4 3 2

∞ The paper used in this publication meets the minimum requirements of the American National Standard for Information Sciences—Permanence of Paper for Printed Library Materials, ANSI Z39.48-1992.

For a listing of books published and distributed by Syracuse University Press, visit https://press.syr.edu.

ISBN: 978-0-8156-3663-2 (hardcover)
978-0-8156-1114-1 (paperback)
978-0-8156-5487-2 (e-book)

Library of Congress Cataloging-in-Publication Data

Names: D'Imperio, Chuck, author. | Beatty, Bob, writer of foreword.
Title: Open house : 35 historic Upstate New York homes / Chuck D'Imperio ; with a foreword by Bob Beatty.
Description: First edition. | Syracuse : Syracuse University Press, 2020. | Includes index. | Summary: "Upstate New York author Chuck D'Imperio takes us behind the scenes of 35 homes throughout the region that are open to the public. Each house boasts of having a famous resident from the past. Whether it be a palatial mansion in the Hudson Valley, or a rustic cabin in the Adirondacks, each home has an interesting and important story to tell. This book is meant to act as a partner to the several other Upstate New York books D'Imperio has published through Syracuse University Press"— Provided by publisher.
Identifiers: LCCN 2019037936 (print) | LCCN 2019037937 (ebook) | ISBN 9780815636632 (hardcover) | ISBN 9780815611141 (paperback) | ISBN 9780815654872 (epub)
Subjects: LCSH: Historic house museums—New York (State)—Upstate New York—Guidebooks. | Upstate New York (N.Y.)—Biography—Anecdotes. | Upstate New York (N.Y.)—Guidebooks.
Classification: LCC F126.8 .D55 2020 (print) | LCC F126.8 (ebook) | DDC 917.47/104—dc23
LC record available at https://lccn.loc.gov/2019037936
LC ebook record available at https://lccn.loc.gov/2019037937

Manufactured in the United States of America

This book is dedicated to the memory of my parents,
Don and Kate D'Imperio.
They always encouraged me to share my stories with others.
I sure would like to have them back for just one more day.

CHUCK D'IMPERIO is a longtime award-winning radio broadcaster, newspaper journalist, and author of nine Upstate New York books. He has been on the air at Townsquare Media in Oneonta since 1989. His columns appear regularly in the Oneonta (NY) *Daily Star* newspaper, and he has written hundreds of articles for publication over the last quarter century. His online Facebook blog, *A Taste of Upstate New York,* is one of the most popular of its kind with more than 75,000 followers. Chuck is a prolific author, with the focus of his books mostly on his native Upstate New York. Among his books currently in print are *Monumental New York, The Unknown Museums of Upstate New York*, and *A Taste of Upstate New York* (all by Syracuse University Press). He is also the author of *Upstate Uncovered* (SUNY Press). Chuck is married to Trish, an educator, and they are the parents of Frances, Katie, Abby, and Joey. The author lives (of course) in Upstate New York.

Chuck can be reached at UpstateBooks@yahoo.com.

Contents

ULSTER COUNTY

WASHINGTON COUNTY

Foreword

Bob Beatty

It's not necessarily easy to determine what makes a structure historically important. I suppose many subscribe to the standard definitions: the structure's age (fifty years, according to the National Register of Historic Places), the building's "look" in relation to its past, and the site's significance to some historical event.

These criteria are valid and important; they have guided the history and preservation professions for years. But I believe there's something more to the historical importance equation, something inherently within us as human beings. Place literally grounds us in the past. It reminds us that people came before us—people who lived and died, succeeded and struggled, loved and grieved, worked and relaxed, just like we do today. Few things remind us of the very act of living more than historic homes.

Each of the sites Chuck D'Imperio features in this book fit the three "standard" criteria of history museums and historic preservation: age, historical integrity, and significance. They take on additional significance when we consider them as actual *homes*. It is then that they fulfill a different function, one nearly as important as the first: they matter deeply to us as *people*.

It is probably not a surprise, then, that I am a big believer in the power of historic houses to connect us to the continuum of life. I've been visiting them for forty-plus years. With more than half of those years spent working in history museums, it has been my job to think deeply about the role historic houses play in understanding the everyday lives of those who preceded us. By touring these sites and reflecting on the lives of the people who lived and worked within, we find that these homes provide meaning to our own lives (if we let them).

"Old places," my friend Tom Mayes writes, "are critical to people's sense of who they are, to their capacity to find meaning in their lives, and to see a future."[1] I have spent much time pondering these very ideas as they relate to my own experiences. I have also kept in mind the emotions these old places evoke in my own family, my friends, and the visitors I have served or encountered along the way. Some thoughts stand out, which I will share below.

When you visit these places, try not to overlook the very humanness found within. Sure, take time to marvel at the architecture, the incredible historic collections, and the stories of the notable person (typically a man), who had the house built. But remember that this was a *home* too. Think about the family who lived there. And rather than thinking of the house as a static entity, try to do so in the context of your own family's life. Remember that the inhabitants cleaned house and washed clothes; they read books and played music. Children played there, laughed there, and (most assuredly) cried there as well. Contemplate how many different generations lived in the house at the same time (or over time), and what their lives must have been like.

Consider also the people who built the home, tended its gardens, cooked meals in its kitchen, and served food in the dining room. Whether the homeowners tended these chores themselves or engaged paid servants or enslaved people is an important part of the home's history. It's easy to miss these seemingly ancillary players, but without them, the house you're visiting simply didn't function and would never have achieved any sense of historical longevity or significance.

When I visit these homes, I also actively seek out objects that speak to me. My criteria for this is somewhat fluid, and the same thing that intrigues

1. Thompson M. Mayes, *Why Old Places Matter: How Historic Places Affect Our Identity and Well-Being* (Lanham, MD: Rowman & Littlefield Press, 2018), xxiv–xxv.

me at one place may not even strike my fancy at the next. Sometimes a piece of furniture interests me—maybe because it helps me understand change over time, or perhaps it reminds me of something my grandmother once had. Other times it's a small item that someone owned and actually used: eyeglasses, a lap desk, a watch, or a small memento. I can find these on my own, but often staff, volunteers, or my family will point out something of interest. (My younger daughter, for example, always gravitates toward things that represent children.) The key is to find something that helps me connect to the people who lived there.

Think also about those who work to save the house as a museum. The act of preservation says as much about those who preserve and commemorate as it does about the past it seeks to protect and honor. What items did they save, collect, display, and highlight? What messages do they convey through the narrative about the house and its importance? What voices do they feature prominently, or exclude altogether? I like to consider what would happen if my own home was turned into a museum—what objects I would want displayed and stories I would want told.

Pondering the answers to these questions as I tour historic houses and sites helps me to understand the decisions made by historical actors who occupied these structures over time—when they were actual homes, through the preservation process, to their current use as house museums. In doing so, they help me feel connected to my own past, and that of others.

One last thing I ask of you. Historic house museums are managed in all sorts of ways. Some are owned by federal, state, or local municipalities; many are managed by private nonprofit organizations; still others are governed by some combination of the two. But all face the same challenge: maintaining old buildings comes with a *significant* financial cost. So, as you finish your visit, make sure you visit the gift shop and take something home with you. And drop a little extra in the donation box if you're so inclined, to help ensure future generations get to experience all of the mysteries within as well.

Above all, I hope you find meaning in your visits to historic places, as they enrich our lives and our communities tremendously.

Ed. Note—Bob Beatty is president of the Lyndhurst Group, a history, museum, and nonprofit consulting firm. From 2007 to 2017 Bob served in senior leadership roles at the American Association for State and Local History and from 1999 to 2007 he directed the Education Department at the Orange County (FL) Regional History Center.

PREFACE

I have written several books focusing on varied fascinating aspects of my native Upstate New York. In these books I have examined the history of one hundred small towns; the quirky roadside attractions that seem to be around every upstate bend in the road; the many "unknown museums" in the region; the heroic (and whimsical) statues and monuments that dot our landscape; and even the scrumptious foods that seem to be localized (and even hyper-localized) in Upstate. Ever hear of "turkey joint candy"? See what I mean?

But one thing has always amazed me as I traveled more than 100,000 miles during the research and writing of these many books: houses. Everywhere you look, from small hamlet to big city, you can see history writ large in the important homes of Upstate New York. Some houses are big, some small. Some are heralded and welcome thousands through their front doors each year. Others sit quietly along a roadside with just a handful of visitors uncovering their DNA through an in-person visit.

I was delighted when the editors at Syracuse University Press allowed me to focus on famous homes for my next book. The list is small, only thirty-five. Of course, I could have made this list about one hundred or even two hundred famous homes, but I came up with some guidelines for the entries. First, and most important, each home must be open to the public—and all of these are. Some on a limited basis, others with a more robust public schedule. Many are seasonal (Memorial Day to Labor Day).

But each home, each residence, has a story worth telling and invites you to come, visit, enjoy, and learn. The stories can be quite unforgettable. Sometimes revealing. Sometimes unusual and poignant. Always important and almost always eye-popping. Some will even give you goosebumps when you read "the rest of the story" I uncovered about the home.

I made the early decision when choosing the homes for this book to look "off the grid" as much as possible. For example, you will not find any of the sprawling lavish mansions that line the Hudson River. These storied homes have been researched, written about, photographed, and visited by millions over the years. They need no reintroduction from me in this book. But fewer people have visited the quiet residential abode of a towering figure in the women's rights movement. That home, located in Fayetteville, outside of Syracuse, is a testimony to the hard work and leadership of one of the suffrage movement's "Big Three." The house tells a little-known story about a great upstate legend.

We did not include the many mansions that line the moneyed neighborhoods of Buffalo, or Rochester either. You can take organized tours of these famous homes any time of the year and, again, they need no more mention from me in this book. But few people have visited a neighborhood home in the Capital District where one of America's most beloved authors lived and wrote some of his most famous works. It is definitely off the grid, but you can find the story in this book.

I visited each of the thirty-five homes in this book, covering twenty-six different upstate counties. Usually, the visit meant a fascinating afternoon spent with the owners, museum directors, veteran docents, and caretakers of the property. They were each passionate in their love for "their houses" and were well-versed on the inside stories about each residence and its owners. Because of this, I believe that this book is unique in that while it is a guidebook to some fascinating public landmarks, it is also a rare opportunity to learn the "inside scoop" about the people who lived there as told by the historians who now oversee these homes.

I found many surprises along the way. I am sure you will be surprised as well. When I began writing this book, I knew very little about historic home designs, architectural aspects, construction techniques, or odd vintage interior flourishes. As you will see, I learned a lot in my travels about things like a "mortgage eye staircase," about why many older homes had so few closets in them, about what a gasolier was, and why a door opening is called a threshold.

I am tempted to tell you here about all of these surprises, but I will let you discover them as you turn the pages of the book. One surprise that I will share now, however, was my favorite. At the end of the tour of one famous house, the museum director pointed me to a window with some markings on it. "As you can see, there are names and dates scrawled on the glass as a sort of guestbook for those who visited this house," he said. I looked carefully at it. Sure enough, there were finely etched "autographs" on the windows scratched in the glass by guests using a diamond. It was a real stunner to see and as I drove away that day, I remember saying to myself, "Wow, I guess I will never see that again."

Not true.

Amazingly, there are three homes in this book where you can see where guests have etched their names with a diamond in old windows. Apparently, it was quite a "thing" back in the day. Surprised? Oh, and one of the diamond-signed "autographs" is that of one of the most famous women in American history.

The range of buildings highlighted in this book is as wide and varying as the people who resided in them. I would have to say the most imposing residence featured here is Hyde Hall. This magnificent mansion sits tucked away on a hill at the north end of Otsego Lake in Cooperstown. Built between 1817 and 1834, it has been called one of the most important neoclassic country mansions in America. While thousands visit Cooperstown each year for baseball and opera, a much smaller crowd finds their way deep into James Fenimore Cooper's Leatherstocking Country to visit this remarkable residence.

Among the simpler, more out-of-the-way homes in this book, I would definitely point you to a small wooden cottage, rough-hewn and anonymous, resting hidden atop Clump Mountain in the Catskills. Here you will find the unvarnished abode of one of our country's most famous and influential conservationists and authors. He lived here for most of his life and is buried near a giant boulder on a knoll behind his cabin.

So many people over the years have told me that they have enjoyed my many Upstate New York books and that they have kept them in the car and used them as guidebooks when visiting the far reaches of our region. My wish is that when you head out on the country road again, you will tuck this book in your glove box. When you pull into a small town or village, take it out and see what adventures await you in a historic house wherever you are.

Happy Travels!

A Note from the Author

As in all my previous Upstate New York books, let me make two observations. First, when setting out to visit any of the homes listed in this book, be sure to plan ahead! Several of the homes can be visited by appointment only and others have fluctuating tour schedules. Many of them rely on the availability of an army of volunteers to keep their doors open so consistency may vary. Each chapter has a link to the home's website or Facebook page, as well as a phone number. Items in the "Visit" section of each chapter may change without warning so please contact the homes before you go, and their staff will be more than happy to give you updated information and to accommodate you.

The title of this book references "Upstate New York." I use the term "upstate" loosely for this and all my other books for a simple reason. I do not write about New York City and the metropolitan New York region. There is always a debate about where "upstate" is exactly. Yes, we have different regions such as the Finger Lakes, the North Country, Western New York, or the Capital District, but to me it is all upstate. I feel I really know Upstate New York: I was born in Delaware County, I went to college in Albany County, my publisher is in Onondaga County, and I live in Otsego County!

Enjoy the book!

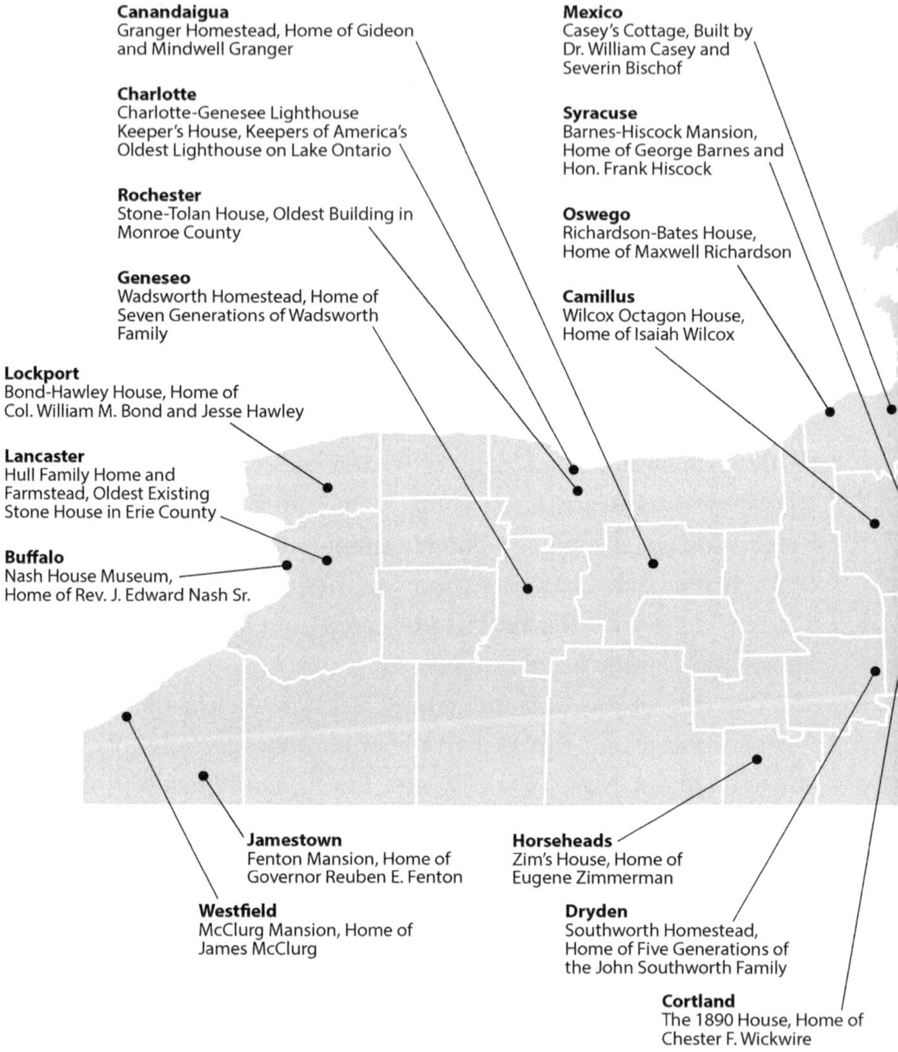

35 Historic Upstate New York Homes

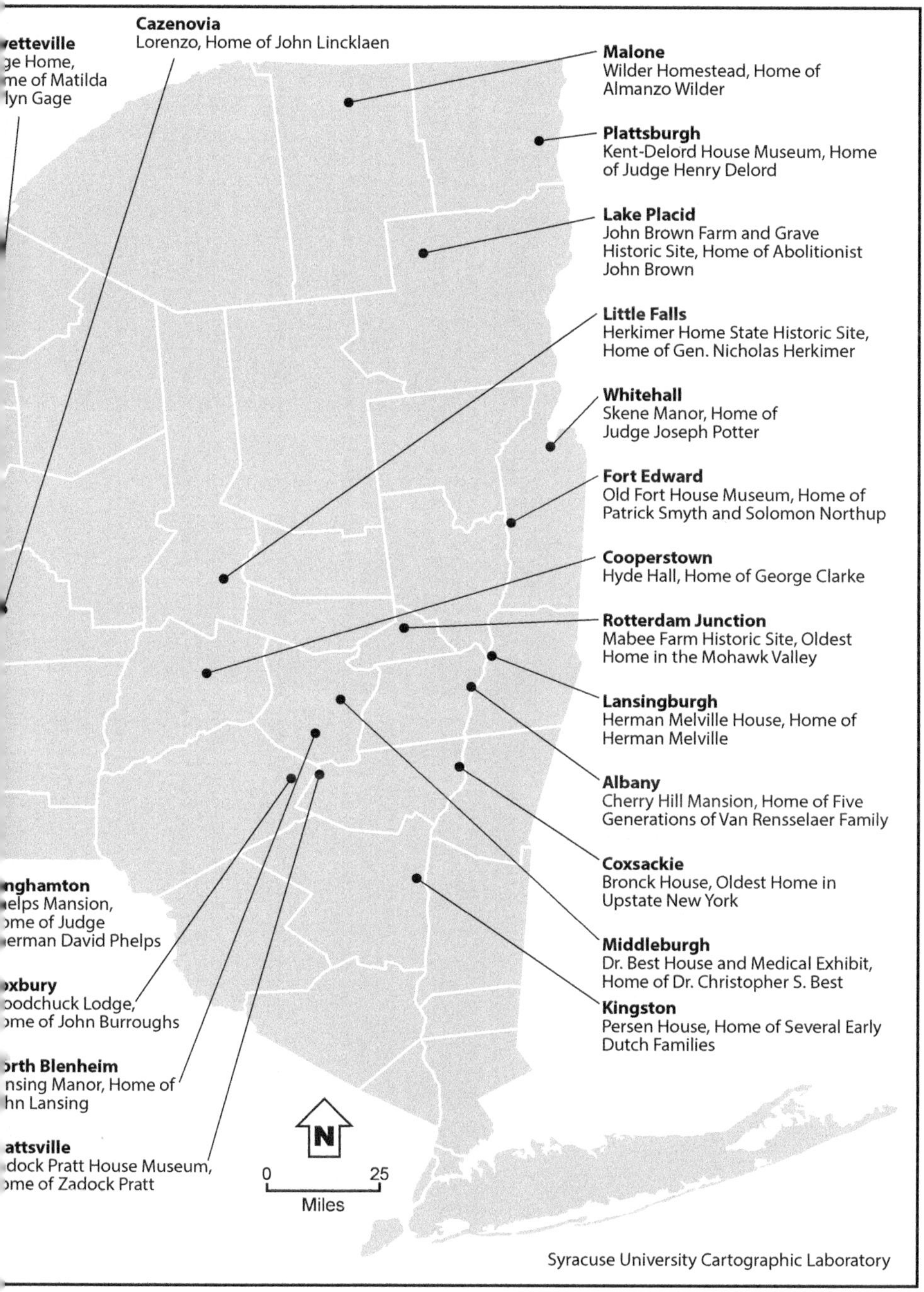

etteville
ge Home,
me of Matilda
lyn Gage
Cazenovia
Lorenzo, Home of John Lincklaen
Malone
Wilder Homestead, Home of Almanzo Wilder
Plattsburgh
Kent-Delord House Museum, Home of Judge Henry Delord
Lake Placid
John Brown Farm and Grave Historic Site, Home of Abolitionist John Brown
Little Falls
Herkimer Home State Historic Site, Home of Gen. Nicholas Herkimer
Whitehall
Skene Manor, Home of Judge Joseph Potter
Fort Edward
Old Fort House Museum, Home of Patrick Smyth and Solomon Northup
Cooperstown
Hyde Hall, Home of George Clarke
Rotterdam Junction
Mabee Farm Historic Site, Oldest Home in the Mohawk Valley
Lansingburgh
Herman Melville House, Home of Herman Melville
Albany
Cherry Hill Mansion, Home of Five Generations of Van Rensselaer Family
Coxsackie
Bronck House, Oldest Home in Upstate New York
Middleburgh
Dr. Best House and Medical Exhibit, Home of Dr. Christopher S. Best
Kingston
Persen House, Home of Several Early Dutch Families
nghamton
elps Mansion,
ome of Judge
erman David Phelps
oxbury
oodchuck Lodge,
ome of John Burroughs
orth Blenheim
nsing Manor, Home of
hn Lansing
attsville
dock Pratt House Museum,
ome of Zadock Pratt
N
0
25
Miles
Syracuse University Cartographic Laboratory

Open HOUSE

1

Cherry Hill Mansion

Home of Five Generations of the Van Rensselaer Family
Albany, Albany County

"Historic Cherry Hill is a Georgian manor that in the eighteenth century would have been typical of those belonging to only the top one percent of society. It is a large sprawling home that was situated on many hundreds of acres at the time. But, despite its substantial size, most visitors feel that the building retains a homey atmosphere. It was, after all, a family home," Deborah Emmons-Andarawis said. She is the director of Historic Cherry Hill.

The house has been tied to many of the great iconic names in Albany's history. And it has a dark secret. A murder took place here!

But more on that later.

The Van Rensselaer family was one of the elite lights at the dawning of Albany's growth. Philip was a descendant of the legendary Dutch patroon Kiliaen van Rensselaer, one of the wealthiest merchants in the Northeast. "Yes, they were one of the premier family names in the city," the director told me. "Philip, and his wife Maria, moved into this home in 1787, the same year our nation's Constitution was ratified. After Philip died in 1798, his widow lived on at the mansion with extended family members, boarders, servants, and one enslaved woman, Dinah Jackson. We believe at one time there were as many as twenty-two residents living here, filling every room in the house from the cellar to the garret."

The house is huge and square, and it mirrors the architectural traits of an eighteenth-century manor house. The original design called for four bedrooms, other private and public rooms, two large center hallways, and

two kitchens in the basement. There was probably no dining room, as the concept of a formal room exclusively for eating was just starting to catch on in homes such as this. And no indoor bathroom facilities.

"Yes, the house duplicates itself from the first floor to the second, and from the left to the right. Two parlors flank a center hall on the first floor, and the upper-level floor plan originally mirrored that of the ground level. Symmetry was key to the eighteenth-century aesthetic," I was told.

The first floor, reached from a large set of steps coming up from a circular driveway, opens into a grand hallway with parlors on each side. A formal parlor was used for entertaining and ceremonies, such as weddings and even funerals. The south parlor served that function for most of the house's history—from the gatherings of Philip and Maria van Rensselaer in the eighteenth century up through the funeral of their great-great-granddaughter, Emily Rankin, in 1963.

"We have the original contract between Philip van Rensselaer and Isaac Packard who was the housewright of the building. There were not a lot of architects in the country at the time. Many of the mansions of that era drew from English architectural pattern books, or they simply replicated the regional styles that the housewright was familiar with.

"Packard was a deft contractor and we can see much of his expertise still today. The original contract called for ten large paneled doors, including four on the first floor, four on the second floor and, of course, the front and back doors. We still have many of these doors, which is remarkable since they date to the original house in 1787. Our front door is an original one," Emmons-Andarawis told me as she slowly opened one of the historic doors.

"The sweeping, curved staircase is a focal point of the home. Philip wanted only the best and this staircase is a highlight. Its banister is made of mahogany, which follows along the curvature of the stairs themselves. A matching chair rail completes the beauty of this feature. The floors are original and are made of wide pine planks, which was typical of that time period," the director continued.

Each room has a fireplace. The mantels in the parlors are Belgian marble—an upgrade added by Solomon van Rensselaer of Cherry Hill's second generation of prestigious occupants. The master bedroom has a Federal-style mantel put in by Catherine Rankin of the fourth generation. "Catherine had nearly lost her family home, having undergone a series of economic setbacks over the years, and this mantel was part of Catherine's restoration of her family home once it was secure in her hands again. She even reinstalled delft tiles around the fireplace that, according to family tradition, were original to the home," Emmons-Andarawis said.

Catherine's eye for design is also evident in the dining room. "The china cupboard is quite beautiful in and of itself," the director told me. "As you can see there are many windows in the cupboard. During the early twentieth century the style was to coordinate the colors of the china, the textiles, and even the flower arrangements in the room. Also, we still have this," she said and opened a door at the bottom of the cupboard to reveal the remains of a dumbwaiter. "When the kitchen was moved from the basement to the first floor, they didn't need a dumbwaiter anymore, so they turned it into a china cupboard. But this is their nod to the past. They didn't want to forget the 'old days.'"

Historic Cherry Hill is a work in progress. Some, though, would call it a labor of love.

"Even before I came to Cherry Hill as curator, the staff had been noticing some troubling structural issues. When the last Cherry Hill Van Rensselaer passed away in 1963 and left the home to be a museum, the entire contents of the house became the museum collection. That's five generations of living and collecting all stored in one house, and mostly in the attic. These collections were literally crushing this house. When you add in water damage and regular wear and tear, we were faced with dangling structural posts, rotting sills, and a foundation that was crumbling in places.

"We had no choice but to empty out the attic. We built the Edward Frisbee Center for Collections and Research and moved most of the 70,000-piece collection there. Now the collections are available to researchers in a way that they couldn't be when they were all crammed into the attic. Now, with the weight of the collections out of the attic we could finally start our restoration.

"It has been slow but satisfying. The house has been stabilized, windows restored, and we look forward to welcoming visitors into a lovingly restored Van Rensselaer home. Few houses of this age and stature can document the minutiae of so many generations of inhabitants. And for that we are thankful. Historic Cherry Hill has quite a story to tell," Emmons-Andarawis assured me.

The name Rensselaer can be found throughout the Capital District. You can find it on street signs and parks as well as iconic venues like Rensselaer Polytechnic Institute in Troy. There is even a county that bears that name as well as a town, Rensselaerville, which has a population of about 2,000 residents.

"We try and tell the story of all the generations of the family that lived here," the director said. "But we really focus on the life and times of the last two generations, Catherine Rankin and her children. She was Philip van Rensselaer's great-granddaughter and she lived here from the age of three to her death in 1948. She was survived by two children who never married, and her daughter, Emily, lived on at Cherry Hill until her death in 1963. Over the years, as society changed and the economic shifts in our country brought a change to the lives of people like the Van Rensselaers, this house found itself on the brink of disaster more than once. When Catherine married a rising lawyer and secured Cherry Hill in family hands, she began to restore it to its former glamour and also began collecting and buying back family items that had left the property years before.

"When I became curator, I felt as I did as a child looking through my grandmother's jewelry box. This house is brimming with great tales. There were so many stories to learn, and I loved them all. For example, when I first researched Emily, I found out that she was a graduate of Smith College. I was a graduate of Barnard College. She was an English major, and so was I. There was a kinship, kind of like two sisters from sister colleges. We were not totally alike, however. For example, I learned that Emily, unlike many of her fellow female college graduates of the time, was fiercely antisuffrage. That was a big surprise to me.

"But I love this house. Outside its sturdy walls and looking out through the tall windows the world changed all around this family over five generations. From high on this hilltop overlooking the Hudson River they watched fortunes ebb and flow, they adapted to industrial shifts and observed social changes. That, and how they responded to those changes, is itself an amazing story," Emmons-Andarawis said.

Author's Notes

This house has everything: great bones, a fantastic history, an amazing collection of 70,000 items directly related to five generations of the same family who lived here, and a wonderful story around every corner.

Two things stick with me after a tour of Historic Cherry Hill. Despite all the glory and grandeur of the past as well as the magnificence of the mansion itself, it is a little piece of wallpaper that touched my heart the most. "Yes, the wallpaper dates back over a century, to about 1910," the director told me. It displays a busy design of green florals and swirls. "But look here a little closer," she said. As I leaned in to observe, I noticed several deep scratches in the paper. "This wall was right outside the family dining room. Emily was very strict when it came to her dog, Dandy. She would not allow the family pet into the dining room while the family was eating dinner. These scratches are from Dandy as if to say, 'Let me in,'" she chuckled. Dog scratches. From 110 years ago. Amazing.

"When we restore this room, we are going to leave them right there," the director told me.

And as if all these stories are not enough, we must get to the murder.

"Yes, there actually was a murder here in the mansion. Jesse Strang was a drifter who lived here for a short while as a hired hand. He became romantically involved with Elsie Whipple, a Van Rensselaer family relative who lived at the mansion with her husband, John Whipple," Emmons-Andarawis said.

Eventually, Strang murdered John Whipple by shooting into his bedroom window from atop a shed roof attached to the mansion's back facade.

The trial had all the elements of a potboiler, with money, sex, social class, and the death penalty all mixed in. Jesse Strang was found guilty of John's death and was hanged on August 24, 1827. It was the last public hanging in Albany.

"We do talk about the murder on our tours. And we try and have a little fun with it, too. In fact, around Halloween we have a tour which focuses on the Cherry Hill Murder. In one room we have a 'corpse' laid out on a table and we read actual quotes from the trial of Jesse Strang. Of course, this is one of the most popular events we have every year," she said.

Visit

Historic Cherry Hill
523 South Pearl Street
Albany, NY 12202
Landmark: Cherry Hill Mansion is located just one block from the I-787 overpass.
518-434-4791
Website: http://www.historiccherryhill.org/

For Further Reference: Jones, Louis C. *Murder at Cherry Hill: The Strang-Whipple Case.* Albany: Cherry Hill Publications, 1980.

While Here: The New York State Museum at the Empire Plaza is an excellent source of Albany and New York State history. It is free.

Tours: April through December
Several different tours are available including house tours, behind the scene restoration tours, and Murder Mystery tours.

Admission:

Adults: $5.00
Seniors and college students: $4.00
Children: $2.00

2

Phelps Mansion

Home of Judge Sherman David Phelps
Binghamton, Broome County

"When this mansion was finished in 1872, it would no doubt have been one of the most magnificent, glamorous homes in Binghamton," Toby Manker told me. She is the executive director of the Phelps Mansion Museum in Binghamton. "The neighboring homes were all wonderful, of course. In fact, some called this 'Millionaire's Row.' But the Phelps Mansion was amazing and elegant without being ostentatious. This home was special."

The mansion, which is now just two blocks from the busy downtown business district, stands out in the landscape as a regal remembrance of Binghamton's heyday.

"The design is Second Empire, and it has many unique features to it," said Joe Schuerch, the house manager. "It has nine bedrooms and four bathrooms, a full kitchen and basement, and fireplaces in almost every room of the house. The architect, Isaac Perry, was one of the most famous of his era and, in fact, he also worked on the New York State Capitol in Albany."

The design of the house is a little bit of an "eye trick." Most of the rooms are not particularly spacious as far as square footage goes, but what they lack in floor space they certainly make up in height. The rooms have soaring seventeen-foot ceilings with towering mirrors and windows all adding to the illusion of their being grand spaces.

Each room in this mansion is a remarkable example of old-fashioned craftsmanship and exquisite attention to detail. "The house cost about $120,000 to build in its day, and everything was the best of the best,"

Manker said as we wandered from room to room. "Each one has its own wonderful surprise."

The rooms are appointed with period furniture (unfortunately, there is not much left of the original Phelps's household belongings). The woodwork is among the finest I have ever seen. There is a grand sweeping staircase that cost $10,000 of the original house's price tag. It is made from American black walnut. The floors in the hall are imported Italian marble. "Perry loved to use combinations of woods and marble in his construction designs. There is no better example of that than here at the Phelps mansion. Almost every room includes a different kind of wood, some of it very rare," Schuerch said.

The fireplace in the front parlor is made from bird's-eye maple and rosewood, the back parlor has walnut throughout, the front doors are mahogany, and the bed in the Judge's suite is a hand-carved work of art created by a local wood carver, Orville Ronk.

The largest room in the house is the ballroom. "It measures approximately sixty feet by forty feet. It was an add-on in 1905. By then all the

Phelpses were gone and the new owners, the Binghamton Monday Afternoon Club, needed a large space for concerts, speakers, theater productions, and fundraisers. Many famous people of that era came and spoke in this ballroom including Ida Tarbell, Jack London, and Jacob Riis," the house manager told me. "The floors are all original, the stage was built in 1931, and the Steinway piano was purchased in 1934." He pointed up to the expansive chandelier overhead. "In 1890, the famous Sherry Hotel in Manhattan sold sixteen of their dining room chandeliers. One man bought all of them for $75,000, and somehow we ended up with one of them. In 1941, the original one came crashing down from the ceiling. This is a replacement."

The mansion is now a museum to the glamour days of the city's past. "We have many items including artifacts, memorabilia, and archival photographs in our collection. But really when asked I always say, 'This house is the most important part of our collection,'" Schuerch commented as he viewed the interior of the residence.

"Mr. Phelps was born in 1814 and arrived here from Pennsylvania in 1854. By then he was already quite successful. He was involved with railroads, banks, a waterworks and gas company as well as being a silent investor in other local endeavors," Schuerch told me. "His success continued in Binghamton and he was a popular member of high society here. He was elected as the city's fifth mayor in 1872."

"At that time things were going smoothly for Judge Phelps," Manker added. "He built this extravagant home not only for his family, but as a showplace for the rewards of his success. Many festive galas and parties were held here over the years, but sadly it didn't last long."

In doing this book I have encountered many stories of people whose lives "went from gold to rust" fairly quickly. The story of this mansion's owner is one of the saddest. Manker, the executive director, shared it with me.

"Mr. Phelps moved into this mansion upon its completion in 1871. By that time he was already a widower twice with his first wife, Susan, having died in 1843. Their daughter, Stella, passed away soon after her mother at the age of five months old. His second wife, Elizabeth Sweet, died in 1863. Phelps himself died in 1878, at the age of sixty-four. He and

Elizabeth had two sons who also died young. By 1882, all of the Phelps family members were gone, and the house was sold. The house was kept up to a livable standard during the next few years by Andrew Jackson, a freed slave who worked as a livery man for Judge Phelps. It had two other owners from 1889 to 1904.

"Finally, the house's future was saved when the Binghamton Ladies Afternoon Club bought it in 1905. The asking price was $20,000. They ended up paying just $15,000 for everything. But they were good stewards of this grand mansion. They were here for exactly one hundred years, from 1905 to 2005, and when they vacated the house it was turned into a public museum. It really is a sad and poignant tale to be told here. All of that money and suddenly everybody was gone," Manker said quietly.

The Honorable Sherman D. Phelps died on November 13, 1878. His body lay in state on the first floor of his mansion for viewing by friends, neighbors, and citizens of Binghamton.

Author's Notes

This is an astounding home. There were a couple of special features that really stood out to me.

In the formal dining room there are many hidden carvings in the elaborate handmade wood furniture, from the tables to the fireplace mantels to the buffet. It is fun trying to find the fox and lion heads and the little gryphons. The gryphon was believed to be a symbol of good luck and manifestations of it can be found all through the house in carvings, images, and even bronze fireplace accessories.

The towering mahogany front doors have no exterior doorknobs or handles. "This was because people just didn't drop in to a house of this stature back then. People were unable to enter the home on their own, but rather they were let in by a servant when they came at a predetermined time. Therefore, no doorknobs were needed," Schuerch told me.

My favorite "find" is in the receiving room. This is where Phelps would entertain his male guests after dinner. "Phelps had served as an associate judge during his time in Wyoming County, Pennsylvania, before moving to Binghamton. He was always proud of that. In this room if you look along the sides of the door entranceways you can see small judge's gavels carved into the woodwork. He did that to make sure his guests knew that he was a jurist at one point in his life," the house manager said as he pointed to the tops of the doorways.

Sure enough, if you look up, all along the wood frames of the entranceways, you can see a series of miniature courtroom gavels replicated in the carvings.

Visit

Phelps Mansion Museum
191 Court Street
Binghamton, NY 13901
Landmark: The mansion is adjacent to the Broome County Public Library.
607-722-4873
Website: https://phelpsmansion.org/tours/

For Further Reference: Gelbert, Doug. *Look Up, Binghamton! A Walking Tour of Binghamton, New York.* Cruden Bay Books, 2010.

While Here: Binghamton is known as the "Carousel Capital of the USA." There are six operating carousels located in various parks throughout the city. They were donated to Binghamton by George F. Johnson (1857–1948), who once owned the largest shoe factory in the world here in the Southern Tier.

Tours: Open Friday, Saturday, and Sunday, 11 a.m. to 5 p.m. Last tour begins at 4:30 p.m.

Admission:

Adults: $7.00
Seniors and students: $5.00
Children under 12: Free

3

Fenton Mansion

Home of Governor Reuben E. Fenton
Jamestown, Chautauqua County

Modern Jamestown has begun to encroach on the grounds of this stunning mansion, but it is still easy to see why, from the time it was built in 1863 through the present day, it has been a showplace for the city.

"Governor Reuben Fenton was one of the most prestigious men to ever come out of this region, serving important political roles in New York and on the national scene, so this house fit him perfectly," said Noah Goodling, the executive director of the Fenton History Center, which operates out of the mansion. "It was the classic prominent man's home high on a hill." The towering Italianate villa house contains fifteen rooms spread over 15,000 square feet. According to Dr. Tom Greer, a Fenton trustee, "What designates the home as Italianate villa design is the tower, or campanile. From that tower, Fenton and his family could have surveyed all of downtown Jamestown. The layout of the house is like when it was built. Unfortunately, we have very few family records of the house so it is kind of a mystery game for us trying to figure out which room was used for what purpose. We do not have the original blueprints for the house, but there were two architectural assessments of it and that helps us a lot.

"Fenton called his home 'Walnut Grove,'" Greer said. "He named it that because of the many walnut trees on the property, none of which remain. We are in the process of planting new walnut trees on the grounds to give the name back its meaning. The architect of the mansion was Aaron Hall, who did many of the most significant homes in Jamestown."

When Fenton died in 1885, his wife, Elizabeth, lived on at the mansion until her death in 1901. Afterward, their children let it sit empty until

it was put up for sale in 1912; there were no takers. Finally, the city of Jamestown bought the home and the grounds in 1921 for $35,000 for use as a Soldiers and Sailors Memorial. The city still owns it, using the house and the surrounding three acres of land as a city park. The property has been on the National Register of Historic Places since 1972.

Inside the home is a variety of exhibits. "After the Fentons died, most of the family's personal items were passed on to descendants so we have very few authentic personal items," Goodling noted. Among the Fenton possessions they do have are fine china and a unique item—the "governor's chair." This is a large oak and leather upholstered chair with the Seal of the State of New York embossed on the high back. Throughout the house you will see many period pieces from the era of the Fentons' residency. The rooms have soaring twelve-foot-tall ceilings and feature original ornamentation such as beautiful hand-carved wooden mantels and gorgeous marble fireplaces.

"Because Mr. Fenton was away a lot, this was very much Mrs. Fenton's house. In fact, Governor Fenton would take one or both of his young daughters with him on his frequent trips to Albany and Washington, and Mrs. Fenton would stay back in Jamestown," Greer commented. Elizabeth Fenton was a supporter of women's rights and the Women's Temperance Movement. "We know that Elizabeth Cady Stanton, Susan B. Anthony, and Lillie Devereux visited here and that suffragette groups met here. Mrs. Fenton was also known for her gardening talents, which were on full display around her home."

One of the larger rooms in the home hosts an exhibit about the history of the furniture-making industry in Jamestown. Given the city's background in the lumber industry, it is perhaps not surprising to find out that the basis for the early industrial boom in this far western New York State city was furniture manufacturing. "Along the back of the exhibit we have a full timeline of chairs that were made in Jamestown," Goodling said as we walked through the room. "The lineup starts with the simple wooden chairs of the 1800s, and moves through the decades showing new styles, material, and manufacturing methods through different eras. Jamestown was once the second largest furniture-making city in the United States, second only to Grand Rapids, Michigan. Our population grew from 400 people in 1827 to over 40,000 people a century later, with a great deal of that growth driven by the furniture-making industry. There were well over one hundred furniture makers in the city with such overall prestige that the Jamestown Royal Company was contracted to make chairs for the US Supreme Court justices."

Beyond this exhibit are many more scattered throughout the mansion. Several rooms in the home are decorated in the Victorian fashion that the Fenton family would recognize. The rooms feature period wallpaper and carpets, and some are lit with chandeliers (several of which are original) that have been refashioned from gas to electric. Portraits of family members and local dignitaries adorn the walls. Beyond these recreations there are other rooms dedicated to specific local topics. A military room, for example, displays many artifacts from the Civil War, highlighting Jamestown's role in this conflict and others. "We have what is believed to be the only New York regimental flag used in the Civil War that is not in control of the state government. It is from the 112th New York State Volunteers that mustered in at Jamestown on September 11, 1862," said Goodling. There are also assorted war-related items from the nineteenth and twentieth centuries lining the walls, including documents, uniforms, paintings, and weapons.

A tour of the Fenton Mansion ends at the very top. On the day I visited, the tall trees surrounding the property were in full foliage so I couldn't quite imagine the sweeping view. There is no doubt, however, that when the leaves fall in October, the city of Jamestown will reveal itself in full view from high atop Fenton's tower.

Reuben E. Fenton may be the most famous New Yorker you have never heard of.

Born on July 4, 1819, his prominence was noted throughout the city on the 200th anniversary of his birthday. Beyond his significant impact on Jamestown, though, where he was a successful and wealthy lumber baron, he also had a notable reputation in the political arena. He served as a member of the US House of Representatives and the US Senate, and was elected governor of New York in 1864 and 1868. He was also a leading contender for the position of vice president of the United States in 1868, but he was passed over. Although initially a member of the Democratic Party, he left to become a founder of the Republican Party, counting another early member of the Republican Party, Abraham Lincoln, as a friend. Dignitaries known to have visited the mansion include Horace Greeley, General William Sherman, General Philip Sheridan, and President William McKinley. After his political career, Fenton returned to Jamestown where he served as a bank president until his death on August 25, 1885. He died of a pulmonary embolism while working at his desk at the bank.

This is one of the grandest mansions in western New York. Although most of the Fentons' possessions were dispersed after Reuben and Elizabeth died, there is still a lot to see. To tour here is to stroll through the Victorian era in the United States and see how it affected the lifestyles, designs, and culture of the time. It is easy to imagine the elaborate soirees held here to celebrate holidays or even any of Reuben's many political victories.

One thing I found fascinating is that the grounds surrounding the mansion are in a seemingly perpetual state of discovery. "With so much unknown about the property and where all of the outbuildings were located, we are conducting an ongoing archeological dig to try and uncover these secrets," said Greer, who also volunteers as the director of archeology here. "We are making headway, but it is a slow process in locating where the carriage house, servants quarters (from an earlier residence), original barn, and other structures were situated."

Behind the Fenton Mansion is another historic home, an 1846 Greek Revival building known as the Hall House, which is owned by the Fenton Historical Center. Director Goodling told me, "That building houses our research and genealogical center. There are experts there six days a week assisting people in tracking down their family roots to the Jamestown area and beyond. Many of our requests are from folks with Swedish lineage, as this area of western New York saw a large influx of immigrants from Sweden arrive here during the 1800s, but we are able and willing to help anyone who wants to search for their family."

One last item I should note is the impressive life-sized statue of Governor Fenton that stands in front of the mansion. The inscription written

Other than Lucille Ball, Gov. Reuben Fenton may be the most famous person ever to come out of the Jamestown area. A life-sized statue of Fenton stands on the front lawn of his mansion.

on the face of the monument describes what may be his most important legacy. It reads:

> During the Civil War he was affectionately known as "The Soldiers' Friend." Your state thanks you and gives you pledge of her lasting gratitude. The people will regard with jealous pride, your welfare and honor, not forgetting the widow and the fatherless.

Visit

Fenton Mansion and Research Center
67 Washington Street
Jamestown, NY 14701
716-664-6256
Website: https://www.fentonhistorycenter.org/

For Further Reference: Lombardi, Peter A. *Jamestown, New York: A Guide to the City and Its Urban Landscape*. Albany: Excelsior Editions, 2014.

While Here: The Fenton Mansion is just a few blocks from the new Lucille Ball-Desi Arnaz Museum and Center for Comedy. Lucille Ball was born in Jamestown.

Tours: Monday through Saturday, 10:00 a.m. to 4:00 p.m.

Admission:
Adults (18 and over): $10.00
Children under 17: Free

Paid admission allows visitor to both tour the mansion and visit the genealogical research center behind the home.

4

McClurg Mansion

Home of James McClurg
Westfield, Chautauqua County

When the McClurg Mansion was built between 1818 and 1820, this part of Chautauqua County sure looked a lot different than it does now.

"The house was definitely outsized," John ("Jack") Horst told me. He is a senior docent at the mansion. "In the early 1800s there were only about 500 voters in the whole county. It was a rough, tree-covered frontier area and most people just eked out an existence in simple log cabins. So, when wealthy James McClurg arrived from Pittsburgh and built this elaborate home, well, let's just say that it really stuck out!"

The residence is thought to be patterned after a Scotch-Irish Manor House, like what the McClurgs would have had in Pittsburgh. There are elements of Federal, Georgian, and Greek revival in the design. The original 6,900-square-foot house had twelve rooms on two main floors and a labyrinth of rooms in the cellar. Four more rooms have been added over the years.

Early locals called the building "McClurg's Folly" because it stood in such contrast to the cabins that surrounded it. The mansion today is a museum, not a period house. Family possessions of Chautauqua County residents and other period artifacts are exhibited throughout the museum. The imposing presence of the mansion in the center of the village of Westfield is a reminder of the early days when the McClurg family home would have been a frontier wonderment.

There was no bathroom in the original plans of the house, and there was no heat, save from the fireplaces. Central heating came to the house

long after the last McClurg and Moore family members were gone (daughter Catherine McClurg had married a local doctor, Edward Moore, and they also resided here).

"The house was beautiful from the beginning, but over time James's daughter, Catherine, made several changes and additions," Horst said. "She brought ideas and items back from her trips to Europe. The large marble fireplace mantel in the front room was put in during the 1880s and is designed like the ones Catherine saw on a European trip. In the dining room you can see beautifully carved wood pieces that carry a 'grapevine' motif. That too was influenced by Mrs. Moore's visits abroad."

The grape design fit right in as Chautauqua County grew to become a center for grape production and the home to Welch's Grape Juice.

One of the house's most striking features is a large, winding staircase that goes from the first floor to the second in the center stair hall. The spiral staircase appears to reach high up to the next floor without any under support.

"I honestly can't figure out what holds that thing up," Horst said. "It is all wood. No steel. It looks like it could fall at any time, but it has been up there for 200 years and is as sturdy as can be. With no pillars, beams, or foundation of any kind under it, that staircase remains a mystery to me," he said.

This elegant house holds much history. As the home of the Chautauqua County Historical Society, the McClurg Museum serves an important role in the society's mission to preserve and interpret objects and archives of historical significance to foster an interest in local history.

One of the most fascinating and historically significant rooms is a unique octagon parlor. This writer has never seen one quite like this.

"The great William Seward, who would become the twelfth governor of New York State, US Senator, and the US Secretary of State under President Lincoln, rented the mansion for several years beginning in 1836. Seward had taken the job of land agent in Westfield and needed a place to live. Mrs. McClurg had gone to New Jersey for health reasons, so James rented the house to Seward for $225 a year," Horst said.

In this room you will find several unique and historical items, from Seward's actual writing desk and papers to smaller items from the county's history. One wall holds a graceful and fancy soapstone fireplace surround. Large portraits of family members and local historical figures done by famous painters hang on other walls. A display case holds items from the era when Chautauqua Lake was the center of high society gatherings. One item is a large lantern from Thomas A. Edison's boat *Olivia*, which won the 1887 first prize during the annual Illumination of the Boats on Chautauqua Lake.

And then there is the fireproof safe. "Local farmers in a dispute with landowners had torn down and burned the nearby Mayville land office. Seward was hired as the new agent to calm things down. At some point, the large fireproof safe was brought to the county, one of the first of its kind in this area," Horst said.

The safe is jet black and the size of an ordinary large floor safe. The front is covered with a series of protruding round hobnails. The trick to opening the safe is to find the secret hobnail and pry it open. It then reveals a lock that you flip to open. Then you must swing the very heavy iron door open to reveal a second door with more hobnails on it. Once you finally find the secret key on this door it will open to a space where papers could be kept safely from fire and thieves.

And finally, the "Ellicott trunk." Joseph Ellicott was the most important land arbiter in the early years of the settlement in western New York. He was the chief land agent for the Holland Land Company headquartered in Batavia and is credited with divvying up tens of thousands of acres of western New York into the small towns and villages that we now know in that area.

"Some years ago, the society found some items that were stored in the attic," Horst said. "It was a bunch of things we had never really given much thought to. I noticed this large trunk in a corner and decided to move it. In doing so, I flipped it over and lo and behold there it was in large script letters: 'Joseph Ellicott.' It turns out that this is the personal trunk of one of the most famous people involved in the development of Upstate New York. And it had been upstairs the whole time!"

The trunk is now proudly displayed in the Octagon Parlor.

Cristie Herbst, president of the Chautauqua County Historical Society, noted, "This grand home is the repository of the society's historical collections. Archivist Kathleen Roe calls these collections the essential evidence of the past. The individual and collective voices that we have in the archives here at McClurg Museum provide us with the source of action and events from our past, and they create what she describes as the thread and fabric of our society.

"As a museum, this historic home enables us to put our visitors in touch with the people who settled our area, the pioneers. And we try to bring them close to county residents from other historic eras. For example, in our military room we encourage visitors to test the heft of one of our original Civil War rifles. Things become quite real to them when they see how heavy this weapon would have been to carry all day on a march or to use in battle," Herbst stated.

James McClurg came to America with his father, Joseph, from Ireland when he was just thirteen years old. The McClurgs eventually settled in the Pittsburgh, Pennsylvania, area where Joseph became a wealthy industrialist. He formed one of the first ironworks in a city that later became known for iron and steel production. He also established a furnace and foundry where many of the cannons used in the War of 1812 were cast. James struck out on his own around 1829 when he was twenty-four years old by moving to Westfield seeking new business ventures.

"Westfield was a small crossroads in the middle of wooded, hilly terrain but it did have access to Barcelona Harbor, a bustling port on Lake Erie. Although it was a total wilderness out here at that time, it did have a profitable, yet small, trading post. McClurg opened a trading store patterned after one his family had owned in Pittsburgh, and eventually he became a very successful merchant here," Horst told me.

James married Martha Eason, the daughter of the first sheriff in Chautauqua County, and they had four children. Their daughter, Catherine, married Dr. Edward J. Moore, a local resident, in 1851. Upon Catherine's death at the age of eighty-nine in 1909, their only son, Dr. William Moore, resided in the home until his death in 1938. He had no children and was the last resident of the home. The mansion was donated to the village of Westfield upon his death. It has been maintained as a museum by the Chautauqua County Historical Society since 1950.

The grounds of the McClurg home are now Moore Park. This park, with the imposing home toward the back, is the centerpiece for community activity in downtown Westfield.

Author's Notes

McClurg Mansion, the oldest brick home in Chautauqua County, is a cornerstone of life in downtown Westfield. Its stately presence watches over all sorts of community events. On the day I toured the mansion the grounds were filled with local sellers accommodating a large farmer's market crowd. The main street in front of the house is New York Route 20, which was once the main pre-Thruway east/west route in New York State.

Few of the homes I visited for this book have as many quality period items as this one does. Thanks to the design sensibilities and historical knowledge of McClurg curator John Paul Wolfe, each room is displayed as if a movie set director had staged it. Copious personal items vie for the attention of visitors and the docents are expert and entertaining.

The house is massive. But the biggest surprise to me was the basement. This is no dark, dirt-floor cellar. The basement is dry and well-lit and has eight-foot-tall ceilings. And it covers the entire footprint of the house. The basement holds hundreds more items including everything from farm equipment to household utensils to ice harvesting machines and more. Several of the rooms in the cellar are set up as exhibit rooms, featuring local history as well as a display of arrowheads and Indian tools from the private collection of Orrie Heath, a well-known local collector. Some of the collection's arrowheads were carbon tested by the University of Buffalo, which showed them to be thousands of years old.

If this house were out in the open, say several miles from town, it would still be spectacular. But the fact that it is right in the middle of all the action makes it special. It gives this old home a feeling of youthfulness. Out front is a playful fountain with a statue of two children trying to stay dry from the jetting water. It is believed that originally McClurg installed a simple fountain shortly after building his home in the 1820s, making it one of the first jet stream fountains in western New York. On the corner, across the street, is a remarkable double bronze statue of President Abraham Lincoln and the little Westfield girl, Grace Bedell, who convinced him to grow his whiskers. Down the block is the tiny 1920s-era Westfield Main Street Diner, and next to the McClurg Mansion is the former headquarters of Welch's Grape Juice, which was formed here by Dr. Thomas Welch in 1897.

Like I said, the McClurg Mansion is right in the middle of all the action in Westfield!

Visit

McClurg Museum
Home of the Chautauqua Historical Society
15 East Main Street
Westfield, NY 14787
716-326-2977
Website: https://www.mcclurgmuseum.org/

For Further Reference: Crocker, Kathleen. *Westfield, N.Y.: Images of America*. Mount Pleasant, SC: Arcadia Publishing, 2006.

While Here: This area is one of Upstate New York's most prolific grape and wine regions. The Grape Discovery Center is the official visitor's center for the Lake Erie Concord Grape Belt. It is located at 8305 West Main Road, Westfield.

Tours: Tours are given all year, Tuesday through Saturday, 10:00 a.m. to 4:00 p.m.

Admission:
Adults: $5.00
Children: Free

5

Zim's House

Home of Eugene Zimmerman
Horseheads, Chemung County

At the time of the peak of his career, Eugene Zimmerman, known to all as "Zim," was one of the most famous illustrators and cartoonists in America.

"The height of Zim's career would be from 1883 on," Marcia Tinker told me. She is the vice president of the Horseheads Historical Society, a group that now oversees Zimmerman's former home and studio. "That is when he was hired by *Puck* magazine, the leading political cartoon and commentary magazine of its day. He originally lived in New York City during the early years of his career, but later moved to Horseheads, his wife's hometown. Zim and his father-in-law designed and built this elegant Queen Anne–style home for them to live in. They began work in 1888 and moved in in 1890."

The house is a tall, sturdy structure with graceful lines, many windows, a high peaked roof, and several sitting porches, both on the first and second levels. The house was designed and constructed using wood, brick, shingles, and roof gables. The interior feels light and open because of the use of wide pocket doors throughout the first floor. Inside there are three bedrooms upstairs, a dining room, a front parlor, and several other smaller rooms. The showpiece of the house is a two-story-tall "great room" that was meant to be the artist's working studio. He later used another room for work and the great room became a place for family gatherings and socializing.

This room is dazzling. The ceiling towers above the hardwood floors. In fact, a second-floor balcony was installed to give a dramatic

overview of the scene below. The great room's walls are cluttered with many unique and unusual artifacts gathered by Zim during the course of his travels. A large fireplace with ceramic tiles is the focus of the room. The walls are covered with a reproduction of the original hand-painted wallpaper. On the walls are Indian items, weapons of all sorts, a Civil War canteen, a Revolutionary War saber and musket, original oil paintings, and an assortment of other items including two stuffed birds—an owl and a heron.

"This great room is very interesting," Tinker said. "Despite all the 'manly' items in here, like the weapons, it also had touches of the Victorian era. One of them is the 'cozy corner.' Here you can see a small sitting area, with a fancy couch tucked up into the corner." This little corner sits in marked contrast to the feel of the rest of the room. Tinker pointed to the balcony overhead. "We believe that is where musicians would have played when the Zimmermans were hosting a party in the house."

Virtually every room in this home has artwork on the walls. Hundreds of pieces. It gives this beautiful private residence the feel of going through an art gallery. The large parlor has many pieces on the wall. "Zim produced over 40,000 illustrations during his lifetime. Many of them were for famous, national magazines. But he also liked to produce original artwork for local businesses and organizations in the Horseheads area. We have many samples of both throughout the house," Tinker said. A large painting on one wall of the parlor was done by James Montgomery Flagg, of the famous "I Want You" Uncle Sam recruitment poster.

"Although Zim was not a musician, he loved music and we have many references throughout in the house," I was told. In the parlor is a large Chase piano made in Norwalk, Ohio. On the music stand is an original piece of sheet music with artwork on the cover by Eugene Zimmerman. It shows a funny dog smoking a pipe. The song title was "The Growler." There is also a Victrola and gramophone in this parlor. "Here is one of the most unusual pieces we have in the house," Tinker said as we walked over to a crowded parlor wall where she pointed to a framed drawing. "This is a caricature of Zim himself and it was done, and signed, by his friend the great opera star Enrico Caruso."

The library is where Zim eventually settled in to do his artwork. "Everything is exactly the way it was on the day that Zim died, in this house no less, on March 26, 1935. His rolltop desk is still filled with personal items as well as his own inks, paints, and artist's tools. Next to his desk you can see a child's desk where he allowed his small daughter to work alongside of her father," Tinker related.

The back wall of the library is covered from end to end with Zim's personal collection of books. These include a complete set of a ninth edition of the *Encyclopedia Britannica*, a set of Mark Twain works, and several items from James Whitcomb Riley, whose poem inspired *Little Orphan Annie*. Zim was a friend of both Twain and Riley.

Other items on the wall of this working room include statues, more weapons including pistols and rifles, and an assortment of oddities. Over the doorway leading out of the room is a long harpoon.

The upstairs bedrooms also are filled with Zim's furniture and belongings. The master bedroom walls are lined with pen and ink drawings, along with the colorful oil painting posters he produced for local businesses. These are funny illustrations with humorous sayings on them. Some of the Horseheads businesses that were favored with these posters included banks, farms, auto supply companies, and even the village blacksmith. There is also a painting in this room of the battleship the USS *Maine*, done by Howard Chandler Christy.

The grounds of the house are meticulously groomed with lawn space and beautiful flower gardens.

The residence was willed to the Horseheads Historical Society by Zim's only child, Laura Zimmerman, in 1980.

This house is a treasure vault of history. The number of personal items of this once internationally famous artist is staggering. With so much to see, don't miss the floor space at the front entranceway. Inlaid into the floor are oak strips that read "ZIM."

Eugene Zimmerman was born in Basel, Switzerland, on May 26, 1862. He arrived in the United States at the age of seven. At sixteen he began an apprenticeship with an Elmira, New York, sign company. He was paid nine dollars a week. This is where he honed his craft for illustrations and caricatures. His original work gained national attention and he was hired by the popular *Puck* magazine, where he worked for over three years. That position led him to *Judge* magazine, and he stayed on their payroll for almost thirty years.

Zim, as he was known and how he signed his works, was an incisive observer of the political scene of the era and no person, no matter what the station, was safe from his scathing, yet always witty, drawings. His illustrations were featured on the cover of hundreds of magazines. Politically, he was a Republican but that did not save his friends Theodore Roosevelt, Calvin Coolidge, or William McKinley from his unrelenting eye and sharp pen.

In 1888, Zim and his wife, Mabel, decided to return to Horseheads, making it their permanent home. A relationship began with this small Southern Tier community that lasted until his death. He was very involved in local organizations and civic events. He continued to work periodically in New York City but hurried home to Horseheads when his work in Manhattan was through.

One block from Zim's home is a village park that he designed, Teal Park. As mentioned, Zimmerman was not a musician, but he enjoyed being in the company of them, and it was at Teal Park that his joy for music was fully manifested. He organized a community band, the "Zim Band," paid for their uniforms and instruments, and even constructed a band gazebo in the park from which they would perform. That gazebo is still in the park. It is unmistakably a Zim creation as it sports colorful, whimsical carvings of cartoonish animals playing horns and stringed instruments.

The family residence was placed on the National Register of Historic Places in 1983.

Eugene Zimmerman died of a heart attack following a short illness in 1935, while working in his upstairs studio at this house. He was seventy-two and is buried in Horseheads.

Cartoonist Eugene Zimmerman created this whimsical bandstand, including insects playing musical instruments, and donated it to the village of Horseheads. It is located in Teal Park near his home.

Author's Notes

Even though the artist was one of the most prolific illustrators of his time, with more than 40,000 known works credited to him, it is still surprising to find such a trove of his original art here in the house. His drawings are on the walls, in boxes, lined up on the floors, and stacked around the furniture. In the basement are thousands of original metal plates from which these cartoons were printed for *Puck, Judge,* and other periodicals.

I must confess that I was not familiar with Eugene Zimmerman or his work until I traveled to his home in Horseheads. After spending several hours researching and visiting his home I have no doubt that he was considered a giant by his peers. In fact, Thomas Edison invited Zim to come to the inventor's studio in Orange, New Jersey, to sketch for him. Edison filmed the artist at work, and it is said that that is the first time sketching was ever captured by a movie camera.

His work is funny and quite clever, and almost always has a bit of ironic social commentary to it. He could do serious work, but it is his humorous depictions of the high and mighty, as well as the average working man and woman, that will remain his greatest legacy.

Visit

Zim's House
601 Pine Street
Horseheads, NY 14845
607-739-3938
Facebook: https://www.facebook.com/pages/Zimmerman-House-Horseheads-New-York/113337332010099

For Further Reference: Zimmerman, Eugene. *Zim: The Autobiography of Eugene Zimmerman*. Selinsgrove, PA: Susquehanna University Press, 1988.

While Here: The town's name comes from the many bleached unearthed horses' skulls that littered the land after the Sullivan Campaign came through in a military operation in 1779. Honoring the memory of the thousands of pack horses that served in the military, today there is a life-sized bronze statue of a military horse in the center of the village.

Tours: Tours are given throughout the year. They are by appointment only. Call ahead for details and hours.

Admission: Free, but donations are appreciated.

6

Kent-Delord House Museum

Home of Judge Henry Delord
Plattsburgh, Clinton County

There are many outstanding old homes in the far northern city of Plattsburgh, and the Kent-Delord House is one of the best. The house, built in 1797, is often referred to as the oldest existing house in the city. It is a stately, Federal-style two-story white clapboard home with impressive 12-over-12 pane windows adorned with New England–style shutters. The windows offer a beautiful view over Cumberland Bay, and Lake Champlain in the distance. It has a one-story pedimented entranceway with an added-on greenhouse on the left side of the front.

The nine rooms in the house are filled with family heirlooms from the Henry and Elizabeth (Betsey) Delord family, who resided here from 1811 until 1913. In fact, all of the items on display throughout the large residence are personal items handed down from over a century of family ownership, including furnishings, accessories, furniture, artwork, War of 1812 and Civil War artifacts, dinnerware, clothing, and personal items including letters and documents.

One of the most impressive aspects of the house is the garden, which dates back almost to the original owners. The formal gardens (open to the public) on the west side of the house were designed by an Army engineer in 1812, Lt. René De Russy, who fashioned them in the image of a French garden. Seven years later, owner Henry Delord hand-drew plans for a larger front garden. He named this 1819 garden after his wife, Betsey, and their daughter, Frances.

There are many family portraits on the walls of the Kent-Delord mansion. They were painted by prominent local artists and are elegantly framed. These portraits act as a guide to the many family members who lived here, from the Delords to the Webbs to the Halls, for over one hundred years.

The residents of this important house entertained a military Who's Who of the time as well as prominent politicians including the president of the United States (James Monroe) along with ordinary visitors to the area. The house was known for its hospitality but in reality, it was the family that was responsible for that. The connections within the house run from James Fenimore Cooper to the Marquis de Lafayette to Robert Fulton and Mathew Brady.

Henry Delord was thirty-five years old when he married fifteen-year-old Elizabeth (Betsey) Ketchum in 1799. Delord was born in France and made his way to America via the French West Indies. In 1810, he bought a small cottage and three acres of land from a prominent lawyer, Judge James Kent. Kent would later become the first chancellor of the state of

New York. In 1811, Delord expanded the small home into the configuration we now see as the Kent-Delord Mansion. Early in the twentieth century, when the house became a museum, Kent's name was more well-known and considered a bigger attraction for the budding museum.

During the War of 1812, Delord and business partner William Bailey agreed to let soldiers stationed in Plattsburgh purchase food and other necessities from their Red Store on credit, with a guarantee that when the government paid the soldiers, they would make good on the IOUs. After the 1814 Battle of Plattsburgh, most of the soldiers were transferred and the IOUs went unpaid, leading to Delord's bankruptcy. He died in 1825 at the age of sixty-one.

His daughter, Frances Henrietta Delord, married Henry Livingston Webb in the front parlor of the house in 1832. Her imported French silk lace wedding dress cost nearly fifty dollars, which was an exorbitant amount for a piece of clothing in those days. The wedding dress is still at the museum. Frances gave birth to a daughter, Fanny, but never recovered from complications of the birth. Frances Webb died on March 15, 1834, at the age of twenty.

Betsey Delord, Henry's widow, remarried in 1829 to William Swetland and continued to live in the mansion until her death in 1870.

Henry Delord's great-granddaughter, Fannie Delord Webb, married Frank Bloodgood Hall on May 14, 1856. Frank was a chaplain of the Sixteenth New York State Regiment during the Civil War and was awarded the Medal of Honor for bravery at the Battle of Salem Heights.

Frank and Fannie Hall became well-known for their social work in the community. Fannie started the local Woman's Christian Temperance Union and remained active in the fight for temperance until her death. She also became a self-taught medical practitioner, focusing on treating the poor. She invented and patented a salve called Fanoline that was produced in an addition built on to the back of the mansion. Today, visitors can still see her medicines, equipment, medical bag used for house calls, scales, and unusual electrical stimulators in this room.

She was the last member of the original family to live in the mansion. She and Frank had no children. Fannie died at the mansion on October 4, 1913, and willed her possessions for use as a museum and the house for use as a hospital. For the next decade, Fannie's loyal housekeeper, Catherine Dowling, maintained the property. William H. Miner, a millionaire inventor from the Plattsburgh area, bought the home in 1924. After renovations the house/museum was opened to the public.

A magnificent towering granite monument to the discoverer of Lake Champlain, Frenchman Samuel de Champlain, is across the street from the Kent-Delord Mansion.

Author's Notes

The house is situated on one of the most attractive lots of any house in this book. Directly across the street from the residence is a short path down to where the Saranac River meets Cumberland Bay. Farther out, the bay joins Lake Champlain. Lording over the scene is the impressive Champlain Monument. This lofty granite and bronze sculpture, erected in 1912, pays tribute to French explorer Samuel de Champlain. The monument features a larger-than-life statue of the explorer, as well as an image of a Native American and some canoes. Steps lead down from the monument to the path to the waterfront.

The mansion keeps a busy schedule of public events all year long.

The house is listed on the National Register of Historic Places.

Visit

The Kent Delord House Museum
17 Cumberland Avenue
Plattsburgh, NY 12901
518-561-1035
Website: http://www.kentdelordhouse.org

For Further Reference: Pratt, Anastasia. *Plattsburgh through Time.* America through Time (series). Mount Pleasant, SC: Arcadia Publishing, 2015.

While Here: Plattsburgh is on the western side of Lake Champlain. The city has constructed an unusually large public beach, with white sand, swimming areas, concessions, and amenities for the enjoyment of visitors and citizens alike. It is really unlike any other beach you will find in this northern region of the state, and it isn't hard to imagine that you are at a beach on the Atlantic shore!

Tours: June 4 through October 7: Tuesday to Saturday, 11:00 a.m. to 3:00 p.m. Other times are available by appointment.

Admission:
Adults: $5.00
Students 18 and under: $3.00
Canadian money is accepted.

7

The 1890 House

Home of Chester F. Wickwire
Cortland, Cortland County

Throughout Upstate New York, you can drive into a village or a city and with very little deep research come up with a name of a family that stood out, both financially and authoritatively, as one of that community's great benefactors. Look to the Coopers or the Clarks of Cooperstown for example. Or the Munson and Williams families of Utica. Or the Eastmans of Rochester. All towering names with storied connections to their hometowns.

Let's add Chester F. Wickwire to that list.

"Mr. Wickwire took over his father's hardware store in McGraw, New York, and became known as a merchant who would barter for the purchase and sale of goods," said Jarrett Zeman, the assistant director and curator of the house. "One day a customer named Rowland Hall came into the store and wanted to trade a carpet loom for a plant stand Wickwire had for sale. Wickwire had no real interest in the contraption, but he was a tinkerer. He fashioned a new machine, based on the loom, which would spin out thin wire instead of thread. It was a great success."

The massive Chateauesque Wickwire residence was completed in 1889. It is a great stone structure consisting of three stories and a cupola. The large boulders were hauled onto the property and were cut to specifications in the back carriage house. The home originally contained five bedrooms, two bathrooms, a kitchen, and a myriad of other rooms including sun rooms, parlors, and servants' quarters. "I like to call it the Clue Mansion," the curator told me. "All the major rooms are here, right down to the secret passages. It's like the board game, only without the murder."

Louis Comfort Tiffany himself advised Wickwire on the design of this house. The exterior of the castle-like residence is the mirror image of a famous home in New York City. Wickwire was visiting New York City once and he saw the mansion owned by James Bailey, of Barnum and Bailey Circus fame. He was so struck by the magnificence of Bailey's home that he walked right up the stairs to the home and called on Bailey. He told the circus mogul he wanted to build a mansion that looked identical to the New York City house. Bailey apparently had no problem with that and that replica is now here in Cortland. (Note: if you want to compare exteriors, the Bailey mansion is still standing in New York City at 10 St. Nicholas Place in Harlem.)

The 1890 House is chock-full of all the gussied-up fancywork you would imagine in a Victorian mansion of this size. The woodwork is among the best I have ever seen. Several banisters, balconies, and pieces of homemade furniture feature carved lion heads, the Wickwire family insignia. There are secret passageways, servant's areas, turret rooms where Mrs. Wickwire would sit and write to her far-flung family, a master bedroom that contains Chester's own bed and clothes, children's areas, a breathtaking staircase, elaborately designed rugs, and magnificent stained-glass windows. "Each room on the first floor is dressed to impress. It is the public part of the house where the Wickwires displayed their wealth, taste and refinement to their guests," Zeman said.

The mansion is very thoughtfully designed so that upon entering for the first time a visitor would be bowled over by the interior. The elite of Cortland society would come calling here for Mrs. Wickwire, usually getting in only as far as the front hallway where they were politely asked to leave just a calling card in a silver bowl. Ardell Wickwire would then take the cards to her parlor, review them, and make social invitation decisions.

The library features elaborate glass pocket doors. The formal dining room displays a full solid silver tea set that was given to Chester by his employees. The children's bedrooms are scattered with century-old toy trains and musical instruments. The second-floor hallway's wallpaper is called Lincrusta. It is the same wallpaper that could be found on the walls of the first-class state room on the *Titanic*. The upstairs bathroom, added nearly a century ago, features an octopus-like ribcage shower. There are four metal pipes that surround the shower stall. Each pipe has a series of smaller pipes from which the water would spray out. "This guaranteed that every inch of your body would get clean. And I do mean every inch," the curator said with a smile as he pointed to the bidet in the center of the shower floor.

This splendid home is surrounded by opulent mansions up and down the city block. This is where the money was. The power. The Wickwire home, known as the 1890 Mansion, is one of the most incredibly extravagant private residences I have seen in Central New York.

Chester Wickwire is referred to as the "Innovator" by the staff at the 1890 House. "He was an inveterate inventor, merchandiser, employer, and builder. I call him the 'Steve Jobs of Cortland,'" Zeman told me. "At one time twenty-five percent of Cortland's population worked in the Wickwire Brothers wire weaving company. They produced horse muzzles, wire popcorn poppers, coal sifters, wire nails, barbed wire for farms and ranches, dish covers to keep bugs away from food, and really almost anything. He had an eye for what folks who lived in the country needed and wanted, and he provided it for them. When he died in 1910, his estate was valued at $1,600,000."

While Chester is known as the "Innovator," the other main characters in this family saga also carry monikers given to them by today's caretakers of their legacy. His wife, Ardell, was the "Boss" for, despite all of her husband's money and influence, this truly was Ardell's house and she ran it with precision and efficiency. They had three children: Raymond is referred to as the "Sickly Child." He died at the age of five of scarlet fever. Charles is the "Romantic." They call him that because there is a great love story behind him: He literally fell in love with the girl next door (Mabel Fitzgerald) and married her. Mabel Fitzgerald's family rivaled, and perhaps even exceeded, the Wickwire family in wealth and prestige. They owned the Cortland Wagon Company, then the largest company in Cortland (the Fitzgerald mansion, now privately owned, is still located next to the 1890 House). Young Frederick is the "Renovator," whose renovations to the house over the years can still be seen today. Long after Chester and Ardell were gone the second family moved in. A now much older Frederick (the "Renovator") was married to Marion, known as the "Poet." "So you see, it gets a bit confusing but these nicknames help sort it all out. We also had Margaret Stack, the Irish cook who lived upstairs in the back of the house. We refer to her as the 'Glue' because she really kept this busy house together," he said.

This splendid home was a real treat for me to explore. I had been in Cortland numerous times, and in fact had family who lived there over the years. But I'd never found this treasure before, and it is a pure delight. The house reminded me of a movie set, perhaps to be used in a 1930s-era Errol Flynn swashbuckler or maybe even a Sherlock Holmes mystery. It is simply dripping with every imaginable architectural and design nuance available in its day.

One of my favorite rooms was the Fernery/Sun Parlor. This spacious, sun-filled room was a family favorite. Its subtle eastern Orient design is a dramatic departure from the Old English castle feel to the rest of the house. The room has tile flooring and a majestic stained-glass ceiling. The lighting is provided by an elaborate chandelier adorned with little naked cherubs. (These cherubs pop up throughout the house.) One end of the room has the feel of a Japanese temple. A statue of a woman is centered against the rear wall. She actually is a fountain with water flowing to a pool beneath her. On either side of her stand two seven-foot-tall metal cranes.

The cranes were imported from Japan. "They are very popular with visitors. In fact, recently we held a social media contest to 'Name the Cranes' and had a tremendous response on our Facebook page. And the result? The cranes are now referred to as Olive and Felix."

By the way, if you are playing along, this room would be the conservatory in the board game Clue.

My favorite feature of this house in the inglenook. *Ingle* was an Old English phrase for fireplace. This "fire nook" is a small sitting room nestled under the giant, curving staircase. Here, the Wickwires could sit on facing wooden benches, in front of a small fire, and enjoy a good book or perhaps a quiet conversation. Overhead is a massive, wooden arch that acts as a separator between the main rooms of the house and this private little warren. The arch is centered with the carving of a lion's head. It is quite elegant and is the first thing a visitor would see when entering the home.

Another interesting vignette told here is the story of Margaret Stack, an Irish cook who worked in the house from 1904 to 1911. Visitors learn about the daily lives of servants and see the contrast between the Wickwires' opulence and the long hours servants worked to sustain their benefactor's lavish lifestyle. Margaret was part of a vibrant Irish community, who socialized together at dances, dinners, and masses.

Also, on the second floor, visitors discover the factory workers who made Chester his fortune. German, Irish, and Russian immigrants made wire products in dangerous conditions—some even lost their fingers. Despite these risks, immigrants came to Cortland hoping to achieve the American dream, and the museum also discusses this and the role of immigrants in today's society through exhibits and presentations.

Visit

The 1890 House
37 Tompkins Street
Cortland, NY 13045

Landmark: This house is located two blocks from Cortland's busy downtown district.
607-756-7551
Website: http://the1890house.org/

For Further Reference: Kane, Mary Anne. *Cortland, New York.* Images of America (series). Mount Pleasant, SC: Arcadia Publishing, 2010.

While Here: One of Upstate New York's newest museums has opened in Cortland. The CNY Living History Museum looks at Cortland's long history as a major central New York manufacturing town. It encompasses three individual museums in one building. It is located at 4386 US Route 11, Cortland.

Tours: Guided tours are given at 12:30 p.m. and 2:30 p.m. daily.

Admission:
Adults: $8.00
Seniors: $5.00
Students and military: $5.00
Children under 10: Free

8

Woodchuck Lodge

Home of John Burroughs
Roxbury, Delaware County

There is something almost lyrical about this small, unadorned cabin located high atop Clump Mountain on Hardscrabble Road in the foothills of the Catskill Mountains. If ever there was a residence that perfectly matched the person who lived in it, this is the place.

This rustic home was built in 1863 by Curtis Burroughs, John Burroughs's brother. At the time, Curtis was running the family farm on Clump Mountain in rural Roxbury. "It's just a cabin. Not much, really," Bill Birns said. He is the president of the board of trustees of Woodchuck Lodge. "It was originally used as a place for the hired hands at the Burroughs farm to stay. The siding is weathered clapboard, with a wide front porch and just five small rooms on the main floor. We give tours of the main floor, as it is a direct reflection of the time that John Burroughs lived here late in his life. The upstairs is not open to the public."

The exterior of the house is completely unspectacular. This was a house that stoically served its purpose. "Burroughs slept almost every night on his front porch. He had his bed out here, a bed that was actually too long to fit on the porch without blocking the front door from opening out. They reworked the door so that it would open in, so as not to interfere with his sleeping arrangement," Birns told me as he showed me the original door, which still swings inward. "All of the shutters have been replaced to the original specifications of the original ones. The porch railings, made out of branches from trees on the property, are original. This porch was the center of life for the writer. He slept out here, wrote

out here, and even ate out here. Its purpose would have been very similar to a modern deck."

Inside the small home, the visitor gains a real sense of the man. Burroughs, certainly the most famous conservationist of his day, lived a spartan life with no unnecessary enhancements to his home. In the living room there is a comfortable rocking chair, also constructed out of tree branches, that was made by Burroughs. Paintings on the wall reflect the glorious outdoor views from the porch overlooking hills and mountains. A Franklin wood stove, a writer's table, a cabinet made with birch branches by Burroughs, and a smattering of personal items are on display in this room. Burroughs would take a lunch basket with him to the hill behind the cabin every day to write. The lunch basket still sits by the door as if waiting for the writer to take it out for a stroll.

"Almost everything Burroughs did in this house was in this room. The left side of the house, not so much," Birns said as we walked into the far side of the small house. "This is what they called a parlor. It is surprising to all of us here that Burroughs, a simple man, would even have had a parlor in his house. But it was almost a cultural commandment of the day to have a formal fancy room in your home for receiving guests and entertaining," I was told. The furniture in this room is decidedly more upscale than in the living room. There is a fussy Victorian couch, a leather chair and ottoman adorned with cow horns, and a large spinning wheel that belonged to his mother.

Other rooms available to the public include a back room filled with pottery, dishes, farm tools, milk cans, and such. "It was a country trait to keep all of these like items in a single room. There is a kitchen which has many vintage household items on display, items owned by the writer. This room is preserved as if John Burroughs just left it. There is a Hoosier cabinet with his personal items in it, and one of the earliest of linoleum floors covering the wood planks. You can see where the flooring is worn where Burroughs walked over it for several years. And this is kind of interesting too, Chuck," he told me as we walked to an old Franklin stove. He opened the cast-iron door. "See, ashes still in the bin. Probably from a fire lit by the great John Burroughs himself."

One room near the front is set aside as the Museum Room. Many of Burroughs's family photos, awards, archival documents, and personal items, such as his original baby cradle, are in this room. One prominently displayed certificate is an award for the Burroughs's family farm winning a "Best Butter Award" at the World's Columbian Exposition.

A bathroom still has the original commode, sink, and tub. The bathroom walls are wainscoted. "We believe that if this wasn't the first indoor bathroom in Roxbury, it certainly was one of the first," I was told.

In the back room you can see his original cot. This was his bed of choice. It is the same cot that was too large to accommodate the front door of the porch. There is a photo hanging on the wall that shows Burroughs resting on this cot on the porch.

"Although he came from nothing, John Burroughs became one of the most famous men in America," said Birns. "He is considered to be the father of American conservation and a founder of the environmental movement, and his writings were among the most popular of his day. There is a large rock out back of the cabin upon which Burroughs, as a child, would view the ever-changing panorama of his beloved Catskill Mountains. He called it Boyhood Rock and it was from here that his inspiration and love for nature's surroundings began and was nurtured. As his fame grew Burroughs bought a property in the Hudson Valley, near Poughkeepsie, as a permanent residence. It is called Slabsides and is still open to the public. Eventually this fame became an impediment to his privacy there (especially from the attention he received 'from those Vassar girls') as admirers and fans constantly were seeking him out for advice and counsel. He sought refuge from this growing spotlight by returning back to the mountains from which he came. This small house, used by farm workers at his family home, was leased to Burroughs by his brother."

This is an autobiographical house. It is unvarnished and unsophisticated, like its owner. Burroughs, a tall thin man who regularly dressed in old worn clothes and a wide-brimmed straw hat, was a familiar sight hiking the hills and paths of this mountain, his long white beard and hair making him unmistakable to neighbors and passersby alike.

But Burroughs was no country bumpkin. "He was at the apogee of his fame around 1890," Birns said. "By then he was turning out countless magazine articles, books, essays, school textbooks, and more. He was also, at this time, quite possibly the most photographed man in America. Also rising on the national landscape were the great titans of industry who were gaining great fame and enormous wealth from their own ingenuity. Great names like Harvey Firestone, Thomas Edison, and Henry Ford. These business legends, seemingly by now having it all, sought out the rural writer that they had become enamored with. In Burroughs these giants saw a glimpse of their own past, of a time when life was simpler. They saw in this plain man an aura of nostalgia. They yearned to escape their trappings of importance and wealth and actually came to Clump Mountain to visit, many times, with John Burroughs. There were no CEOs in those days. These guys were master inventors, creators on a very large scale. Henry Ford alone held over 1,000 patents. Burroughs became great friends with all of them. They visited here, and he visited and traveled with them.

"Despite the fact that he was hobnobbing with some of the most important men in America, John Burroughs never stopped being just a simple mountain guy from rural Delaware County. To me he is the presiding spirit over the entire Catskill Mountain region. He gave us the language of the people up here. He was a good neighbor, too. One time a man who had lost his team of horses came to this house and asked for $800 to buy a new one. Burroughs listened intently to his neighbor's woeful tale. After a while he simply turned his head and called out to Clara Barrus, his biographer who was working in the house, 'Clara, draw up a draft for $800 for this good man.'

"One of my favorite John Burroughs quotes, spoken at the height of his notoriety, is: 'My soul is redolent with the breath of cows.' A true mountain man to the very end."

Author's Notes

This small house in the Catskills is a poignant souvenir of the life of a very famous man. Despite his worldwide fame, the building reflects the plain, no-nonsense lifestyle of its owner. The furniture is simple and in many cases homemade. The walls are bare save for a few paintings of the beauty outside his front door. The tools are basic, the family belongings are practical. They used everything, saved everything, and wasted nothing here.

Perhaps the most telling item of the house for me is a chair. A worn chair made of branches. The chair's covering tells a remarkable story.

"Once, after Henry Ford visited the house, it was discovered that he had left behind his jacket," Birns told me. "Since there was no way to get it back to him Burroughs simply fashioned the jacket into a chair slipcover." And there it is, a century later, in the front room of this cabin up on Clump Mountain. Billionaire Henry Ford's jacket, buttons and all, stuffed with padding and covering an old rocking chair!

Just a few yards up from Woodchuck Lodge is Memorial Field. No visit would be complete without walking up there. There are picnic tables and signage about the author/conservationist plus walking paths that lead to Boyhood Rock, the place where it all started. This is also Burroughs's final resting place.

Visit

Woodchuck Lodge
1633 Burroughs Memorial Road
Roxbury, NY 12474
Website: http://jbwoodchucklodge.org/

For Further Reference: Renehan, Edward. *John Burroughs: An American Naturalist*. Delmar, NY: Black Dome Press, 1998.

While Here: Infamous Wall Street financier Jay Gould was also from Roxbury. A church, erected by his children in his memory, on Main Street is well worth a visit. There are several stunning original Louis Comfort Tiffany windows within. The Jay Gould Memorial Reformed Church is located at 53837 NY Route 30, Roxbury.

Tours: Free, guided tours of Woodchuck Lodge are offered the first weekend of the month, May to October, Saturday and Sunday, 11 a.m. to 3 p.m.

Admission: Free

9

Nash House Museum

Home of Rev. J. Edward Nash Sr.
Buffalo, Erie County

The area around the Nash residence was once the beating heart of the Buffalo African American community. The neighborhood was busy with family homes, retail businesses, professional offices, schools, manufacturing, and social venues.

"I know it is hard to believe, but this area was popping," George Arthur exclaimed. He is the treasurer of the Michigan Street Preservation Corporation. From the front porch he swept his arms out across the neighborhood. "Houses were lined right up one after another all the way down the block. They were big houses, usually two-family dwellings with the owner living on one floor and a renter on the other. But they had no driveways back then, around 1900 or so. No garages either. They used horse and buggies and had a separate entranceway on the side where the wagon would pull up and let the riders out. The horses were kept elsewhere. Down the street was a large stable where the city constables kept their police horses and across the street was the New York Sixty-Fifth Regimental Armory.

"There were shops of all kinds and it was a lively, busy, and exciting time. Everybody got along famously. Blacks, whites, and all ethnicities. There were at least seven Jewish synagogues right around here. In fact, the famous songwriter Harold Arlen, then known as Hyman Arluck, lived three blocks away. His father was a cantor at a major synagogue nearby on Pine Street. This was the first integrated neighborhood in Buffalo. We also had the first Chinatown and many businesses were owned by European immigrants. But this was always the heart of the African American

community. Everybody got along so well. It was a role model for the nation," Arthur told me.

Oh, how things have changed.

Today, Rev. J. Edward Nash's home is the only residence left standing on the block. Wide open green swaths mark the areas where the rows of houses once stood. At the end of the block, a brick building appears to be abandoned and falling in on itself. Across the street is the former armory, now used as a city property for housing vehicles, and it is in serious disrepair. Many of the windows have been broken out. Very little traffic makes it way up and down the street.

"We are hoping the revival of the Nash House as a museum will be the beginning of a new life for the street and the neighborhood as a whole," Arthur said. "We truly believe it to be so."

Rev. J. Edward Nash Sr. was a leading citizen of Buffalo. He ministered at the Michigan Avenue Baptist Church from 1892 to 1953. The red brick church, still used as a house of worship, is located behind the house. Nash was a leader in the Civil Rights movement both in the city and nationally. Many said that he was the most important black man in Buffalo and was so influential that he had direct access to several different mayors. The street in front of the house was once Potter Street but was changed to Nash Street to honor the minister in 1953.

The house is an unassuming, tall Queen Anne–style residence. A long porch spreads across the front. It is three stories tall including a large attic on top. The exterior reveals intricate woodwork designs around the porch, a large bay window on the second floor, and a four-window configuration at the attic peak. Like the other neighborhood homes, this was a two-family dwelling with Rev. Nash and his family living on the second floor and renters living below.

Despite the rather plain and ordinary exterior of the residence, there is nothing ordinary about what you will find inside.

"After Rev. Nash died in 1957, his widow, Frances Jackson Nash, let the lease of the renters below expire and she moved downstairs where she lived until 1985 when she entered a nursing home," Arthur began. "Imagine this. One day Mrs. Nash simply locked the door to the upstairs apartment—all of the belongings still inside—and moved downstairs for the last twenty-six years of her life. When she passed in 1987, Nash's son allowed the pastor of the Michigan Street church to live downstairs for free so as to watch and protect the property. In 1999, the newly formed Michigan Street Preservation Corporation bought it and moved in for their offices. To everybody's absolute shock, when they first opened the upstairs apartment they found it filled with hundreds of Nash's personal items, each room set up exactly as it was when she locked it up decades before. It was a museum just waiting to be found," he said.

The main floor of the Nash house today is a small visitor's center, gift shop, and gathering place for public events such as public speakers and meetings. There are many one-of-a-kind pieces of Buffalo ephemera in display cases. "The Nashes had one son, Jesse, born in 1926, and we have many of his items from when he was a small child," Arthur said. In this room is a small toy ride-upon Spirit of St. Louis airplane that belonged to the boy. "Look here. We even have Jesse's high chair. I mean who saves a high chair? That thing is ninety-two years old," laughed Arthur.

The big reveal happens once you go up the back stairs to the Nash's residence. It is a jaw-dropper for sure.

"Every single item you see in this apartment belonged to the family," Arthur announced as we began to go from room to room. The bathroom still has bottles of shampoo, Dr. Lyons foot powder, hairbrushes, bars of soap, the family toothbrushes and linens, all now seventy-five years old and in pristine condition. The kitchen is set up as if dinner is about to be served. There is a coal and gas stove, the family plates and silverware are all lined up on a shelf, and a Hoosier cabinet with flour and sugar bins sits ready for the family baking needs.

A small room off the kitchen is Mrs. Nash's sewing room. "You can see here that there is a sewing machine, all the accessories she needed, reels of fabric, and a storage closet. The walls are lined with elaborate, handmade hats. Being a minister's wife, Mrs. Nash would never go to a Sunday service with the same hat on, as it would have been shocking to her friends and parishioners. So she made a new hat every week and made them right in this little room," I was told.

Jesse's bedroom contains a variety of musical instruments. He was a talented horn player and was an influential member of the African American music scene. Mrs. Nash's bedroom contains her personal belongings and a small suitcase with the monogram "F. J. N." on it.

Rev. Nash slept in a separate bedroom as he had great difficulty sleeping. His bed is cluttered with pillows that he positioned to help him rest better. Hanging on the wall is his original black silk minister's robe.

"When Jesse graduated from college, he wore his father's ministerial robe when he accepted his diploma," my guide said. It should be noted that Jesse Nash went on to become an esteemed professor at Canisius College in Buffalo, and a guest lecturer at such highly regarded schools as Cornell, Yale, and Harvard universities. He passed away in 2016 at the age of ninety.

The last room of the upstairs residence is Rev. Nash's office. All of the furniture is original, the walls are lined with his books, and the furniture is positioned exactly as it was when it was last used. This is the office where Nash would welcome his friends and business associates such as

Rev. Adam Clayton Powell Sr. of the Harlem Abyssinian Baptist Church. A life-like mannequin of Rev. Nash, dressed in his original suit, shirt, and tie, and wearing his original spectacles, appears to be hard at work writing correspondence. The visual is quite startling and emotional.

"When we first opened this house up to the public, we brought Jesse and his family in the night before for a preview. When he entered this room and saw his father working at his desk he broke down and cried," Arthur said.

From the plain exterior to the amazing upstairs apartment, this is a home unique among all of the others in this book. The second floor here has been called one of the most significant collections of African American home furnishings from the pre–World War II era as well as a "virtual museum."

Rev. Nash and his wife purchased this home in 1925. Nash was the minister of the Michigan Avenue Baptist Church located behind the residence. Nash was a highly regarded Buffalonian and he dedicated his life to the advancement of the black community in his city. He hosted many famous African Americans in his home and at his church. He is credited with indelibly changing the course of the twentieth-century Civil Rights movement both nationally and locally. Papers found in his upstairs office revealed that Rev. Nash was at the center of many historic African American events in the Buffalo area that were conceptualized and executed right from this house.

Author's Notes

This unassuming home, located on a small side street just outside of the Buffalo business district, is one of the true "hidden gems" in this book.

One thing I really enjoyed was the outside property surrounding the house. There is a large lot next to the home (where other homes stood a long time ago) that has now been dubbed the Michigan Avenue Heritage Corridor (Michigan Avenue runs parallel to Nash Street behind the house). Here you can meander along a winding brick pathway that leads directly to the church where Rev. Nash ministered for over six decades. Along this path are narrative plaques with archival photographs, explaining the history of the area and some of the remarkable African Americans who lived here or who came through here. These include Mary Burnett Talbert, an activist and suffragette who some Buffalo historians have called the most famous colored woman in the United States at the time, and William Wells Brown, America's first published African American playwright.

The Michigan Avenue Baptist Church played host to both Frederick Douglass and Booker T. Washington and was a stop along the Underground Railroad.

Visit

The Nash House Museum
36 Nash Street
Buffalo, NY 14204
716-856-4490
Website: http://www.nashhousemuseum.org

For Further Reference: A substantial library of Rev. Nash's personal papers are archived at the Department of History at the E. H. Butler Library, SUNY Buffalo State (716-878-6300).

While Here: Buffalo is one of New York's greatest cities. I suggest the newcomer take a guided tour of the city as a first step, then have a lunch of hot chicken wings at the Anchor Bar (they invented them), and then spend the afternoon at the wonderful Albright-Knox Art Gallery.

Tours:
Thursday: 11:30 a.m. to 4:00 p.m.
Saturday: 11:30 a.m. to 4:00 p.m.

Other days, group tours and special arrangements can be made by calling the Nash House.

Admission: $10.00 (special group rates are available)

10

Hull Family Home and Farmstead

Oldest Existing Stone House in Erie County
Lancaster, Erie County

Like so many other older, historic homes in this book, the origins of this house remain a blank slate. "Unfortunately, we do not have any primary sources or documents surrounding the founding of Hull House, but we believe it was built around 1815," Gary Costello told me. He is the president of the Hull House Foundation.

The house today is rather unspectacular in comparison to many of the other homes featured in this book. Still, it would have been considered a substantial home on the western frontier of New York back in the early 1800s. "It is a large house consisting of nine rooms and a full cellar and attic. It was a typical structure of the day, one suitable for a large family and for being the center of a working farm. Warren Hull was in his fifties when he built the house, and he and Polly had a family numbering twelve children. In fact, when he bought the property in 1804, Polly was pregnant with their tenth child. That, of course, was also not uncommon at a time when a man's children were a main source of labor on a farm. The Hull farm covered almost 340 acres and they grew mostly grains—wheat and barley. It was a difficult life in this then-remote area. Remember that at the time Buffalo, located about fifteen miles to our west, only had about fifty or sixty buildings in it and only a few hundred residents," Costello said.

Although there are no possessions of the original Hull family in the house, it is a house whose plain walls and bare floors reveal a long and storied family timeline. "We interpret this house in the earliest years of the family, from about 1815 to 1825. It is of an early Federal-style design

and features double-hung windows, oval moldings, and oval windows in the attic. The Federal style was very popular at the time, signifying a break from previous designs and manifesting the feeling of our country's newfound independence. Actually, this would have been a typical upper middle class dwelling for the time," Costello said.

A large entrance hall greets the visitor, and the first room on the right was known as a common room. "We believe that this room was utilized as a place for travelers to stop and rest and perhaps even take a meal as they journeyed through this unpopulated area." There is a large fireplace with a limestone hearth. There was a side door, separate from the main entrance, which would have been used for guests to enter to dine or to stay over. It is possible that the great land developer Joseph Ellicott, agent for the Holland Land Company, visited this room while attending to his business. Off this room is a small pantry, brightened by a large 12-over-12 pane glass window. The room is stocked with traditional pantry items of the day such as chinaware, candlesticks, woven baskets, pewter tankards, and more.

In the room interpreted as Warren Hull's office we can see a very old writing desk from the early 1800s. "This item was donated to us and couldn't be a better fit for the home," Costello said. Again, this room is full of antique items appropriate for the intended use as an office.

A sitting room is appointed with period furniture and replicated 1815 newspapers.

The front parlor is the last room on the first floor. The furniture is not big but is comfortable. The room, which is located in the front of the house, features two large, tall windows. "Notice how deep the windowsills are," Costello said. "We find it rather curious, actually. We cannot find any signs of hangers or shutters or curtain appliances for these windows. Just no evidence at all. So, this room would have been open to the outside at all times. Curious. But maybe they just liked a lot of light," he said with a smile.

As we climb to the second floor, we notice a stunning seven-foot-tall grandfather clock on the landing. "This clock was made by local craftsmen and was recently donated to our foundation. It is dedicated to Iris Drzewiecki. She was a school librarian who really was key to the saving of Hull House. She founded the Hull Restoration Committee and really got the ball rolling for all that you see here today. She passed away recently, and the clock was given to us in her memory by her husband," said Costello.

The second floor contains a boy's bedchamber, girl's bedchamber, a master bedchamber, and a "mystery room." Costello said, "As I mentioned, we really had no original plans for the house or knowledge how these rooms were used. We use this room to exhibit a weaving display. We have wool, a large antique loom, and other examples of what one of the responsibilities of this farm would have been like. But, truly, it really is a mystery room to us."

The children's bedchambers have vintage toys and games on display and each bedroom includes a rope bed like those used at the time. "Since the Hulls had twelve children, nine of them girls, the girl's room is the largest in the house. The room stretches from the front to the back of the house and has three large rope beds in it," Costello told me.

There is a large set of Palladian windows casting light throughout the second-floor hallway. There is also a curious "shoe in a box" on display.

"Yes, it is quite unusual. It is a lady's Victorian shoe we found tucked away high in the rafter of the attic ceiling. Folklore tells us this was done to bring good luck? We don't know who put it there many, many years ago," Costello said.

The third-floor attic is quite a revelation. "Actually, this is my favorite room of the house. As you can see it is rough and in a primitive state. This is about as original as it gets at Hull House. The walls are still of the unplastered stone facing dating back to 1815. Large oval windows allow sunlight into the dark attic space. It is almost as if the original owners just blew out a lamp, closed the doors, and went downstairs. The attic covers the entire length and width of the house and is structurally intact. It is quite a remarkable room."

A steep staircase with a low overhang takes the visitor to the cellar kitchen. The room is surprisingly large with an eight-foot ceiling. There is a large cooking hearth with a long mantel and a brick baking oven. A scullery and a larder are off the kitchen, two small rooms where much of the food production took place in the house.

The entire home is kept warm through radiant heat, which was installed below the floorboards during restoration.

"We appreciate the story of Warren Hull and his family here in the early wilderness. He was not a celebrity, not a general. He was a typical Revolutionary War soldier who served, did his duty for his country, and continued on with his life. He purchased the property from the Holland Land Office. He was not a personality. People are surprised when they hear about the size of the Hull family, living in a house this size. We do know that all fourteen Hulls did not live here at once, with the older children eventually moving on, but it still would have been a busy, productive home and farm. Polly Hull died in 1834, and her husband died four years later. Warren, Polly, and at least three of their children are buried in the small family burying ground located a few hundred yards behind the house," Costello said.

After the Hulls passed away, five or six other owners took possession of the house down through the decades, including two of their daughters. It was acquired by the Landmark Society of the Niagara Frontier in 1992. What was acquired at that time consisted of less than one acre, but subsequent purchases have expanded the holdings to twenty-eight acres. "The Hull House Foundation was formed in 2006 to save the house for future generations. The residence was in very rough condition when we got it but fortunately it was structurally intact. While the restoration of the inside is mostly complete, there is still much work to be done outside. Although they are no longer in existence, we know there were other buildings on the property. We hope to investigate their locations and reconstruct the outbuildings, which include a smokehouse, root cellar, threshing barn and a privy," Costello explained.

I asked Costello how it felt to be a part of such a venerable place as Hull House. "It is the timeline that really gets me," he began. "It is so fascinating and interesting that this home was lived in by a Revolutionary War veteran. I shudder when I think about Mr. Hull just picking up a rifle and walking off to fight for the independence of his country. Now we get to be in his home. The timeline of this house and the history of its

On the day of the author's visit, a group of young people were doing an archeological dig on the centuries-old property.

residents runs from that war to the War of 1812, which impacted this area immensely, to the burning of nearby Buffalo by the British, to the building of the Erie Canal, to the history of the Native Americans who lived close by, to the westward migration through here, to the Hull grandchildren fighting in the Civil War, and more. To me, every great American story for over a century goes right through this house. That means something to me. And to think that this is the oldest existing stone structure in Erie County. Amazing."

Author's Notes

There are two things (among many) that really impressed me during my visit to the Hull House and Farmstead. One is tangible and the other is not.

The tangible thing? The rock.

"The ground out here is solid with limestone," Costello told me. "You just have to dig a foot or two to discover that. The Onondaga Escarpment is a massive shelf of limestone that runs throughout the region including through the Hull property. Because of that, it was used as a primary construction material for the house." This can be seen in the seven impressive fireplaces throughout. Although each is different in style and decoration, they are all made out of solid Onondaga limestone.

The intangible thing? A feeling.

I was deeply impressed with the ongoing involvement of the small group of foundation members with the local community. On the day of my visit the front lawn was abuzz with activity. Several wooden contraptions had been erected over piles of freshly dug dirt. Young people of all ages were busy with a very serious hands-on project. Costello explained what was going on.

"Recently we needed to move and reset the front steps to the home. In doing this, we uncovered earth that hadn't been touched in many, many years. So we decided to do an archeological dig with the help of the Department of Anthropology at University of Buffalo. We set up several excavation stations in the front yard. You can see the students, some high school age and some from UB, filling sifting grates with fresh dirt and trying to uncover any mysteries that the ground holds. It is fun, it is a learning experience for them, and on top of it all they earn school service credit hours."

Before I left from my visit, I stood near a tree out of sight of the excavating group and watched. It was heartwarming to see so many young people excitedly exclaiming, "I found something!" as they worked the large sifters back and forth. It may have been just a cork or maybe a piece of broken chinaware, but to them it was discovering a real piece of history. Or unraveling a piece of a puzzle. A mystery. And all of this in the shadow of a 200-year-old home.

As a writer whose books cover many Upstate New York topics, I felt strangely comforted knowing that the younger generation may just be willing to take up the cause of local history and historical renovation.

Visit

Hull Family House and Farmstead
5976 Genesee Street (at Pavement Road)
Lancaster, NY 14086
716-681-6451
Website: http://www.hullfamilyhome.org

For Further Reference: Monnin, Mary Jo. *Lancaster Memories: A Pictorial History*. Lancaster, NY: Dick Young Service Publishing, 2016.

While Here: Technically, Lancaster is considered to be along the "outer ring of suburbs" of Buffalo. There are many historical buildings in Lancaster. One of the most famous is the Liebler-Rohl Gasoline Station, built in 1935. It is a classic example of twentieth-century Tudor-style commercial architecture and at the publication of this book was being operated as an ice cream stand.

Tours: Hull House is generally open on two Saturdays each month from May through September, from noon to 4:00 p.m. Tours can always be arranged for other times by calling in advance.

Admission: $5.00 for all visitors

11

John Brown Farm and Grave Historic Site

Home of Abolitionist John Brown
Lake Placid, Essex County

For better or for worse, abolitionist John Brown was one of the most famous men of the mid-1800s. His passionate antislavery beliefs and his ability to marshal supporters throughout parts of the country brought him great fame and ultimately led to his violent denouement. Many of us learned the story of John Brown, "Bleeding Kansas," the fiery orator with the Moses beard, his Adirondack refuge for black Americans called "Timbuctoo," his ill-fated attempt to arm a black liberation army by raiding the US military arsenal at Harper's Ferry, the fiery gun battle that ended the raid, his capture and trial, his hanging, the long funeral procession from the south to the north, and finally his burial in the High Peaks region of Upstate New York. These stories are familiar to generations who learned of this messianic leader in their history books. And through song.

"Yes, many people are surprised to learn that 'John Brown's body lies a-moldering in the grave' . . . in Lake Placid, New York," Brendan Mills told me. He is the site manager for the John Brown Farm State Historic Site. "That marching song from the Civil War made his name well known. He came here in the late 1840s with dreams of building a home and farm for his growing family. He would eventually father twenty children, eleven who survived to adulthood. His son-in-law, Henry Thorpe, built him a sturdy frame house on the site. Brown was not entirely happy with that choice saying, 'Why build a frame house when the logs on my property are free for the having and cut timber costs money?'"

The property, situated on 277 acres of pristine Adirondack property, includes the six-room frame house (built by Thorpe with no design plans), a large two-story barn, a pond, and the John Brown gravesite, which is enclosed by an iron fence.

"The property hasn't really changed much over the years," Mills told me. "One big change was the location, though. In 1923, the barn, built in 1861 to 1862, was moved far back from the front of the property to the back. Today, the original location holds a large statue of Brown with a small child in the middle of a circular driveway. A tall flagpole now marks the spot where the original barn was located."

A tour here includes both structures. The exterior of the house is basically in original condition. The changes in the interior are few but significant. There were no fireplaces, with the family choosing to heat the home with stoves instead. "With just a wood stove to heat the lower level, Mary Brown always complained that 'it was cold in here' so she insisted that the walls be plastered over to make it more efficient than it originally was. I like to say that was the first home improvement of this house," Mills told me.

There was an outhouse, as well as chamber pots located in the bedrooms.

On the main floor, two of the original rooms have been combined into one. They served as the dining room and parlor. Only a few of the Brown family possessions are left to see, but one fine item is on display in the living room. It is the tall top piece of a sturdy bookshelf that was used by John Brown as a writing desk. Brown's personal wicker rocking chair sits next to the bookshelf.

"We have filled the Brown house with period pieces reflecting the lifestyles of the 1850s. There is no known photograph of the interior of the house when they lived here, so we have used our expertise to surmise what was located where. In the Browns' kitchen, we have placed items that would have been found in a kitchen of that period, including candle molds, tools, soap-making equipment, and more. Provisions were precious to the Browns' living in such a remote location. A large barrel which held both salt pork and flour was an important part of their existence. The Browns, with a large family, got by the best they could. When Brown received a request for monetary assistance from either a friend or family member, he sent flour or pork salt instead, realizing the value of those items during hard times," Mills said.

The large barn at the rear of the property is the location of a fascinating exhibit on John Brown's life. In the lower level of the barn you can view a professionally produced video, with actors in period clothing, telling of Brown's importance in the antislavery movement and how he strove most of his adult life to help blacks reach whatever level of equality they could in those harsh times of slavery and segregation. Exhibits, archival photographs, and maps along the walls of this level tell a compelling story of his trials and tribulations. It is all extremely well done.

Although it is unverified, it is believed that the Brown farm did in fact shepherd some escaping slaves on their way to Canada. "Yes, Brown was fond of saying, 'There was never a day I didn't work on the railroad, and it was not in an engine or a caboose,'" Mills told me.

The upper level of this large barn holds changing exhibits. On the day I toured it an exhibit exploring the concept and foundation of a free black community named Timbuctoo, championed by John Brown and located near his farm, is illustrated with informative panels and exhibits.

"John Brown came to Essex County early, in 1849. He was given the plot of land he built his home on from abolitionist Gerrit Smith in exchange for advising the settlers with his farming experience. At the time, Smith was offering plots of land here for free blacks to settle. By New York State law, black Americans had to own at least $250 in real estate to gain the right to vote.

"Called Timbuctoo, the concept was not a success, with roughly a dozen black families moving to the area. In any case, John Brown didn't stay here long. In fact, from 1855 to 1859, he only came to the farm for a few short visits. By this time, he was in Kansas joining antislavery forces, including his sons, in the fight to determine if Kansas would become a free state or a slave state. Most of the male members of Brown's large family joined him in this cause. The women stayed home. This was a critical time for John Brown. He got more and more involved in the violence in the Kansas Territory and his public image began to change from crusader to instigator. It is important to remember that violence brought John Brown to Kansas, and not the other way around," Mills told me.

The raid on Harper's Ferry was a debacle. Nine of Brown's raiders were killed, including two of his sons.

Mary Brown, John's second wife, stayed at the farm following Brown's execution but eventually found the notoriety to be too much for her in the Adirondacks. She finally joined a wagon train headed west in 1863 where she eventually settled and died in 1884. She is buried in Saratoga, California.

Several of John Brown's male family members are buried in the impressive gravesite in front of the residence.

I asked Mills what it was like to work at such an important place in American history. "I have been here for more than seventeen years," he began. "I am originally from Long Island and I remember that I did a middle school book report on John Brown. And now I am here telling others his story. I try and do my best because this is a true and exciting part of our heritage. I am honored to participate in that history by guiding people around John Brown's home and farm."

A larger-than-life statue of John Brown, with his arm draped over the shoulders of a young African-American boy, stands at the entrance to the historical site.

Author's Notes

The first thing a visitor notices when pulling around the circular drive at the entrance to this historic site is the juxtaposition of the tall statue of John Brown with his arm draped around the shoulders of an African American boy, and in the near distance, towering over the scene, stands the tall Olympic ski slopes at the Olympic Winter Training Facility. Yes, Lake Placid may be best known for its hosting of two winter Olympics, one in 1932 and again in 1980, but as far as American history goes it is hard to beat the experience of visiting the John Brown Historic National Site located near the edge of the Olympic Village.

The grounds are impeccably cared for and quite beautiful with a curtain of deep green Adirondack Mountains in the distance. Brendan Mills, who lives on the property, is a font of Brown history and a very engaging tour guide. And, although there are few real personal possessions of Brown to view, the story here is both compelling and inspirational at the same time. The exhibits in the barn near the back of the grounds are among the most impressive I have seen in a home/museum during research for this book. And there are a few oddities along the way. One of the most startling is seen on the second floor of the residence. In a glass display case you can see a Civil War soldier's shaving mug made out of an actual piece of wood taken from the scaffolding John Brown climbed on the day of his hanging. This unusual souvenir carries the inscription, "Made and carried by Sgt. A. F. Stahl." My guide told me that items like this were not uncommon as men in the Union Army carried them proudly as reminders of the slavery issue that was the cause of the war.

I cannot fully describe both the impact and the majesty of the John Brown gravesite. A huge boulder carries descriptive plaques honoring those who are buried here, and there are many in the ground in this plot. Among the many names and graves are Captain John Brown (John Brown's grandfather), John Brown, sons Frederick, Oliver, and Watson, and other members of the infamous Harper's Ferry raiding party. All are buried inside the elegant black wrought-iron fence that surrounds the family plot.

One important note is that the layout at this historic site lends itself beautifully for self-guided tours. There are many plaques and diagrams around the grounds that tell the timeline of John Brown's life both here at the farm and elsewhere. There are also useful "audio hot spots" marked along the paths that allow visitors to use their phones and listen to audio stories of the history of the Brown farm.

Visit

John Brown Farm State Historic Site
115 John Brown Road
Lake Placid, NY 12946
518-523-3900
Website: https://parks.ny.gov/historic-sites/29/details.aspx

For Further Reference: Quarles, Benjamin. *Allies for Freedom and Blacks on John Brown*. Boston: Da Capo Press, 2001.

While Here: Lake Placid has enough interesting sites to explore that it makes for a great weekend visit in any season. The site of two Winter Olympics, the history of these fabled winter contests is written in many places throughout the small village. The Lake Placid Olympic Ski Jumping Complex can clearly be seen rising into the sky near the John Brown farm.

Tours: May 1 through October 31, grounds are open during daylight hours for self-guided tours, guided tours start every half hour at 10:00 a.m. and the last tour begins at 4:30 p.m.

The house is closed on Tuesday.

Special tours can be arranged at other times by appointment.

Admission: Free

12

The Wilder Homestead

Home of Almanzo Wilder
Malone, Franklin County

Famed writer Laura Ingalls Wilder wrote the classic *Farmer Boy* in 1933. The *Little House on the Prairie* author wrote the story based on the boyhood tales told to her by her husband Almanzo Wilder. He grew up on a farm in Malone in the northern part of Upstate New York.

"We call this the Little House in the North Country," Jim Lusk told me with a smile. He has been a tour guide at the Wilder Homestead for eight years and has been researching "everything Wilder" for more than three decades. "The story is so sentimental, and it all took place right here on these eighty-eight acres. When you read the book, which millions of people have, you will recognize all the places in the book as being right here for all to see. The barns where he did his daily chores, the house where the family lived, the pump house, the fields, the orchard, the land. It is all right here. When you go between the barns you have to realize that you are standing on the actual ground where a young Almanzo trained his oxen, Star and Bright. Even those old apple trees, as crooked as they are, could be ones that were actually planted by Almanzo. People who love this book are just awestruck when they are here. It is all so real to them. And it is real."

The book, one of Laura Ingalls Wilder's most enduring tales, tells the charming story of a vanishing era long before cell phones and television. Life on the farm consisted of hard work, fun times, and strong family values. "We view the homestead as a living museum," Lusk told me. "We have visitors who come here from all over the country, and even around the world. They are all familiar with the book and want to visit this place

for the ultimate experience. Some of them even arrive holding the book in their hands. This is the only Little House structure that is still standing on its original site, and we are proud of that. There are, of course, many Wilder sites across the country, mainly in the Midwest, and I have been to them all." With that Lusk brought out a thick photo album describing in pictures and words all of his travels while chasing down his passion, the story of Laura Ingalls Wilder. There are photos of her other homes, some substantial and some not, with documentation from Jim's visits to each. Pepin, Wisconsin; Independence, Kansas; Walnut Grove, Minnesota; De Smet, South Dakota; and others.

James M. Wilder bought this farm in November of 1840 for $342 and moved in during the spring of 1841. They grew barley, wheat, oats, Canada peas, and even hops on the farm. "This was farming country back then, and the Wilders were quite successful," Lusk told me. "In fact, this was one of the top five most successful farms in the region."

The house is plain in detail and practical in design. "There was no architect. The house was built by the men of the family. It is a simple farmhouse now, but originally they added some fancy Greek touches to it. It is your basic wood-frame house, two stories tall, with four bedrooms and an outhouse. It had no fireplaces but was heated by two large wood stoves."

The barns are reconstructions of the original buildings, which were lost to lightning and fires. "We had an archeological dig performed here by students from the State University of New York at Potsdam, and they found the original foundation. When the barns were rebuilt, they used the actual drawings that Almanzo did for Laura for her book. Wilder was pretty exact as to where he remembered the location of everything, and the builders used his notes extensively. The reconstructed barns had been built to within one foot of the exact location of where they were first built," Lusk said.

Although there are few actual personal items from the time Almanzo lived here, the house is filled with period furnishings and artifacts that evoke that precise time. The bedrooms have the old rope beds that were common at the time, the kitchen has old appliances and accessories, and other items from the past like toys, sleds, and clothing can be found throughout. The floors of the second level are original to the home's construction and you can see the old square nails still holding the boards together.

Although this is an important puzzle piece of the entire Laura Ingalls Wilder story, the writer actually never stepped foot on the property. James and Angeline Wilder had six children, with Almanzo being their fifth born (1857). Almanzo left the farm at the age of eighteen when his family moved west. He eventually settled in what is now De Smet, South Dakota. Here he met Laura Ingalls, ten years younger than he, in 1882 and they were married in 1885.

Although the Wilder family moved from Malone when Almanzo was very young, he took with him the precious memories of growing up in the rural North Country of New York and it is those stories from which his wife would later create the immortal book *Farmer Boy.*

Author's Notes

Laura Ingalls Wilder was one of America's most popular novelists. Millions of copies of her Little House books have been printed since 1933. And, of course, the hit television series starring Michael Landon (1974–1983) brought her wider, even international, fame.

Whole legions of her admirers have made the trek to Malone to visit the farmhouse. "Many of them bring along the book when they visit here," Lusk told me. "They whisper to each other as they go from room to room, both in the house and in the outbuildings, recalling their favorite passages in the book. They all have favorite chapters and they positively squeal when they get to a certain favorite room. The most anticipated place in the house is the front parlor where the famous 'black mark incident' took place."

As the fans of *Farmer Boy* know, there is a scene in the chapter titled "Keeping House" where Almanzo and his overbearing older sister Liza Jane are hurriedly cleaning the house in anticipation of their parents' arrival. In his hurry, young Almanzo let slip a stove blacking brush, which flew at his sister, missed her, and hit a wall leaving a large black mark.

"Oftentimes, the first thing our guests say when we bring them in the house for a tour is, 'Where is the black mark room?' or 'We want to see the smudge from the blacking brush incident.' They all remember that scene vividly. Unfortunately, we do not have that black mark to show them," Lusk said.

The backstory is that when the house was renovated several years ago, workmen stripping away the wallpaper and layers of paint in the parlor came to a place that had a black smudge mark on it. The workers, all well-versed in the story of *Farmer Boy*, froze and called for their superiors. The mark was photographed and, relying on the description from the book, everyone agreed that this was, most likely, the legendary black mark caused by young Almanzo 150 years ago. "Sadly, we do not know what ever happened to that mark. It may have been covered over again. Maybe that section was taken out and is stored somewhere," Lusk said. "Still, when I get to this part of the tour I go through the whole story of the throwing of the blacking brush and everybody listens wide-eyed. Without a doubt that is the most requested part of the book that visitors want to see."

One thing I liked in particular is that as you roam the grounds, barns, and house, each room is recalled with displays of the original, lovable book illustrations done by the great Garth Williams. The illustrator, one of America's most famous, also illustrated *Stuart Little, Charlotte's Web,* and countless Little Golden Books. These drawings bring each room and each incident from Almanzo's youth to life as if they were a silent narrator along the tour. Whether it is milking a cow or shearing a sheep or visiting a county fair, or yes, even throwing a blacking brush, these drawings are an important and irreplaceable part of a visit to the historic Wilder homestead.

For those who are interested in the history of New York's literary past, this is a must.

Visit

The Almanzo Wilder Homestead
177 Stacy Road
Malone, NY 12853
518-483-1207
Website: https://almanzowilderfarm.com/

For Further Reference: Anderson, William. *The Story of the Wilders: A Biography of Almanzo Wilder and the Family from* Farmer Boy. William Anderson, 1983.

While Here: For true fans of the book, visit the home of the Franklin County Fair in Malone. The entrance looks similar to what it was in Wilder's time. A historic marker in front reads: "Franklin County Fair. Held here since 1852 and described by L. Wilder in *Farmer Boy*."

Tours:

Open Memorial Day through end of September
Monday to Saturday: 10:00 a.m. to 4:00 p.m.
Sunday: Noon to 4:00 p.m.
Check the website for their many annual family events.

Admission:

Adults: $9.00
Children: Free

13

The Bronck House

The Oldest Home in Upstate New York
Coxsackie, Greene County

In these chapters you will find homes that are old and homes that are older. This one beats them all.

"This house tells a remarkable story about a remarkable family. The house was built in 1663. Today there are eleven structures on the property. Our tours take visitors through each of the rooms and down the timeline of history back to the original owner Pieter Bronck," Shelby Mattice told me. She is the curator of the Bronck House Museum. "I am an archeologist and anthropologist by profession, so I just love this old house. I started here as a volunteer in 1972 when I was just twenty-five years old. And I never left," she laughed. "When I arrived, I was astonished to find the extent of the collection that was here. For many years I have documented the house's contents. My great interest is exploring the history of the first several Bronck generations to live here, up until about the 1830s. But it is all so fascinating. This house has many tales to tell."

A tour here, in the oldest house in all of Upstate New York, is an eye-opener.

In January 1662, Pieter Bronck entered into a contract to purchase from the Katskill Indians a tract of land known by the Indian name "Koix-hackung." Today we know the village as Coxsackie. Choosing a site at the base of the Kalkberg Ridge, Pieter built his dwelling, a small single-room structure with cellar and storage garret. From the first generation to live here, all in one room, to a more extensive residence completed by the grandson of the original builder, the house itself, in its unfolding history,

tells an amazing story of early Dutch life in what is now New York's Capital District.

The rooms are sparsely appointed, much as they would have been in the 1600s and 1700s. There was not a lot of space for the fancy things in life.

"This was a working farm and a very busy house," Mattice told me as we looked around in the oldest portion of the house. "Just imagine, wherever you see an empty space it would have been filled with cooking utensils and sleeping places. Everywhere. People slept two or three to a bed, sharing body heat for warmth. Some raised their beds to get away from the dampness. The rooms were small and there could be anywhere from five to fifteen people living in the house at one time, including adults, children, and slaves. By modern standards it would be considered a difficult living environment to say the least."

Each room boasts an impressive fireplace that was used for heating and cooking. Open beams recall the early Dutch influence of the original owners. Dutch customs were strictly adhered to in this house, and Dutch was spoken by its occupants, at least until the American Revolution. Exposed walls show aging stones and bricks. Later a large porch was placed on the front of the house where the Broncks could conduct business in good weather.

An exterior kitchen was added by the fifth generation, that of Judge Leonard Bronk (as Dutch influence in the region waned, the *c* was dropped from the family last name). "The kitchen is a stand-alone brick building just a couple of steps away from the main house," Mattice told me. "It was a miserable place and people really didn't spend any unnecessary time here. This was not a place where one would come for a cup of coffee or to do the *New York Times* crossword puzzle," she said. "In the summer it was hot, stinky, and thick with flies and rodents. In the early nineteenth century there were little or no sanitary codes by which to prepare food. They used wooden bowls, which were just wiped off after use. This invited food poisoning to originate from here. People in earlier times routinely just dumped waste out of the windows so there was literally a mini-garbage dump under many windowsills. Still, the kitchen dependency building, they called it, did serve a purpose. It brought all of this misery, the smells, heat, bugs, and everything out from the main home, making the residence a cleaner, safer, and more livable place."

A guided tour of the structures and grounds of the Bronck House is really quite unlike anything in Upstate New York. There is a 1663 stone house, a 1685 stone expansion house, a 1738 attached brick house, and a New World Dutch barn as well as a thirteen-sided barn that is the oldest multi-sided barn in New York, plus many other structures and features to explore.

It is hard to comprehend the fact that many of the massive hand-hewn beams, wide plank floors, cellar trap doors and hatchways, and Dutch doors are still intact, surviving from the 1600s. This is one of the few homes in this book I can readily suggest you allow several hours for a visit. To say there is a lot to see here is a monument to understatement.

To know the residents of this home, you must really visit it, look at the exhibits and time lines, study the photos, and take a tour. Seven generations of Bronck family lived in this dwelling over the past 355 years or so. Many were just hard-working laborers and farm hands, especially in the earliest generations. Later generations saw family members that were local officials, judges, and others in esteemed positions.

There are countless Bronck descendants scattered around the world. "We get many descendants of Pieter Bronck who come to this house each year. And it is a delight when they come. I've met family descendants from all over the United States who toured the house, as well as Broncks from far-flung places like Australia and Brazil," Mattice told me.

Owner Pieter Bronck was related to Jonas Bronck, for whom the Bronx is named.

Author's Notes

This is one of the most significant houses I have ever been to. Not so much for the period architecture or antique furnishings, but for the wonderful DNA it has in its old bones. There is no better way to describe this feeling than the answer I got to a question I posed to Shelby Mattice. She is one of the most passionate docents and administrators of any of the houses in this book that I met. I asked her, simply, "What is your favorite item in this house?"

Mattice closed her eyes and thought for a moment. She then opened her eyes and cast her gaze across the room from where we were sitting. "Right here," she said as she motioned her hands around the room. "This 1663 house itself is my favorite thing.

"This house is a survivor. When I come in during the early morning hours to get ready for tours, I sometimes just look around and think about all it has 'seen.' I try and imagine all the people, down through the years, old people and young people, famous visitors and passersby, who have walked through this space. I wonder what they talked about, what they thought about, and how they met the troubles in their lives. Remember, the 1663 Bronck House was already 113 years old when the Declaration of Independence was signed! Amazing. This venerable old Dutch house has been witness to the entire history of the United States and more. Yet, somehow, here it sits, in this quiet little corner of the Hudson Valley, still watching over us all centuries later. Yes, a survivor, I say."

Visit

Pieter Bronck House
90 County Route 42
Coxsackie, NY 12051
518-731-6490
Website: https://www.gchistory.org/bronck-museum-directions/

For Further Reference: Meeske, Harrison. *The Hudson Valley Dutch and Their Houses.* Fleischmanns, NY: Harbor Hill Books, 1999.

While Here: A side trip to Athens, New York, is interesting. The village, located on the Hudson River, is just five miles south of Coxsackie. There are many historic buildings in the village as well as the Hudson-Athens Lighthouse, one of the river's most beautiful. Tours are offered.

Tours:

House is open seasonally, Memorial Day weekend to mid-October
Closed all Mondays and Tuesdays
Wednesday: 12:00 p.m. to 4:00 p.m.

Thursday: 12:00 p.m. to 4:00 p.m.
Friday: 12:00 p.m. to 4:00 p.m.
Saturday: 10:00 a.m. to 4:00 p.m.
Sunday: 1:00 p.m. to 4:00 p.m.

Admission:

Adults: $7.00
Youth 12–15: $3.00
Children 5–11: $2.00
Children under 5: Free

14

Zadock Pratt House Museum

Home of Zadock Pratt
Prattsville, Greene County

"Zadock Pratt built this home in 1828. He planned the design and built it himself," Carolyn Bennett said. She is the director of the Zadock Pratt Museum. "Originally it was built as a two-story, white clapboard five-bay Federal-style home. That would be the front part of the structure. Two rooms downstairs and four rooms up. Later, his fourth wife, Mary, wanted to make the home more presentable for the times. She modernized it by removing the balcony, which originally spanned the entire length of the second floor, and added a peak roof in the front. This transformed the house into the Greek Revival building seen today. The six octagonal columns are the home's signature exterior feature. The house originally had four fireplaces and no indoor bathroom."

The Pratt home is remarkable for several reasons. The first is that it was built by Pratt himself. He was one of the most important people ever to come out of the Catskill region. At one time he owned the largest tannery in the world, with its factory located in Prattsville, a town he founded.

"Pratt was a master planner and a master builder. He knew the strength and durability of the hemlock trees that proliferated in this area and he built his own home out of hemlock timbers cut at his sawmill across the street. At the time, consumption (now known as tuberculosis) was a leading cause of death and many people believed the illness was borne on drafts entering one's home. This house is as tight as can be with the hemlock timbers acting as a lock against any outside drafts. And that was by Pratt's design because his first two wives both died of the disease.

He built this for his third wife, Abigail. She died in 1834, shortly after giving birth to their third child, a daughter. Abigail was only thirty-three years old when she died," Suzanne Walsh told me. She is the house's curator and archivist. She also pointed out, "Unlike his other wives, Abigail did not die of consumption."

It can all be quite confusing when trying to explore Pratt's family line. He married five times, including two sets of sisters. But more on that later.

The house, still standing on the same spot where it was built, is spare inside but has a wonderful story. "Pratt was a fabulously wealthy and famous man, but he came from Puritan roots and he was not an ostentatious person. We can see that in the center entrance hallway. Pratt could have built the most elegant staircase imaginable, but as you can see, it is plain, unadorned, and just thirty-three inches wide. Pratt had many employees, friends, and neighbors in the village, and he welcomed them all into his home. His simple taste was a tribute to his Puritan upbringing but also because Pratt was a man of the people and he never wanted any visitor to be inhibited by the entrance to his home. The staircase railing is of a simple handmade Shaker design. The chandelier overhead, perhaps one of the only 'fancy' items of his remaining in the house, is original to the Pratt family. It has four hand-painted reverse glazed glass panels around the light, each one depicting a different season," Walsh said.

The downstairs contains two rooms that mirror each other, and they too are spare and simple. One room holds a prized possession of the museum's collection, though. "Pratt was always building his little town up, and expanding it out from the center. To document this, he commissioned painters to create and add to a large narrative painting of the village's growth. We have no idea how many painters contributed to this. If someone was passing through town Pratt would ask them if they could paint. If they said yes he would invite them to add a new building or road or object to the painting," Walsh explained.

The resulting painting is quite unlike anything this writer has seen. It is a very large (five-foot by eight-foot) hand-painted depiction of the village done on three attached panels. The colors, though almost 200 years old, are vibrant, and the depiction of the buildings, forests, animals, rivers, and even people is an accurate narrative of the village he founded. You can pick out Pratt's tannery, a hotel, an academy, and many other long-gone buildings. Pratt himself can be seen on horseback riding through town. You can even see a woman going into a small church. "Pratt helped to rebuild the Old Dutch Church in Prattsville and for many years women were not allowed to enter the church through the right front door, which was for men only. So when they finally allowed women to enter this door to worship alongside the men, Pratt found an itinerant painter and asked him to paint the woman you can now see entering the church through the correct door for the first time to document the momentous occasion," Walsh said.

The front parlor was a busy place. "Pratt was always inviting guests into his home. He really loved people and he was fond of entertaining here. Everybody was invited, people from all over the globe. Pratt never had slaves, but he did have servants. He treated them fairly and they were like part of his family," Walsh said.

The wide plank floors are all original to the construction of the house, and large 12-over-12 windows allow much welcome light in through the hundreds of old windowpanes. One pane is of special consideration.

"Yes, Zadock's son, George, always presumed he would be famous someday. So, like other young people might do, he liked to practice writing his autograph. In fact, he even practiced it by scrawling his initials across a windowpane, perhaps with a diamond," Walsh told me as we walked over to a windowpane that has been framed in place for safekeeping. Here, the visitor can clearly see the initials "G. W. P" written into the glass.

"Of course, there was another reason Zadock wanted his son to master his autograph. Zadock owned the only bank in town and was always giving out loans to the residents of Prattsville and people who came through town. He wanted his son to be able to cosign on these loans," I was told.

Pratt was a true renaissance man. He was a banker, a member of Congress, a tanner, a builder, an investor, a soldier, a visionary, and a newspaperman. His tannery brought him worldwide fame and a hefty fortune. In fact, at one time Zadock Pratt, of tiny Prattsville, New York, was the seventh richest man in America. His influence was felt across the country. He was a powerful legislator and financier. Among the initiatives that he was heavily involved in were the construction of the Trans-Continental Railroad, the building of the Washington Monument, and the founding of the Smithsonian Institution.

He was married five times. His first and second wives were sisters, Beda and Esther Dickerman. His second and third wives were also sisters, Abigail and Mary Watson. His fifth wife was Susie Grimm. His first four wives died while married to Pratt. Zadock Pratt passed away in 1871 at the age of eighty-one leaving his widow, Susie.

Pratt's crowning achievement was the village that the residents named after him. He designed and built one hundred structures for his employees in the little town, plus everything from a racetrack to businesses to churches. His tannery employed 400 people from the region, and his benevolence was felt throughout Greene County.

"It's a little sad that nobody really learns about Mr. Pratt anymore," Walsh told me. "Up until about the 1950s his name and story were in all the history books in the local schools. That is no longer the case. 'The Greene County Tanner' has slowly faded away in people's minds, but we aim to change all that and continue to tell the extraordinary story of this remarkable genius right here in his very own home."

Pratt Rock has been called "New York's Mount Rushmore."

Author's Notes

I cannot tell the story of the Pratt House Museum without telling the story of Hurricane Irene.

It roared through the Atlantic Ocean in 2011 and then raked Upstate New York as an epic tropical storm for several days in August. When the storm dissipated and horror-struck residents crept out to see the damage, the results were unimaginable. The Schoharie Creek, usually a timid stream of water arcing around this and other northern Catskill communities, became a monster that shredded the village. Every structure in Prattsville was damaged, with more than twenty of them destroyed. Businesses, churches, homes, schools, and even his museum were severely damaged. Governor Andrew Cuomo called Prattsville the hardest-hit community in the state.

"The water came up four feet in the house," Walsh told me, pointing to the fifth step of the staircase to illustrate the level it reached. "We had incredible damage to hundreds of items in our collection and lost almost all of our documents. All we could do was store everything in a large off-site freeze-dry facility and start over. Fortunately, because of Mr. Pratt's insistence of building this home out of his sturdy hemlock trees, the house never moved an inch off its foundation, unlike many other homes which were damaged, destroyed, or simply washed away."

Over the years the house has come back to life and is now open to the public once more. Walsh said, "Every once in a while we will bring out a damaged Pratt item and raise money for its restoration. I remember the first item we did this for was our giant three-panel wall painting of Prattsville that is so precious to us. We raised $14,000 to have that single item alone repaired and restored. The first Pratt family item we chose to repair was Zadock's personal writing desk. Miraculously, descendants of Pratt from Paris and London stepped forward to aid in its restoration. We have it on display now and it is beautiful. We will continue to do this until all of our items are back as they once were before the nightmare of Hurricane Irene tried to steal it all away from us. Like Zadock Pratt, we are a resilient group here at his house."

Visit

Zadock Pratt Museum
14540 NY Route 23 (Main Street)
Prattsville, NY 12468
518-299-3395
Website: https://zadockprattmuseum.com/

For Further Reference: Capen, Nahum. *Biography of Zadock Pratt of Prattsville, New York*. Whitefish, MT: Kessinger Publishing LLC, 2010.

While Here: No visit to the Zadock Pratt House would be complete without stopping at Pratt Rock, just one-half mile south of the village on Route 23 (Main Street). Here, after a short hike up the mountain, you can see massive bluestone carvings done by stone carvers employed by Zadock Pratt on the rock walls. They depict a horse, hemlock trees, significant dates, and other iconic imagery. One image is a tribute to his son George who was killed in the Civil War. Known as "New

York's Mount Rushmore," this oddity is also important as being recognized as the first man-made Civil War memorial in America, as Pratt's son was memorialized here soon after receiving his mortal wound at the Second Battle of Bull Run, three years before the war ended.

Tours: Saturday and Sunday, 10:00 a.m. to 5:00 p.m.; tours available every hour

Admission:
Adults: $5.00
Children: Free

15

Herkimer Home State Historic Site

Home of General Nicholas Herkimer
Little Falls, Herkimer County

The home of Revolutionary War hero General Nicholas Herkimer is a tall red-brick Georgian Manor house. "Over time there have been many changes to the building. Today we find three large rooms on the first floor and three on the second. We find a large center hall on both floors as well, as is typical of the Georgian concept. After General Herkimer's family moved on from the house, several subsequent owners made substantial renovations to the structure and New York State itself undertook a comprehensive restoration in the 1960s. Still, the house is a real treasure to behold. Today it sits on 169 acres," Michael Roets told me. He is the site manager at the Herkimer Home State Historic Site.

"This would have been one of the most impressive homes of that era in the Mohawk Valley. Imagine this substantial residence standing alone in the wilderness right along the banks of the busy Mohawk River. This was a real frontier during that period and the Herkimers were important to the well-being of the area. As time went by, they controlled the commerce and water traffic along the Mohawk River, and they had a business in moving goods around the falls west of here at Little Falls. Later, a river portage went through the Herkimer property, which provided a steady income for the family. They were major agricultural producers, land owners, and they supervised a large network of tenant farmers. This all would have combined to make them one of the wealthiest families in the area. Nicholas was also a civic leader and a military officer of great repute."

Although there are but few Herkimer family possessions in the house today, the residence is set up to reflect eighteenth-century life in the Mohawk Valley. The large center hall on the first floor would have been the heart of the house's activities. In the summer, the doors on both ends of the hall would be opened to take advantage of the cool breezes coming up from the river, and this would have also been where the general entertained his many guests. "This was a very busy house," Roets told me. "Because of General Herkimer's stature, there was a constant stream of visitors coming through the house including Sir William Johnson, Native American leader Joseph Brandt, Major-General Philip Schuyler, and many others. Add to this a collection of area businessmen, Native Americans, tenant farmers, soldiers, and neighboring farmers and you can see that this house could get quite crowded at times."

The "best parlor" located on the first floor would have contained the family's best furniture and furnishings, and the general and his wife would have welcomed guests here to showcase the high position and regard in which he was held. At his death General Herkimer willed the exclusive rights to this lone room to his second wife, Maria, for as long as she remained unmarried. To get as close as possible to the original wallpaper as that of Herkimer's time, a color analysis was done, and the paper was closely matched by using the historic samples from the Colonial Williamsburg catalog. This room, like all rooms in the house, was heated by a fireplace.

Here we find a beautiful and rare piece of furniture whose lineage can be traced to General Herkimer. It is his personal writing desk. "Yes, we actually found written documentation affixed to the top drawer of the writing desk which traces the ownership of the piece back to the general. We are very lucky. You just don't find that kind of documentation anywhere," the site manager said.

A second large room, probably another parlor, is interpreted on the tour as Herkimer's office. "This is where he would have tended his business, both personal and military. This is also the room that General Herkimer died in."

The largest room in the house was once two separate rooms. "We believe that one room was a formal dining room. In a corner of the room we have a doorway that leads to the cellar. It makes sense that it would have been used by the servants to ferry food from the downstairs kitchen up to the dining area." (Herkimer had thirty-two enslaved and indentured servants.) The large formal dining table belonged to the Herkimer family. "Actually, it is two tables joined together. They were made of birch but stained to look like a much more expensive mahogany wood. The Herkimers were of German Palatine origin and because of that the house is rather plain with not a lot of extravagance or fanciness. Although here we do see a heart motif carved into the chair backs, a rare nod to fashionable design," Roets explained.

The other part of this large room exhibits a whole different dimension to Herkimer Home. "General Herkimer was a militia leader. He was responsible for the defense of the region during the Revolutionary War. Because of that many officers and soldiers were housed here for long periods of time. Records show that the house was attacked by Tories and native warriors on several occasions. Documents tell of the soldiers taking out all of the windows on the main floor and boarding them up with wood, with rifle holes to shoot through. Because the house was large and solidly made from bricks, it was seen as a bit of a fortress in the Mohawk Valley. The portage around the falls of the Mohawk River behind the house was strategically important for the passage of men and material and Herkimer's militia had to defend it several times. The house would have been a formidable challenge for any attackers. Along with the strength of the house itself and the size of the garrison, eight fierce bulldogs were on duty, a pair chained to each of the four corners, as an extra deterrent," Roets said.

The exhibits in this part of the room interpret how the house would have been used during war. A display of vintage surgical tools gives grim evidence as to what went on here. General Herkimer's own mortal wounds were addressed in this room. The display of bone saws, vises, drills, bloodletters, and knives bespeaks the horrors of war that visited this place.

The top floor is scattered with knapsacks and bedding to evoke the area where refugees and soldiers would have slept while seeking sanctuary in the house.

General Nicholas Herkimer lived here with his first wife, Maria Dygert, until her death around 1774. After, he married another woman from the same family, also named Maria Dygert (not uncommon in those days). The second Maria Dygert outlived the general.

Nicholas Herkimer is one of the great epic stories to come out of the Revolutionary War. An inspiring leader who commanded the Tryon County Militia, Herkimer led his soldiers on a mission to relieve the siege of Fort Stanwix, almost thirty miles west of Herkimer Home. On August 6, 1777, his soldiers were ambushed by a larger contingent of British, Tory, and Mohawk forces. During this massacre, known as the Battle of Oriskany, General Herkimer's horse was shot out from under him and his leg was shattered. He continued to bravely direct his forces in battle while resting upon his saddle, which was leaning on a tree in the middle of the battlefield. After, he was carried to his home where attempts were made to save his life. He died in the front parlor of Herkimer Home on August 16, 1777, at the age of forty-nine.

Author's Notes

This place is so well done. There is a visitor's center where much can be learned about the Mohawk Valley, the German Palatines who were among the early settlers, and the impact of the Revolutionary War along the river valley.

The house is spare and yet tells a vivid story of life in this remote wilderness. For me there are several unforgettable highpoints to look for during a tour.

One of them is a small porch that juts out from the front of the house and overlooks the Herkimer property. This stunning vista tells its own panoramic history of the region. In the distance you can see the Mohawk River and the Adirondack foothills. In front of that is the Erie Canal towpath. In front of that is a railroad bed where a train would come by several times a day as the canal went out of favor. Closer to the house you see the fertile farmlands that were worked by Herkimer family members and their enslaved servants and finally a lush raised garden near the perimeter of the house. This view is a painter's dream and is a hallmark of the tour of Herkimer Home.

Not to be missed is one of the most graceful and beautiful family burial grounds I have seen in writing this book. The Herkimer family cemetery, located just a few yards from the house, is filled with family members ranging from 250 years ago to more current burials (as recently as two decades ago). The "Hero of Oriskany" is buried beneath a soaring sixty-foot-tall obelisk bearing his name and biographical information.

Visit

Herkimer Home State Historic Site
200 NY Route 169
Little Falls, NY 13365
315-823-0398
Website: https://parks.ny.gov/historic-sites/14/details.aspx

For Further Reference: Boehlert, Paul A. *The Battle of Oriskany and General Nicholas Herkimer: Revolution in the Mohawk Valley.* Charleston, SC: The History Press, 2013.

While Here: Just six miles east of the Herkimer Home State Historic Site is the village that bears his name. Here, in Myers Park, is a dynamic statue of the general, lying mortally wounded yet still directing his troops in battle, positioned on a giant boulder that was taken from the battlefield in Oriskany.

Tours: Memorial Day through Labor Day: 9:30 a.m. to 5:00 p.m. (last tour begins at 4:30 p.m.). Closed Monday and Tuesday.

Note: The museum is housed in a modern building on site. It is accessible and has restrooms. The original house itself is not accessible.

Admission:

Adults: $4.00
Seniors: $3.00
Children under 12: Free

16

Wadsworth Homestead

Home of Seven Generations of the Wadsworth Family
Geneseo, Livingston County

This is one of those grand old homes that can take your breath away.

Geneseo's Main Street is dotted with small mom-and-pop businesses, some college stores for those attending SUNY Geneseo, a few taverns and eateries, an exquisite hotel, and a whimsical fountain featuring a dancing bear, which is located smack in the middle of town. And at the very end of the street, out of sight behind a curtain of leafy trees and hidden behind a long stone wall, is the home of Geneseo's founder, James Wadsworth, and seven generations of his family.

You enter a stone gate and proceed up a long winding driveway. On the left you will see many of the property's 300 acres. On the right you will see an old cobblestone gate house, then some gardens, and then a circular driveway. This leads up to one of the most magnificent mansions in Upstate New York.

"James Wadsworth and his brother, William, came to the Genesee Valley in 1790 to settle this land and they built this home in 1804," William Wadsworth told me. The property is owned by Will's father Austin and Austin's children and grandchildren. Will is the current caretaker of the property and is a sixth-generation Wadsworth. "They originally built a log cabin just west of here. This larger home was built in 1804 in the style of the Four-Square Federal homes of the day. The home has had several major additions over the years, including 1815, 1823, and in 1874 when the entire house was moved back 130 yards from Geneseo's Main Street for added privacy. Apparently, this house-moving endeavor was

quite the public attraction as it required more than twenty teams of oxen to move the large house on long timber beams and rollers. The original Wadsworths owned a large tract of land in the region, and the property included over 250,000 acres of western New York wilderness. Today this property consists of about 300 remaining acres."

The Wadsworth Homestead contains forty-four rooms, including twelve bedrooms and eight bathrooms, and was constructed with solid three-inch oak planks. "Yes, it was built almost like a ship. And it was very solid, as it was constructed to withstand gunfire during the wild and uncertain times of the early frontier out here. The Senecas were the previous inhabitants of the land and they were pushed out following the Clinton-Sullivan Campaign of 1779, during the American Revolution. Many of them resettled in Canada, which is not very far from here. So, there was some worry that outside forces would rile them up in Canada and encourage them to return here and reclaim their ancestral land. That is why this house was built strong, like a ship or fort. You just never knew," Wadsworth told me.

The interior of the house appears as if some of the earliest generations of Wadsworths simply locked the door and left. Each room is overflowing with family furniture, antiques, and possessions. The walls are museum-packed with large portraits of family members down through the years, as well as hunting scenes and landscape paintings by some of the most well-known early American artists.

There are fourteen fireplaces in the mansion, all of them working. "We have seven fireplace flues and four chimneys. Each mantel and fireplace surround is unique. Most of them are carved wood, with one carved out of Vermont marble," I was told.

There are hundreds of large, hand-poured glass windowpanes, many of them installed in sweeping bay windows, which make the house seem light and airy. The wallpaper, carpets, silver objects, piano, books, and personal items all belonged to any and all of the family generations. This was a home lived in by wealthy, important people. "One of my early grandmothers concocted an intricate bell system to call the servants. There are buttons (some secret), which you could push in almost any room for an attendant to come," Wadsworth said. He demonstrated this system for me. After pushing a button in the library, we walked to the servants' quarters and looked at a large glass box with many little white arrows and labels in it. And sure enough, the little white arrow for the library was pointing up signaling that a Wadsworth was waiting for a servant to call. All of the rooms in the house are listed in this call box, including the drawing room, kitchen, Mrs. Wadsworth's bedroom, and front parlor.

Perhaps the showstopper of the house is the large, ornate three-story staircase that winds its way up to the third floor. It is painted all white, including the banisters and the railings. It gleams in the glow of a large hanging chandelier, which is itself reflected in round antique mirrors. A tall grandfather clock stands sentinel on a landing. The whole scene is highlighted by a large, stunning stained glass window depicting the Atlantic Ocean. It was done by John La Farge, a contemporary of Louis Comfort Tiffany. It is quite spectacular.

This massive home is set off by two large porches. The front porch is glassed in for all-weather enjoyment and faces the tall porte cochere, which would welcome guests in their horse carriages or early automobiles as they rounded the circular driveway. The rear or west porch is open air and accommodates several outdoor seating areas overlooking an expanse of lawn, gardens, and trees.

While strolling the west porch, I asked Will Wadsworth what it felt like to be the caretaker of something that has such a long and glorious family attachment for him.

"You know, sometimes I come out on this porch and watch the magnificent sunset in the Genesee Valley below. It is not hard for me to understand that just a few layers of paint under my shoes separate me from my ancestors who stood at this very spot and saw the same sunset. I take the responsibility to keep the family name and legacy alive in this home very seriously."

James and William Wadsworth were the seed from which great wealth, importance, and civic responsibility sprang. Over a span of six generations, each family member left his or her mark on the homestead. Some were little marks and others were epic. The family has deep roots to Geneseo. In fact, they donated the land for a school, which is now the State University of New York at Geneseo, the economic engine that drives the success of the village and the surrounding area. Even today, Will Wadsworth, a current owner, is involved in Geneseo's daily life as he acts as the town supervisor.

The Wadsworth brothers' uncle, Jeremiah, originally purchased 4,000 acres of western New York wilderness and convinced his two younger cousins to invest in this land and to take it upon themselves to market it to future buyers. The Wadsworth brothers paid eight cents an acre to their cousin for 2,000 acres and moved here to an Indian village named Big Tree (today's Geneseo). The return on the sale of the land to arriving settlers made the brothers wealthy.

Big Tree was named after an enormous swamp oak, which was a famous landmark that served as a treaty meeting place for the Seneca Indians. Eventually the tree itself became property of the Wadsworth family. The big tree fell in 1857, but it is remembered here at the homestead in a colorful landscape scene painted by Hudson River School painter John Kensett.

Over the many generations, some Wadsworth men married women of means and high standing from Boston. Because of their frequent shopping trips to Boston, the house has many fine period furnishings from some of that city's premier furniture makers. "Yes, the visits back and forth to Boston were so frequent that it was said my grandfather actually developed a Bostonian accent," the owner chuckled.

There are too many great stories from the Wadsworth family tree to list here, but one sticks out as quite remarkable. "James S. Wadsworth, the first son of this house, was a friend of Abraham Lincoln. Despite having had no military experience whatsoever, he went to Lincoln and asked to serve in the Union Army during the Civil War. Although he was fifty-six years old, President Lincoln agreed, making my ancestor General Grant's oldest commanding officer. Major General James S. Wadsworth served gallantly in the war, fought at Gettysburg, and was killed in the Battle of the Wilderness on May 8, 1864," he told me.

Many of the Wadsworth family tales are told throughout this house through portraits, possessions, and house documents.

The Wadsworth family were the founders of Geneseo, New York. In a downtown park sits this replica of the founders' original cabin they built in the wilderness.

Author's Notes

When taking a tour of the Wadsworth Homestead, there is no doubt that you will be thinking, "What a lovely museum." Except this is not a museum, this is a home, and has been for the same family for over two centuries. The hundreds of items you see as you walk through each room are not items donated by history-minded patrons. These are Wadsworth belongings, seemingly left where they were as one generation slipped on to the next. There are walls lined with family chinaware, children's toys, military weapons used by the family's men in war, hundreds of books (the oldest being a 1634 tome titled "How to be a Justice for the King"), silver candlesticks, embroidered pillows, and hundreds of other items.

On a table in a corner is a letter from 1909. The letter is a personal invitation asking Austin Wadsworth to "stay overnight at the White House during his next visit to Washington, DC." It is signed by President Theodore Roosevelt. On another table is a 200-year-old Seneca war club that played a significant part in the first generation's safety at the homestead. On a shelf is a brass button from the prestigious Genesee Valley Hunt Club. This club was well known for its elaborate fox hunts, of which several generations of Wadsworths were key participants. A similar button was taken to the moon and back by astronaut Pete Conrad, who belonged to the club. Lining the walls are a dozen dramatic, snarling stuffed fox heads glaring down on visitors as prize reminders from these heralded social hunts.

In the entranceway is an epic hat rack, made from Adirondack elk horns. On each horn hangs a hat from a Wadsworth family member, including stylish fedoras, women's hats, and even an Army helmet. History lived in this house and history visited this house. In fact, both Roosevelts, Theodore and Franklin, were overnight guests here.

To complete your visit here, a quick side trip to the downtown village park is a must. There you will see a replica of James and William's first log cabin from 1790.

Visit

Wadsworth Homestead
4 South Street
Geneseo, NY 14454

Landmark: Just outside the walls of the Wadsworth Homestead, two blocks down Main Street, is the village's beloved mascot, "Emmeline." Situated on a pole coming up from a round fountain in the middle of the street is a statue of a bear holding on to a lamppost, that has brought smiles to visitors ever since it was erected in 1888. It is named Emmeline to honor its benefactor, Mrs. Emmeline Austin Wadsworth.

585-764-9005

Website: http://www.wadsworthhomestead.com

For Further Reference: Cook, William and Daniel Schultz. *Around Geneseo.* Mount Pleasant, SC: Arcadia Publishing, 2004.

While Here: The National Warplane Museum is located at the Geneseo Airport. Austin Wadsworth was an early organizer and president of the museum.

Tours:

Tuesday: 10:00 a.m., 11:00 a.m., and 1:00 p.m.
Thursday: 10:00 a.m. and 11:00 a.m.

Call in advance to arrange for other tour times.

Note: All tours are led by Will Wadsworth, sixth generation of the family.

Admission: $15.00 per person (groups of 20 or more are welcome, with special group rates offered).

17

LORENZO

Home of John Lincklaen
Cazenovia, Madison County

This regal mansion, situated at the southern end of Cazenovia Lake, was built in 1807 in the Federal style. "This is a magnificent home, but there is no architect on record for its design," Jackie Roshia commented. She is the curator of Lorenzo. "John Lincklaen designed the home and named it Lorenzo after Lorenzo di Medici's villa in Florence, Italy. It was built by local craftsmen. It is a solid brick house, both inside and out. There are two full floors for living space as well as a basement and attic. The house has over twenty-five rooms including five bedrooms and three baths open for public viewing. We also have nine of the ten original fireplaces. The front part of the house was for the family and the back was the servants' wing. Our current visitors' center was a carriage house built in 1892. Four generations of the same family lived in this house."

Like so many of the grand homes in this book, the entranceway into the mansion is gorgeous. "We have 160 years of original furnishings and household items on display. Everything is original to the family," Roshia said. The main hall features portraits of the builder and his wife, John and Helen Ledyard Lincklaen. All of the brightly colored wallpaper, carpets, and draperies are historic reproductions of those of the time of the third generation of residents. The hallway is a kaleidoscope of busy red and white patterned wallpaper of birds and landscaping contrasting with a tricolor Minton tile floor. Much of the furniture from the builder's time period was made by craftsmen in Cazenovia.

The house is restored to the time period of the third owners, 1894 to 1931. Photographs taken of the first-floor rooms in 1906 were of great value in the process of restoration and they offer visitors the opportunity to see how the rooms would have looked a hundred or so years ago.

A large formal dining room features an Austrian crystal chandelier, highlighted by brass stags, dating to 1841. There is a beautiful oil painting of family member Mary Ledyard Foreman Seymour on the wall. In the portrait, Mrs. Seymour can be seen wearing jeweled earrings. Below the painting, the original earrings have been framed and are on display. An interesting side note to Mary Seymour is that she was the mother of Horatio Seymour, the eighteenth governor of New York and the Democratic candidate for the presidency in 1868.

There are several signed photos on the wall as well. One of them is an image of President Grover Cleveland, bearing his signature below.

The drawing room has more family portraits, an 1867 square grand piano, and a sofa and twelve chairs that date to 1808.

The next room on the tour is the library. This room was utilized by the gentlemen. The large bookcase was purchased by the builder of the home and the books in it are part of the approximately three thousand in the historic collection. Two chairs and a bookcase, given as wedding gifts to the third owner in 1871, are also among the objects in this room. Among the paintings collected by the families is a Cazenovia landscape by local artist William Boardman. There is also a statue of a mountain lion on display. It is a small-scale version of Edward Kemeys's sculpture "Still Hunt," which can be seen in New York City's Central Park.

The breakfast room features more oil paintings, including one by Hudson River School painter Jasper Cropsey. Here we also see family silver items, including tea services, chinaware, and Chinese export items that were wedding gifts to the original Lincklaen family.

The large "flying staircase" that takes you from the first to the second floor is both graceful and dramatic. It shows no visible sign of underneath support and the stairs are wide and the woodwork is elaborate. "Notice this little ivory button at the bottom," Roshia pointed out. "This is called the mortgage eye and it traditionally capped a hollow spindle on the staircase. Inside that spindle the owner would place the ashes of the burnt mortgage papers, signifying their home was paid for." I asked her what was inside this mortgage eye. "Probably nothing," she grinned. "John Lincklaen paid for this house as construction progressed so there was never a mortgage."

The second-floor contains the family bedrooms. One is a guest bedroom and has a special story. In 1887, President Grover Cleveland, then in his first term as president, visited Lorenzo during a wedding trip through the region with his new bride, Frances Folsom. They spent the night here on July 18 at the suggestion of the president's Secretary of the Treasury Charles Fairchild. Fairchild's wife, Helen, was a member of the Lincklaen family. According to a family member's diary, the First Couple stood at the front door of Lorenzo and greeted each of the four thousand people who came to see them. The people lined up at the front door and exited out the back door of the main hallway.

"We think this guest bedroom is special because this is where the president and his wife spent the night. It is a special room, not the least because it has a 1949 Otis elevator in it, installed more than a half century after the president's visit," I was told.

John Lincklaen, the founder of Cazenovia, was born in Amsterdam and had a budding career in the Dutch navy when he decided to come to the New York region to act as a land agent for the Holland Land Company. The company was tasked with buying, selling, trading, carving up, and naming hundreds of tracts of land that now comprise much of central and western New York. In 1792, his business duties found him in the area of present-day Cazenovia where he eventually settled and began planning his future. Within a decade, he had completed Lorenzo.

John married Helen Ledyard, and they had no children. However, they brought several young family members into the household to raise, including Helen's brother, Jonathan Ledyard. "Jonathan's son, whose given name was Lincklaen Ledyard, would become Lorenzo's second owner. In an attempt to preserve the Lincklaen surname he legally changed his name to Ledyard Lincklaen just prior to inheriting the property. In fact, you can see several places throughout the house the initials "L.L.," which were placed there by Ledyard Lincklaen during renovations of the home," the curator told me. "Ledyard Lincklaen had one child, a daughter named Helen Lincklaen Fairchild, who would become Lorenzo's third owner."

The last sole owner of the house was Jane Ledyard Remington, who had married into the famous Remington arms family. "She lived in this house from 1931 to 1953. After she passed away the house went to her nine heirs. They were the ones who jointly made the decision to keep the house exactly as it was and donate it and all of its contents for the purpose of establishing it as a museum."

Author's Notes

The setting of this house is majestic. It stands tall and proud at the foot of Cazenovia Lake. Behind the house are the family's prizewinning gardens with border beds restored to 1914 garden plans, which are set apart from the surrounding landscape by a dramatic "dark aisle." This stand of trees acts as a windbreak for both the house and garden. A sky-reaching black locust tree was planted on the grounds in 1819.

Some of the surprises that I found interesting in this house included a servant's call box that connected each room to the kitchen area, as well as the many oil paintings that give several of the rooms the air of a famous art museum. My favorite was one by Dwight Williams Jr. It is an 1884 landscape that depicts the lake view from the entranceway of Lorenzo. The scene includes a Norway spruce that was planted in 1845. It is highlighted in the painting and still stands on Lorenzo's front lawn.

In the kitchen, a chalkboard shows a menu served at a dinner party given by the Fairchilds for President and Mrs. Grover Cleveland: raw oysters, consommé, terrapins, sweetbreads, thick chops, hot ham, grouse with crumb sauce, and salad.

Visit

Lorenzo State Historic Site
17 Rippleton Road
Cazenovia, NY 13035
315-655-3200
Websites: http://www.friendsoflorenzo.org/ or http://www.nysparks.com

For Further Reference: Atwell, Christine. *Cazenovia Past and Present: A Descriptive and Historical History of the Village*. Bowie, MD: Heritage Books, Inc., 2012.

While Here: Visit the Cazenovia Library at 100 Albany Street. Upstairs is the Museum of Oddities. Fun museum with an actual mummy!

Tours: Early May until mid-October, Wednesday through Sunday, and holiday Mondays: 10:00 a.m. to 4:00 p.m.

Admission:
Adults: $5.00
Seniors and students: $4.00
Children 12 and under: Free

18

Charlotte-Genesee Lighthouse Keeper's House

Home of Keepers of America's Oldest Surviving Lighthouse on Lake Ontario
Charlotte, Monroe County

When I was drawing up the list for this book, I didn't want it to be just a litany of splendid mansions and sprawling estates, although there is a large segment of the book dedicated to those residences. I also wanted the list to include houses with a different profile, a different history. That is why there are chapters featuring a rare octagon house, a rough-hewn cabin in the woods, a farm, and a doctor's office.

And then this lighthouse keeper's residence.

"This lighthouse played an important part in the history of Rochester," Fred Amato told me. He is the president of the Charlotte-Genesee Lighthouse Historical Society. "In the beginning this was way out in the wilderness. It was then part of the Town of Greece. Over the years the Port of Rochester grew up. Lake Ontario and the Genesee River come together at this point, making this a very busy area for shipping and water travel. So, it was decided to establish a lighthouse here in 1822 to oversee it all.

"The early lighthouse keepers, the civilians, had a difficult life out here. They had serious responsibilities and were pretty much alone. Except for their families, of course. In fact, we know that an early keeper was Giles Holden who lived here in the original two-room stone cottage with twelve of his children. Hard to imagine," Amato said with a smile. The original house was twenty by thirty-four feet, its two rooms separated by a large

fireplace, and included a fifty-two-foot-deep well. The cost to build the house and the original tower was $3,301. David Denman, an elderly veteran, was the first keeper to live in the cottage, but he died within a year. He was followed by the first permanent keeper, Giles Holden, who lasted from 1823 to 1835. The keeper's pay was $350 annually.

Today's adjoining lighthouse residence was built in 1863. It is a fine, sturdy brick structure with three floors, eight rooms, and a basement. What would have been the bedrooms and kitchen have now been turned into exhibit areas for those wanting to explore the history of the lighthouse. The basement had a coal bin and an open cistern that collected rain water for house use. There was an outhouse (privy).

The land upon which the tower and the keeper's house were built was owned by Mehitabel Hincher who, with her late husband William, a Revolutionary War veteran, was among the first settlers in this area north of Rochester. She sold the four-acre property to the US government after her husband's death in 1817, for the purpose of building a lighthouse and a keeper's residence for a total of $400.

The port dates from 1805, when President Thomas Jefferson established the Port of the Genesee at Charlotte, a tiny hamlet where the river met the lake, and appointed Samuel Latta as the first customs collector. His 1806 house is still standing just a block away from the lighthouse property. This immediate area was attacked by the British four different times during the War of 1812, a mere ten years before the lighthouse was built.

The first keepers were originally employed by the US Lighthouse Service until it merged with the Revenue Cutter Service in 1915. Then they became government employees as new rules were put into place that stated that the lighthouse keepers at all US lighthouse towers had to belong to the US Coast Guard. On July 1, 1939, the Coast Guard merged with the Lighthouse Service and the Revenue Cutter Service and assumed all responsibilities for the operation of the lighthouses, thus ending the era of civilian keepers.

This house has been home to eighteen different keepers and their families. From David Denman in 1822 to the last keeper, Wilbur L. Folwell Sr. who lived here from 1940 to 1947, the house has seen few changes in its design and integrity. The tower has seen many changes, structurally, architecturally, and technologically. In fact, the tower, which is only forty inches from the house, was once connected to the house by an interior walkway for the keeper's convenience.

Although the life of the very earliest keepers was routine—keeping lamps lit and watching for errant ships approaching sandbars—that duty changed to a much more dangerous role in a few short years.

In 1829, conditions had caused the waterfront area to shift along the shoreline. Two 2,600-foot-long piers were laid out, reaching far offshore. These parallel piers represented the new entrance to the Genesee River and the port.

In 1838, an inspection report was sent to the Secretary of the US Treasury stating that after the pier installation, conditions at the lighthouse had changed dramatically. In the water, the marshy opening of the Genesee River had shifted significantly, making the lighthouse's octagonal tower even farther from the water than it had been. Also, the condition of the tower itself had deteriorated drastically and needed repairs. To remedy all of this, the government decided to place automatic beacon lights at the end of the piers to supplement the beam being thrown off by the lighthouse itself. These new beacons were added to the responsibilities of the lighthouse keeper, as was the new elevated walkway that had been erected stretching out to the beacons for the keepers to use for maintenance and repair purposes.

On August 18, 1853, lighthouse keeper Samuel Phillips was rowing through a heavy storm to reach the pier beacon, which had gone out. Twice thwarted by roiling waters, he made a third attempt to reach the end of the pier, this time accompanied by his cousin Cuyler Cook, who was an assistant lighthouse keeper himself. After they successfully lit the beacon, a large wave capsized their boat. Phillips survived by clinging to the pier's beacon all night long. Cook, who made it safely back up the pier, was then washed away by a large wave at the height of the storm. His body was found days later.

Reportedly, there are other stories of lighthouse keepers who died while working this dangerous job.

Author's Notes

I have always been fascinated with the job of a lighthouse keeper. Not so much for the technical duties, the science of the light itself, or the comings and goings of the nautical life below. But more for the commitment to solitude it must have taken to be at a remote lighthouse far from people. Some lighthouses are out in the water (in the Hudson River, for example) and others are precariously positioned on rocky peninsulas. But no matter where they are located, the life of the keeper must have been pretty much the same.

I imagine it must have taken a person who was comfortable being alone, although many had families with them (with even as many as twelve children). Some keepers mixed with their local communities and sent their children to local schools. And they had farms they tended. But others were far from provisions, far from assistance in emergencies, far from schools for their children and, well, just far from everything.

The importance of this occupation cannot be denied. For a time, ships were alerted to dangerous sandbars here on Lake Ontario by merely following a lantern swinging from a butternut tree branch along the shore (there is an example of this setup in the first room of the tour). But a human was really needed in these early, dangerous days, and the lighthouse keeper's role was created. They were officials, they were the men in charge. This was not something done lightly. They had uniforms with brass buttons, double-breasted coats, and a cap with an official lighthouse keeper's badge in the middle. They kept meticulous records and many times were called upon to go above and beyond the call of duty (witness the death of Cuyler Cook).

It is just a house, for sure, but one that is a capsule of a time gone by, of a job no longer needed, and of men who were respected and responsible. Men of courage. Perhaps my feelings for them can be summed up by the epitaph on the gravestone of Cuyler Cook, who perished while tending this very light. He is buried nearby in the Charlotte Cemetery.

> To God above, His spirit yield,
> He took him in his strength and bloom
> When struggling with the seas and waves,
> He wove his garland for his tomb.

Visit

Genesee-Charlotte Lighthouse
70 Lighthouse Street
Rochester, NY 14612
585-621-6179
Website: http://www.geneseelighthouse.org

Note: For a view from atop the lighthouse, a weather video camera affixed to the top streams live 24 hours a day at https://www.weatherbug.com/weather-camera/?cam=RCGLH.

For Further Reference: Muller, Robert G. *New York State Lighthouses.* Mount Pleasant, SC: Arcadia Publishing, 2006.

While Here: Charlotte is a suburb of Rochester. Located just five miles to the south, that city has many interesting museums, theaters, historic sites, and restaurants to explore.

Tours: By appointment. Children must be older than 7 years of age, must be accompanied by an adult, and must be over 4 feet tall to climb the tower.

Admission:

Adults 18 and older: $5.00
Youth 5 to 17: $2.00
Children 4 and under: Free
Group rates available on request

19

Stone-Tolan House

Oldest Building in Monroe County
Rochester, Monroe County

"Although this area around Rochester seems very busy right now, at the time of the building of this home (rear wing in 1792; front section in 1805), this was in a rural, remote area. However, two major Seneca Indian trails came through here, so the founders erected not only a home, but a tavern at this spot," Cindy Boyer told me. She is the director of public programs of the Landmark Society of Western New York. "Orringh and Elizabeth Stone built, lived in, and worked in this home. They were smart business people and built a tavern in their home that provided food and a place to sleep for the travelers who came through on their way west."

The house, built in the classic vernacular Federal Style, has two sections. They are constructed of post and plank materials covered over with clapboard siding. Originally, the Stones worked this as a family farm, but seeing the necessity for a small inn, they added a tavern in the front room and provisions for overnight stays. It was a busy place. In fact, there are stories about the Marquis de Lafayette staying here as well as Aaron Burr, Mohawk leader Joseph Brant, and Louis-Phillippe, who would later become the King of France.

Originally, there were seven rooms on the first floor and sleeping rooms upstairs and in a loft. There is a fireplace in every room. Although there are very few possessions dating back to the original Stone family left in this house, it is set up to give a realistic look at what it would have been like carving out an existence in the wilderness.

Everything for all of the family's needs was done on the property. The kitchen has a large brick fireplace with two side cubbyholes to hold wood and a bake oven. There is a pantry off the kitchen where all the foodstuffs were held and next to that is a spare workroom that substituted for a traveler's guest room when the house was full. "Oddly, the kitchen fireplace hearth stretches under a wall and well into the guest bedroom. We really can't understand why. Not the fireplace, mind you, just the hearth," Boyer told me.

Since the second floor of this historic home is not open to the general public, one of the rooms downstairs is set up as a period bedroom to give visitors a sense of the era.

Clearly, the highlight of this house tour is the tavern room in the front. It is staged as if it is open to the guests who might have wandered down a wilderness trail some two centuries ago. The family did the cooking and cleaning in the back, and the front shows a small yet comfortable meeting place. And, in fact, meetings were held here for many years. Some say the legal papers for setting up the Town of Brighton were planned and executed here in Stone's Tavern.

A table is set with mock foods of the era, including eggs placed in wine glasses rather than egg holders. Antique parlor games are set up on a table in front of the fireplace. In one corner of the room a triangle bar is set up. It is separated from the main room by a high counter, a door, and a drop-down wooden grill gate. One curious item is a chalk-drawn calendar above the door allowing visitors to keep track of their days on the road. This was a tavern custom as seen in several early American paintings.

"Obviously this is the most popular room in the house," Boyer told me. "We have public events in here. One of the most anticipated of those is our 'Tavern Takeover Nights.' On these nights we invite local craft brewers to come in and serve their beers from behind this 200-year-old bar. We have to get a one-night liquor license for those events, but it is worth it. They usually sell out, the public loves it, and the craft brewers really enjoy serving up their brews in what would be the oldest tavern in the county."

The original property consisted of about 200 acres. Now the plot consists of about four acres. Outside there are several points of interest. You can see the large "summer kitchen" attached to the outside of the house. This is where they could cook in the warm months, do laundry, and make apple butter from their own apples. "The orchard today consists of nineteenth-century historical varieties of apples grafted onto twentieth-century stock. We have about forty trees on the property," Boyer said.

Also on the property is a large boulder known as Council Rock. "Yes, although it appears to be huge, believe it or not, there is twice as much rock underground as there is above ground. It was a Seneca Indian gathering place. 'Meet at the rock,' they would say," Boyer related.

A large barn in the back of the property now holds an orientation center for visitors, family diagrams, and timelines, as well as some items that have surfaced during the years on the property. These items include jaw harps, animal bones (which helped historians learn what the early families ate), knives, spoons, plates, and ceramic tiles. "We did a lot of work to make this a place nice for our visitors. These are the original floorboards from the 1880s. They look so nice because when we fixed this barn up we simply flipped the original floorboards over to the side that was never walked on," Boyer said.

Orringh Stone had ten children; eight with his first wife Elizabeth and two with his second wife, Sally West. Out of the ten children he had seven girls and three sons. Elizabeth died shortly after giving birth to her final child, a boy, and that son lived only a few short months. The surviving son, Enos, left Brighton to join the California Gold Rush of 1849 and was absent for many years. "Orringh Stone died in 1839 and there were several short-term owners between the Stone family and up to when John A. Tolan bought the house on December 17, 1860," I was told.

Tolan had two daughters. One, Mary, was a nun who joined the Sisters of Mercy and who gave much of the property to their convent. Fearing the house would be razed, and with an eye for historical preservation, the remaining daughter, Ellen, sold the house to the Landmark Society of Western New York in 1956 with a stipulation that she be allowed to live in it until her death. Ellen, the last surviving Tolan to live in the house, died in 1965 at the age of ninety-nine.

The house was first opened for public tours in 1976, to celebrate our nation's bicentennial.

The designers of the Stone-Tolan House fashioned the corners of the house to look like stone blocks to impress visitors. They are actually all wood.

Author's Notes

As an Upstate New York writer, there are several reasons why I liked the Stone-Tolan House so much. I think the biggest reason for me is the fact that it is the oldest structure in Monroe County. When you factor in that there can only be sixty-two buildings in the entire state that can claim the title of oldest in their county, it is sure to catch a historian's eye. Also, this house, unlike several others even in this book, has never been moved. The front porch, the back orchard, the outside summer kitchen—all are facing the exact same views as they did more than two centuries ago.

Visitors should note the exterior paint scheme. The house is painted barn red but the corners are painted gray as if to give the impression that the house is cornered in stone block columns. Not so. It might take you a short walk up to the structure and a few knocks on the "stone" corner columns to realize it was all an architectural ruse. The entire exterior is in fact all wood. This was a common ploy in fancier Federal-style houses. The corners are called coigns, from the French for corner.

It appears that at a couple of times through this old house's timeline, there was an opportunity to sell it off to developers or others. It is satisfying to see that those opportunities were denied and that it continues to operate as a historic vessel for future generations.

Lastly, this house continues to play an active role in the community. And with Stone-Tolan also having been the first tavern in the county, that certainly is a real plus.

"When we have our tavern nights it is so wonderful to see so many young people attend and see, perhaps for the first time, what we have here. We bring on docents who are adept at starting conversations with people and let them mingle among the twenty-, twenty-five-, and thirty-year-olds who attend. It gives all of us great pleasure to see this old 200-year-old home come alive again with laughter and smiling faces," Boyer told me.

Visit

Stone-Tolan House
2370 East Avenue
Rochester (Town of Brighton), NY 14610

Landmark: Stone-Tolan House is located in a heavily residential area and is set back from the road. Watch for a small red sign alerting you to the driveway.
585-546-7029
Website: http://landmarksociety.org/

For Further Reference: Grenier, Mary and Emily Morry. *Rochester Through Time.* America Through Time (series). Mount Pleasant, SC: Arcadia Publishing, 2015.

While Here: Brighton, New York, is three miles from the Stone-Tolan House. Brighton once was one of the largest brickmaking centers in New York. Today there are seventeen existing structures in the "Bricks of Brighton" historic district. They were all constructed of bricks made in Brighton in the 1800s.

Tours: The house is open for drop-in tours on the fourth Friday of every month. Other tours, including group tours, are welcome and can be arranged by calling the Landmark Society in advance.

Admission:
Adults: $5.00
Children: $2.00

20

The Bond-Hawley House

Home of Col. William M. Bond and Jesse Hawley
Lockport, Niagara County

"The Colonel Bond House was built in 1823. Bond and his wife, Nancy, arrived in Lockport from New Hampshire in 1821 with several members of their family to take part in the growth of both Lockport and the Erie Canal. The canal reached Lockport about the same time as the Bonds arrived," Rebecca Pittler told me. She is a volunteer docent at the house and has been involved in the Niagara Historical Society for many years. "Although the house appears crowded in the middle of the city block it inhabits today, in 1823 it would have been a grand home situated on nearly 200 acres."

The Bond House was the first brick house built in the city of Lockport and one of the first in the entire county. It is a three-story late Federal/early Greek Revival–style home with a total of twelve rooms. There are four original rooms on the first floor including a parlor, dining room, library, and kitchen (there is also a second kitchen that was added later). The second floor has four rooms plus a maid's room. There are three rooms on the third floor.

A formal entrance welcomes guests into the home. "We have had to do a bit of rearranging this house in our minds," Pittler told me. "In more recent years, the house had been portioned off into several apartments and after the Niagara County Historical Society took possession of it in 1968, they wanted to restore it back to its original configuration."

Immediately to the left upon entering is the most formal room in the house. This parlor was used for entertaining guests and for special

occasions. Although there is little that can be traced back to the original Bond family, the historical society (which owns the house) has done a wonderful job of furnishing it with attractive antique furniture and items that reflect the early to mid-1800s era. In the parlor is one of the most unique items in the house. It is an oddly beautiful multi-tiered black curio shelf. "Yes, we think this is a great item. It is actually made of papier-mâché and has painted gilded edges and inlaid mother-of-pearl. It is quite a rare item," Pittler told me. The walls are lined with old portraits. At the time of my visit the room was festooned with Christmas finery and was a nostalgic tribute to a bygone era.

The library, located off the dining room, was also used as an office. Again, there are many portraits lining the walls of this room. Many of them are of people with local connections who gained fame in other places. One, Solon M. N. Whitney, of Niagara Falls, New York, was manager of that city's famous Cataract Hotel and a civic leader, served on several prestigious boards, served as mayor of Niagara Falls, and at the time of his death was the oldest resident in the city.

This room was also believed to be used as a music room. Here you will find a beautiful early-1800s music box. "We love this," Pittler said. "When we got it, it didn't work but after a while it was discovered that all it needed was a spring. It is a lovely addition to this room and demonstrates an early innovation when music could be heard without actually playing an instrument." This room also holds one of the several rare Eli Terry mantel clocks to be found in the house. It features a painting of a young couple on the front. Terry was a master clockmaker from Connecticut who taught Seth Thomas and others his craft.

The dining room is set up as if to welcome a family together to enjoy a formal dinner. This room also contains the only piece of furniture that can be dated back to the Bond family, a beautiful sideboard.

The kitchen evokes a family cooking area of the mid-nineteenth century. There is a dry sink, some old cooking implements, and a large original cooking hearth.

A servant's room, sewing room, nanny's room, and several bedrooms complete the house. Each is appointed with period furnishings appropriate to that room. For example, in the "boy's room" there are several different vintage toys of the era when the Bond family children grew up.

The entire house is beautifully decorated and filled to overflowing with interesting antiques and curiosity pieces. The first thing you will discover when entering the house, for instance, is an antique walking stick that opens to reveal a saber.

The Niagara County Historical Society narrates this structure as a house museum, and they do an excellent job of it. The house was placed on the National Register of Historic Places in 1995.

Although Col. Bond built this home, he only lived in it briefly, from 1823 to 1831. He was an early investor in the growth of Lockport, during the heyday of the beginning of the Erie Canal activity. He was not always an adroit dealmaker, however; by 1831 he was buried in debt and New York State seized his holdings. At this point the ownership of the Bond house passed to his brother-in-law Jesse Hawley. Therefore, the house is referred to often as the Bond-Hawley House.

Jesse Hawley has a fascinating story. A failed business venture landed Hawley in jail for twenty months. During his incarceration, Hawley, who had an intense interest in the benefits of water trade and canal technology, wrote fourteen articles to a local newspaper, the *Canandaigua Messenger*, which laid out his thoughts on the advantages of an east-west New York State canal as well as examining the pros and cons of different canal routes. These were serious discussions and caught the attention of legislators in Albany who were just beginning to imagine a canal from the state capital to the Great Lakes. Because of this, Hawley is considered by many to be one of the originators of the Erie Canal.

It was descendant Kate Chase Seymour who divided the house up into apartments while she was still living there, to ease the financial burden of owning such a large residence. She died in 1955 and left the property to her adopted son, Erdman MacDonald. When he died in 1968 the Niagara County Historical Society bought the house.

Author's Notes

The Bond House has a timeline like so many of the other homes that I have researched for this book. The house, obviously of great import to the city of Lockport, was handed down through the years to eight different owners. As is the norm, over the years expenses grew, repairs were needed (and oftentimes neglected), changes were made to keep the structure viable in private hands (such as fashioning this house into several apartments) and then, ultimately, the house came to its final crossroads. I have heard many stories over my travels of houses that have come to this understandable crossroad to meet the fate of falling into irretrievable disrepair and many even having to be demolished.

The Niagara County Historical Society has rescued a piece of Lockport (and New York State) history since the time they "saved" the Bond House in 1968. "All of us are so committed to the viability of the house. It has so many wonderful stories. We are part of the local historical society, and we try and hold events and give tours that will show off these stories. Of course, like so many other older historic homes, there is always something that needs to be repaired or replaced. And that can be a bit of a struggle. But we keep on with our mission, we keep our doors open, and we look forward to sharing our rich history with any and all that come here," Pittler said.

I strongly suggest that you put Lockport on your New York State history "bucket list." Come for the locks but start your visit at the historic Col. Bond House just a few blocks away.

Visit

The Col. William M. Bond House (aka The Bond-Hawley House)
143 Ontario Street
Lockport, NY 14094
Niagara County Historical Society: 716-434-7433
Website: http://www.niagarahistory.org

For Further Reference: Linnabery, Ann Marie. *Historic Postcards of Lockport,* N.Y. Lockport, NY: Niagara County Historical Society, 2012.

While Here: Lockport has many great sights to see when coming here for a visit. Of course, the famous Erie Canal locks are the top tourist draw. The Bond House is located just a few blocks from the "Flight of Five." This is a series of five canal locks on top of each other that carried the canal up and over the daunting Niagara Escarpment, the greatest impediment in the construction of the canal. These locks were one of the greatest engineering marvels of their day. An underground cave tour explains much about the construction of the canal, and includes a subterranean boat ride.

Tours: The Bond House is open by appointment only from the beginning of June through Christmas. It has no set hours, but arrangements can be made to visit by calling the Niagara County Historical Society.

Admission: Free, but donations are welcome.

21

Wilcox Octagon House

Home of Isaiah Wilcox
Camillus, Onondaga County

Octagon houses are a rare breed of homes.

They sprouted up in the 1850s, championed by a man named Orson Squire Fowler. He was a phrenologist, writer, and amateur architect. He believed that the most efficient and inexpensive way to build a substantial house was to make it eight sided. He believed that this type of design led to convenient heating in the winter and cooling in the summer and, because of all the angled walls, would allow the maximum amount of light into the residence. His concept took off briefly, and at one time there were hundreds of octagon homes built around the country. Today many of them are gone, fallen victim to changing times, deterioration, neglect, and neighborhood transformations. Still, you can find them if you look hard enough. You can find them in large places like metropolitan New York City and in tiny villages like Unadilla. In New York State there are nearly fifty known octagon houses, maybe more.

One of the finest is the Wilcox Octagon House in Camillus, New York.

"Our house is quite large for an octagon," Joy Flood told me. She is the first vice president of the volunteers of the Octagon House. "It is a full six-story house, from sub-basement all the way up to the cupola. The house was constructed using materials found on the Wilcox farm, including wood, stone, and bricks. They also made their own mortar. It took two and a half years to build and was finished in 1856. The sub-basement is quite remarkable. This is where the servants would store and prepare food.

The walls are twenty-two inches thick down there, making it a perfect cold storage area to keep produce, meat, and dairy products."

Each of the eight sides is seventeen feet long, and the house consists of ten square rooms and eight triangular rooms. "Each room has a unique closet in it. Back in the day, taxes were based on the number of rooms; closets with doors were considered rooms. Having closets altogether in this house was unusual since most farmhouses didn't have closets or windows in every room. Fowler emphasized that having windows in every room afforded a healthier way of living since you would have more light and cross ventilation when you open the windows. Fresh air! Also, a kind of central air conditioning if you open the upstairs windows and draw the cool air of the basement," I was told.

Only two families lived in this house over a period encompassing more than a century. The property surrounding the house was once a 138-acre working farm. The Wilcoxes had a large orchard behind the house where they grew five different varieties of apples. Although there are few remaining personal possessions belonging to the two families (Wilcox and Fox), the house itself is the main attraction here.

Unlike smaller octagon houses, this one is large enough that some visitors might not ever get a sense of disorientation. The rooms, although angled into octagonal corners, are as large as those would be in a regular home. There are no fireplaces. The house was comfortably heated by cast-iron wood and coal stoves on the main floor. The family moved their sleeping quarters down to this floor during the winter months and the second-floor rooms were simply closed off.

The living room, two parlors, kitchen, and pantry are all staged in period items to evoke the lifestyle of the original family. There are old oil paintings on the wall, a fireplace mantel in the back parlor (no fireplace, though), a vintage organ, hand-poured glass windows, and ceiling lamps that were once gas- and oil-fed but are now electrified.

"The house is pretty much set up as it would have been for the Wilcox family. The upstairs bathroom is quite unique. The water for the sink and tub was pumped into the house by a windmill located in the backyard. The family used a lead-lined bathtub (now gone), which was situated under a large window overlooking the orchards. The water came into the basement where it would have been heated up by the servants and then carried all the way up several floors to pour into the tub for a bath. That was a lot of work," Flood told me.

The pantry was the real workhorse of the house. Located in the basement, this was where the servants baked and cooked, killed chickens, smoked meats, and prepared the meals that would later be sent upstairs by a dumbwaiter. The original door from the pantry opens to the backyard. Remnants of an old cistern can also be seen here, basically a large stone-walled pool of water for household use.

The original front door was built extra wide to accompany female guests who arrived dressed in fancy hoop skirts. An eight-sided front porch rings the house. In several places throughout the house, panels have been installed to show original house wallpapers, paint, and construction materials. One floor, leading to the basement, was left uncovered to display the architectural beginnings of the house.

"The home became empty and began to deteriorate around 1968. As demolition loomed large, a local woman, Betty Campbell, who was related to the Fox family, helped raise funds to preserve it. She became the first director of the Volunteers of the Octagon House. She saved it and for that we are most grateful to her," Flood said.

The house is today owned by the Town of Camillus and is operated by the volunteers.

Isaiah and Ann Wilcox were farmers who built this house and tended their adjoining apple orchards, gardens, and livestock. They had two children and have no known living descendants. Isaiah Wilcox was a fervent abolitionist. "Although we have no proof, we believe that this house acted as a way station on the Underground Railroad. Mr. Wilcox was against slavery, the house is near the Erie Canal for quick passage to Buffalo and on to Canada, and our sub-basement which had its own exterior door would have made a perfect hiding place. Sadly, no documentation of that exists, however," Flood told.

Descendants of the second occupants, the Fox family, have visited the Octagon House. "The second-generation members of their family came to visit us about four years ago. We were so pleased to meet them. They came on Mother's Day and showed us how the family utilized the rooms and celebrated holidays in the house many years ago. Before they left, they presented us with the original deed to the house. We were thrilled," she said.

Author's Notes

This is the first octagon house I have ever been in. I was surprised how spread out the rooms were. They are not small, busy, or kaleidoscopic as I imagined. Even though the Wilcoxes had only two children, it was easy to imagine a large family living here.

Joy Flood did an excellent job as tour guide. She was smart. She took me way down to the sub-basement at the beginning of my visit. From there we worked our way all the way up to the cupola. She does this on purpose so as to give a visitor the maximum effect of how tall this house really is. You follow a circular staircase up sixty-two steps to the top, getting off to explore at each landing. The glass cupola offers a reward for the climb by showcasing a beautiful view of the surrounding Camillus landscape (the cupola is the tallest spot in the town).

Of the many surprises along the way, one that I found most interesting was the staircase itself. Wilcox really had an infatuation with the whole octagon concept. The winding wooden stair banister and its balusters are carved with eight sides, all the way from the bottom to the top!

Visit

Wilcox Octagon House Museum
5420 West Genesee Street
Camillus, NY 13031
315-488-7800
Website: http://www.octagonhouseofcamillus.org

For Further Reference: Fowler, Orson Squire. *The Octagon House: A Home for All.* Mineola, NY: Dover Publishing, 1973.

While Here: The Camillus Erie Canal Park is nearby. Be sure and visit the Sims Museum, which is a replica of an Erie Canal general merchandise store.

Tours: 1:00 p.m. to 5:00 p.m. (April to November). For other dates, group tours, and events call the Octagon House.

Admission: The tours are free, but all donations are greatly appreciated.

22

Barnes-Hiscock Mansion

Home of George Barnes and Hon. Frank Hiscock
Syracuse, Onondaga County

You can still see the ghosts of the Gilded Age along Syracuse's tony James Street. Many of the fine old mansions have now been turned into corporate offices, nonprofit headquarters, and multiple family dwellings. A handful still stand alone, exactly as they looked over a century and a half ago. The Barnes-Hiscock mansion is perhaps the best example of this.

"The home was built in 1854 for George and Rebecca Barnes. Barnes was a wealthy civic leader, industrialist, and abolition leader. It was later the home of Frank Hiscock, who married George's daughter, Mary Elizabeth Barnes. Frank Hiscock was the chief judge of the New York State Court of Appeals. There were many important people connected to this historic house, and many important events took place here," Arlene Stewart told me. She is a founder and first president of the George and Rebecca Barnes Foundation.

The house was originally built in the Italianate villa design style and was later converted to a three-story antebellum-style home in 1894. It was the first residence built on the hill at the top of James Street. "People thought George was crazy to build up here. At the time this was far from the center of Syracuse. He already had a beautiful home in the city. When this mansion was completed, he advertised his other home for sale in the newspaper he owned, the *Syracuse Evening Chronicle*. Anxious to get it sold and move into his new showplace, George drew up an ad declaring the house for sale to be 'one of the city's finest, including an attached

outhouse.' The house sold in quick order and the Barneses moved into the new home," Stewart said.

The house underwent several design changes from the original concept. During the residency of Frank and Mary Hiscock it was refashioned in the Colonial Revival style popular in the late nineteenth century. After the renovations were completed by Frank and Bessie (his wife, Mary Elizabeth) Hiscock, the house became known for its six towering Corinthian columns in the front. When the home was sold to a woman's club in 1949, it became known as the Syracuse Corinthian Club. The club maintained ownership of the home until 2009 when it sold the property to the George and Rebecca Barnes Foundation.

A long circular driveway would deposit guests at the front door. Many of those guests were among the top tier of Syracuse and, in fact, New York State society.

A sweeping graceful staircase connects the first two floors. The rooms are spacious, featuring stained glass windows, fifteen-foot-tall ceilings, and elaborate woodwork throughout. The mansion originally had a fireplace in each of the eight bedrooms, with a total of a dozen fireplaces in the entire home.

The dining room is perhaps the most spectacular room in the house. The walls are topped with rare canvas panels created by Italian artist Tommaso Juglaris printed with landscape scenes and cherubs at play. "One vignette shows children at play. One is African American as you can see," Stewart pointed out. "That was Mr. Barnes's nod to his abolitionist activities."

The walls are dark and paneled with mahogany imported from England. The chair rails and wall panels reveal carved lion's head designs, a pattern found in the house. The carvings were all done by craftsmen in the Syracuse area. A unique feature is a back bar set up with six arched glass compartments. These glass doors lifted to reveal house wines and liqueurs.

"Mr. Barnes delighted in entertaining in this room," Stewart said. "In the center of the room would have been his large dining table. He would sit at the middle of the table and when time came that he needed the attention of one of the servants he simply reached his foot under the table and stepped on a small gold button, which alerted the staff to come to the dining room." The button is still on the floor.

A gathering room was used as a ceremonial room. Four weddings were held in this room as well as the Hiscocks' fiftieth anniversary celebration. Archival family photos are scattered around the room as if to introduce us to the important members of both the Barnes and Hiscock families.

In a room referred to as George's office, we can only guess at the important and sometimes secret meetings that took place here. "As you can see, the two large rooms across from each other here are almost identical. One of the rooms was known as the 'ladies' room,' where Mrs. Barnes and her female friends would gather and discuss topical issues of the day, especially women's rights. Across the hall, in the 'men's room,' George Barnes and his colleagues would meet at the same time and draw up plans for their abolitionist goals," Stewart said. Among the many male visitors that would huddle in this room were several of the leading abolition leaders of the day, including Gerrit Smith and Henry Stanton.

There are several large bedrooms upstairs. The Judge's bedroom had a joined bathroom with his wife's bedroom across the hall. "No matter what was going on, Judge Hiscock would retire to this room at nine o'clock every night. His bed was always located in the center of the room," Stewart explained. The original bed is still located in the center of the room.

Perhaps the most surprising room of all is a large bedroom on the second floor. It once had a very special and very important visitor.

"We call this the Taft Bedroom. President William Howard Taft spent many evenings at this house," Stewart said. "He was by then the chief justice of the United States Supreme Court. At the same time, Frank H. Hiscock was the chief judge of the New York State Court of Appeals. So, they had much in common. Judge Hiscock would meet Taft at the train station in his horse-drawn carriage and they would ride to the Barnes-Hiscock mansion together.

"A token that we cherish in this house is a solid silver tea service gifted to Judge Hiscock. It is inscribed to him by all of the sitting judges on the New York State Court of Appeals dated June 7, 1917." The tea service can be seen in an upstairs room that holds a collection of the family's personal possessions.

Another item that makes this house so special is that it has an elevator in it. Stewart said, "We believe that this might be the oldest residential elevator in the United States. It was installed here in 1894. We do know that the famous Greenbrier Hotel in West Virginia has one of approximately the same age, but that would be for commercial use. So, we think ours is pretty special." The mansion was also one of the first homes in Syracuse to be fully electrified.

Also on the grounds is the original carriage house. "Mr. Hiscock never owned or drove a car. He had a collection of coaches and carriages he kept in the carriage house. Even at the end of his life in 1946, when he was almost ninety years old and when everybody seemed to own an automobile, the judge could still be seen being carried about the city in his horse-drawn carriage," Stewart related.

The members of the two families who owned this residence were influential, powerful, and wealthy leaders of the Syracuse community.

George R. Barnes was born in England in 1827 and moved to Syracuse in 1844. He was a prominent lawyer, newspaperman, and businessman and a leader in the Underground Railroad activities in the city. "It is unclear how many freedom seekers he and his wife, Rebecca, helped shepherd on the route to Canada. We do know that George owned a lumberyard in St. Catharines, Canada, and that he secreted slaves from New York State to Canada hidden aboard his lumber barges," Stewart told me. In October of 1851, at the height of the Fugitive Slave Act controversy, a freed slave, William Henry (known as Jerry), was targeted by slave catchers in Syracuse, caught, and imprisoned. The city rose up and a mob physically freed him from captivity and spirited him away. George Barnes personally paid the bail for each of the three white men arrested for freeing "Jerry."

Frank Hiscock was born in Tully, New York, just south of Syracuse in 1856. His law career is one of the most stellar of any Upstate New Yorker. He was a justice on the New York State Supreme Court from 1896 to 1913 and then served as chief judge of the New York State Court of Appeals from 1917 to 1926.

He was married to Mary Elizabeth Barnes, George Barnes's daughter. She was very active in social and civic affairs in the city and was known for her prizewinning gardens on the back lawn of the mansion. She lived to be eighty, dying on her husband's eighty-first birthday. Judge Hiscock lived to be ninety years old.

Author's Notes

This very old home is very much alive today. The Corinthian Club, an all-women's organization, meets here regularly and holds private and public functions. This author has done several book presentations at the mansion.

There are many small things to notice as you take a guided walking tour of the mansion. For example, you will notice that in some of the front rooms there are tiny lights dotting the ceiling. These were placed there to evoke a starry night sky when entertaining guests. In the formal dressing room hangs a family wedding dress, long train and all. "You can just imagine how beautiful the bride would be wearing this gown while descending our large, curved staircase," Stewart commented.

And then there are the fireplaces. Although none of them is currently in use, each one is of a different design, color, and texture to reflect the room it is in. The array is quite beautiful. In the children's bedroom the fireplace is of white brick; in the Judge's bedroom the fireplace tiles are bright red. The fireplace in the dressing room is emerald green and others are pink and a mixed marble. The fireplace in the Taft Bedroom is cobalt blue.

The house is exquisitely elegant. But the main dining room, with its mahogany walls and illustrated canvas panels, is still the highlight. Roxanne Dawson, the mansion's office manager, accompanied Ms. Stewart and me on our tour. I asked her which room was her favorite.

"Without a doubt, the dining room. It is just so beautiful. I am passionate about this house and my job. I see so many wonderful people and enjoy being a part of the rich history of the mansion. I just love it here, and I guess you could say this is my home away from home. Everything about the house is magnificent but this dining room is special to me. The canvas panels, the stained glass, the dark wood, the elaborate fireplace. It is wonderful."

Visit

Barnes-Hiscock Mansion
920 James Street
Syracuse, NY 13203
315-422-2445
Website: http://www.grbarnes.org

For Further Reference: Hardin, Eva Maria. *Syracuse Landmarks: A Guide to Downtown and Historic Neighborhoods.* Syracuse, NY: Syracuse University Press, 1993.

While Here: Clinton Square in downtown Syracuse is one of the great urban squares in Upstate New York. The former location of the Erie Canal pass-through, today the square is ringed with magnificent buildings dating back to the mid-1800s. There are several significant monuments and statues here (including the Jerry Rescue Monument) and it is a great gathering place for public events, concerts, and festivals.

Tours: The mansion is open for tours on Saturday and Sundays all year long. Tours may be arranged for other times by calling ahead for an appointment.

This is one of the few massive old homes in this book that remains totally accessible due to the early installation of an elevator. There are restrooms located on all three floors.

Admission:

Adults: $5.00
Seniors, military, and students with ID: $3.00
Children: $2.00

23

The Gage Home

Home of Matilda Joslyn Gage
Fayetteville, Onondaga County

Ask any student of history to name the three most prominent women who were the founders of the women's rights movement in America and you will quickly get the answers of Susan B. Anthony and Elizabeth Cady Stanton. But the third one many times is a puzzler. Although you might not know the name of Matilda Joslyn Gage, she is nonetheless a towering figure in the history of the women's rights movement and was an activist who showed a steely fortitude in her passion for equal rights, Native American rights, abolition, women's suffrage, and religious issues.

"Matilda Joslyn Gage is one of the 'big three,'" Colleen Pilcher told me. She is the deputy director of the Gage Center for Social Justice Dialogue in Fayetteville. "Actually, the three formed a formidable triumvirate when it came to action in the women's rights movement," she said as she pointed to three portraits on the wall of the Women's Rights Room. Gage was in the center. "A lot of the foundation of the movement began right in this house."

Matilda and her husband, Henry Gage, moved into their home in this suburb of Syracuse in 1854 and it is where most of her social justice work was done while she lived here for forty-four years. The house is of Greek Revival design and while added on to over the years, it was brought back to its original design using photos taken by Wizard of Oz author L. Frank Baum, Gage's son-in-law, while he lived in the house in 1889.

Each of the rooms is dedicated to a segment of Gage's work for justice. The rooms are titled Underground Railroad, Women's Rights, and

Religious Freedom, among others. "We also have the Haudenosaunee Room. This room is dedicated to the influence of the Haudenosaunee (Iroquois), where women had full equality, on Gage and other women's rights leaders. Gage supported treaty rights and Native sovereignty. She was given an honorary adoption into the Wolf Clan of the Mohawk Nation and given the name of 'Ka-ron-ien-ha-wi,' which translates to 'Sky Carrier,'" I was told. The room has many artifacts on display including the beautiful clothing of Haudenosaunee women and nineteenth-century women.

The narration in each room, through photographs, personal items, and period furnishings, is a guidebook to this important woman's life. The home was an Underground Railroad station and the room that highlights this is fascinating. There is a collection of abolition ephemera, a recreated "hiding place" behind a wall bookshelf, and a pair of heavy iron slave shackles. "The kids who go on our tours are pretty surprised when they get to this room. We let them hold the shackles to see how heavy they were. The room's ceiling depicts what the night sky would have been like on Juneteenth (the day of emancipation for American slaves in 1865) over Central New York, and among the stars and clouds are the names of actual enslaved peoples who fled from the south through the area to freedom," Pilcher said as she pointed to a name near the edge of the ceiling: Harriet Tubman.

"The center of the house's spirit can be found in the Women's Rights Room, which was the back parlor. This is where Matilda did most of her writing. We have her writing desk in this room. We allow visitors to sit at her desk and write a note to her. We keep them in hopes of preserving them in a book in the future. This is a highlight of our tour as people can channel the women's rights leader while sitting at her very own private desk." I noticed many of the single-page notes in the cubbyholes and asked if I could read one. Pilcher picked one that was unsigned and handed it to me. It was written by a visitor on May 1, 2017. It read, "Dear Matilda. My grandmother was so glad to vote in the first election that women could vote in that she rode from her home in a horse and buggy to cast her ballot in 1920. Thank you!"

One room is known as the Oz Room. "Matilda's daughter, Maud, married L. Frank Baum in 1882. He was traveling with his play at the time and of course went on to great fame as the author of The Wonderful Wizard of Oz books. Maud and Frank actually got married in the front parlor of this home," Pilcher said. The room is amazing due to the fact that there is a replica of a photograph on display here that was taken when the Baum family lived in the house in the summer of 1887. It is the only known photograph of the house's interior and it clearly shows how this room was set up nearly 150 years ago. Although there is only one photo of the interior, other photos that Baum took showing the exterior of the house were used when the foundation was renovated.

Some of the furnishings are original to the time of the photograph. An exact twin of the ornate chandelier hanging in the photograph was found in Ohio and was purchased during the restoration of the house. "The room is to honor the influence Gage had on the Oz books. Telling Frank to write the stories, she influenced the strong female heroine Dorothy and the social justice themes found in the series.

"Also, in this room we have a painting done by Matilda, titled 'Apple Branch,' on the wall, as well as a photograph of her painting it," Pilcher said.

A recent Welcome Center was added to the rear of the home as the formal visitor's entrance. This addition is modeled after the original wood shed that was on the Gage property.

"There is so much history in this house. And we almost lost it. When our foundation acquired the home in 2002 it had been repurposed into three apartments. It was a lot of work to get it back to its original configuration, but we believe the house will stand for many years as a testament to one of America's greatest women's rights pioneers. It is also the only home left that is open to the public where L. Frank Baum lived."

Despite the impressive history that exists in this house, it was after all a home. Matilda and Henry raised four children here. The house was built on a gentle rise that offered a beautiful view to the west. They named their home "Sunset View."

Matilda Joslyn Gage was an equal to Anthony and Stanton. With them she coedited the first three volumes of the History of Women's Suffrage. She was much more progressive than either of her two colleagues and this caused her to branch out later in her career. The three women had organized the National Woman Suffrage Association and later Gage, disappointed at the slow movement toward suffrage, went out on her own and formed the Women's National Liberal Union in 1890.

Gage was inducted into the National Women's Hall of Fame in 1995. Her induction entry reads: "Matilda Joslyn Gage holds a significant position in history as a radical feminist thinker and historian whose writings shaped her times."

Author's Notes

The homes in this book have significant historical value. A few of them take that value to the next level when you consider the famous Americans who were actually in the homes. And that is what really made this such a special place for me.

The upstairs bedroom here is identified as the Anthony Room. "We know that Susan B. Anthony was a frequent overnight guest in this house," Pilcher said as we climbed the stairs to the library, where Anthony slept. Inside this small simple bedroom are a bed, some basic furniture, and a few items encompassing the house's history.

For the second time in researching this book, however, I was surprised to observe something most unusual. I had seen it once before at the Lansing Manor in Blenheim. And now here.

"If you look at this old window carefully you can see where Anthony actually scratched her signature into the glass," Pilcher told me as we leaned up to the window and squinted in the afternoon sun. It was faint and dainty, but it was clearly a Susan B. Anthony "autograph." I asked her how she did this. "Family history tells us Anthony scratched her name into the glass window using her diamond ring."

What was once the dining room on the main floor is where Gage did most of her research and writing. It is not hard for me to imagine Matilda hunched over a stack of papers, writing furiously away in the glow of a dim light, when all of a sudden Susan B. Anthony comes padding down the stairs and enters the room. The two perhaps share a quiet cup of tea together and then sit and collaborate deep into the night on the future role of women in America.

It is not impossible for me to imagine that happening in this house at all.

Visit

The Gage Home
Home of the Matilda Joslyn Gage Foundation
210 East Genesee Street
Fayetteville, NY 13066
315-637-9511
Website: http://www.matildajoslyngage.org

For Further Reference: Carpenter, Angelica Shirley. *Born Criminal: Matilda Joslyn Gage, Radical Suffragist.* Pierre, SD: South Dakota Historical Society Press, 2018.

While Here: Just three blocks east of the Gage house, at 109 Academy Street, is the home of President Grover Cleveland. He was born in New Jersey in 1837 but moved to Fayetteville before he was five years old. He attended Fayetteville schools. The house is now a private residence, but a historical marker tells of its significance.

Tours: Monday through Friday, 10:00 a.m. to 3:00 p.m. Also, the first and last Saturday of the month, 10:00 a.m. to 3:00 p.m.

Note: The house is accessible and has restrooms.

Admission: Free but donations are greatly appreciated.

24

Granger Homestead

Home of Gideon and Mindwell Granger
Canandaigua, Ontario County

This large, imposing three-story Federal-style wood home is situated on a park-like plot of land nestled into a neighborhood of homes just up the street from Canandaigua's busy business district. The main part of the home went up in 1816 and other sections were added later, including a north wing added around 1860. The home is graceful and features a large cast-iron one-story porch. The home has fifteen rooms, of which nine are shown on a tour.

"This is a magnificent home, for sure," Carla DeMeco said. She has been involved with the Granger Homestead for over a quarter of a century and is now one of their senior docents. "Canandaigua was one of New York's first planned communities and this residence was one of the first homes built in this area of it. It was unique in that it was a working farm located in the city. The house was built by local laborers with all local materials. It is a very large home. In fact, it is 13,000 square feet and it cost $13,000 for them to build it in 1816," she said with a smile.

The home is tall and stately and is crowned with a wood balustrade that outlines the entire top portion of the house. The architect is unknown. The house has undergone different configurations over the years and there are several different outbuildings, which include an 1816 barn and a gashousc that provided acetylene gas to light the house. The gashouse was built around 1903.

"When the last Granger to live here, Antoinette, died in 1930, her will stated that the house was not to be sold for residential use. It was her

intention that it be used as a home for retired ministers and in fact Ms. Granger willed the homestead to the Congregational Church. When it was discovered that our local school district wanted to buy the home and tear it down for a new school there was much consternation among those interested in preserving the historic structure. Judge Joseph W. Cribb, an Ontario County Surrogate Court justice, came to the rescue. He raised over $25,000 to buy the home and keep it from being torn down. He literally went door to door trying to raise funds and many of his contributions came in nickels and dimes. He really was a savior," DeMeco said.

Judge Cribb died in 2013 and his will allotted funds for the maintenance and upkeep of the Granger Homestead.

The rooms inside the home have many Granger possessions and exude a great deal of country sophistication. The hand-carved wooden fireplace mantels and room enhancements were done by a local artisan, Stephen Wood. On the main floor the two front parlors mirror each other in the Federal style. Waterford crystal chandeliers now provide light for the rooms and each sports a Rumford fireplace, which was tall and narrow to better reflect heat into a room. Thomas Jefferson had Rumford fireplaces at his home, Monticello.

The height of the ceilings in each room, eleven feet, gives the house a feeling of being much larger than it is. A long center hallway separates the two main parlors, permitting a refreshing flow of air to waft from front to back. One of the parlors features an original Granger family chair. "We looked on the bottom and we found a piece of paper attached to it that said it belonged to 'Mindwell Granger, Canandaigua.' Notice it didn't say Canandaigua, New York, since this was pre-1788 and we were not a state yet," DeMeco told me.

The colorful carpets are reproductions of the originals but are historically correct as to patterns. One room has an ornate gasolier. These were chandeliers that used gas instead of electricity. This gasolier is brass and extremely ornate, featuring depictions of people, wildlife, and mythological images. The three large images at the top represent Art, Industry, and Science.

The dining room features period furniture and a china cabinet that contains some of the Granger family china. "This large dining room table has a fun story to it," DeMeco said. "Mrs. Granger liked to call it the White House table. It was once said that Gideon Granger got this table from Dolley Madison herself when she was in the White House. Of course, after we dated this table, we realized that the First Lady famously fled the British attack and burning of the White House on August 23, 1814, taking with her only the Gilbert Stuart painting of George Washington, so our White House table really isn't so. Of course, we do like to tell the truth about the house and its possessions, but I think this is a fun story anyway," she said.

You reach the second floor by climbing a sweeping flying staircase. The elegant staircase banister is original, now over 200 years old, and goes on to reach the third floor. The second floor has more bedrooms, an office, and a bathroom with a chain pull gravity toilet.

The Granger family lived here from 1816 to 1830. The guest bedroom is called the Helen Keller Room. "Helen Keller came to Canandaigua once to give a speech. Mrs. Granger did not want someone that famous to stay at any hotel, so she invited her to stay here. Apparently, she had a wonderful visit here, as you can see," the docent said as she led me to a large photograph on the wall. It was an image of Helen Keller and the inscription read: "To Dear Mrs. Granger. With all kind love and 'mindfulness,' Sincerely, Helen Keller, 1926."

Another impressive guest photograph is in the hallway. It is of Secretary of State Edward Everett, who is now most famous as being the long-winded orator who immediately preceded Abraham Lincoln when he gave his Gettysburg Address in 1863. His handwritten inscription reads: "Dear Mrs. Gideon Granger: In grateful remembrance of December 26, 1861."

As impressive as this regal home is, the outbuildings here are just as fascinating. The Granger barns hold the largest and most extensive collection of carriages in Upstate New York. More than one hundred of them

The grounds of the Granger Homestead hold many interesting buildings, including this small law office where Stephen Douglas (famed for his debates with Abraham Lincoln) once clerked.

are on display in revolving exhibits in the two barns in the rear of the property. Also, a small columned building was moved to this property from a couple of blocks down the street and was the original law office of a local attorney, Walter Hubbell. In 1832, Stephen Douglas of Illinois first studied law under Hubbell in this very building. "Of course, we know Douglas most famously today for his political debates and campaign for the presidency in 1860 against Abraham Lincoln," DeMeco told me.

Gideon Granger was born in Connecticut in 1767. He had a storied career in that state in business and in politics. He later became the longest-serving United States postmaster general in history, serving under both Presidents Jefferson and Madison. With wealth and a stellar reputation secured he moved from Connecticut to Canandaigua where he vowed to build a "home unrivaled in all the nation." He married Mindwell Pease in 1790. Granger was a highly respected man in his new hometown of Canandaigua but lived only briefly at his new home. He died in 1822. Mindwell lived on at the homestead for many decades after, passing away near her ninetieth birthday in 1860. They had three sons, Ralph, Francis, and John, who helped their father build the home in Canandaigua. Daughter Antoinette was the last direct descendant of Gideon and Mindwell Granger to live in this home. She died in 1930.

Visit

The Granger Homestead
295 North Main Street
Canandaigua, NY 14424
585-394-1472
Website: http://www.grangerhomestead.org

For Further Reference: Hotra, Lynda M. *Canandaigua 1850–1930—A Photographic History of the Village and the Lake.* Canandaigua, NY: Ontario County Historical Society, 1982.

While Here: Canandaigua Pier is just a mile from the Granger Homestead. This pier offers a stunning view of Canandaigua Lake. Notice all of the fancy, colorful boathouses along the pier. No doubt you will see artists and photographers capturing this idyllic scene.

Tours:

Tuesday, Wednesday, Sunday: 1:00 p.m. to 5:00 p.m.
Thursday through Saturday: 11:00 a.m. to 5:00 p.m.

Last full tour of the mansion and the carriage museum barns begins at 3:00 p.m.

Admission:

Adults: $6.00
Seniors: $5.00
Students K–12: $2.00

The mansion is accessible to the first floor via an elevator lift. The carriage barns and museum are also accessible.

25

Casey's Cottage

Built by Dr. William Casey and Severin Bischof
Mexico, Oswego County

Never judge a book by its cover!

This is without a doubt the oddest home featured in this book. Well, maybe not home. Cottage, maybe. Hideaway? Part-time home? Labor of love? A getaway in the pines? Call it what you want—it is a strange house with a charming backstory and it has been a hidden jewel located near the former mouth of the Little Salmon River at Lake Ontario for over 110 years.

"This is now called Mexico Point State Park," Sandy Scott told me. She was my guide for the day. She is an author and retired educator, and a founder, charter member, and trustee of the Friends of Mexico Point. "As you can see, today the park is a lovely, quiet place for families and visitors to enjoy a day on the shores of Lake Ontario. But back in the day, this was one of the most vibrant places in the whole area. There was a large resort here called the Mexico Point Club, built in 1906. The beach was much larger then, over ninety feet long. The club was elegant and attracted families as well as the rich and famous of the area and even a few celebrities. Two famous upstate boxers, Carmen Basilio and Joey DeJohn, trained here and great crowds came to watch them. The club sent horse-drawn carriages to the local railroad station to bring guests up to the large stone clubhouse. Many of the women and children stayed all week while the men would leave to go to work on Sunday night and come back up on Friday. It was very popular. If you didn't have a reservation you didn't get in," Scott told me.

The glory days of the Mexico Point Club ended when it was destroyed by a fire in 1952. All that remains now are the thick stone wall foundations, the stone kitchen chimney, and some thick heavy chains holding up stone pillars.

And the carriage house.

"Luckily, the carriage house was located far enough from the club house that it was not damaged by the fire. It sat slowly disintegrating over the years when two friends, Dr. William Casey, a professor at Columbia University and Severin Bischof, a well-known artist, teamed up to turn the structure into their concept of an eleventh-century Norman manor house. That was 1930," Scott said.

The labor of love that is now referred to as Casey's Cottage is wonderful. The exterior of the house (although it is not a traditional home) is unassuming, and frankly quite unattractive. Vertical siding clashes clumsily with horizontal siding. Narrow "gun slits" inexplicably pock the exterior. A moss-covered roof slopes low over the building. An odd addition on the top level carries a façade of large Adirondack timbers.

"Local folklore says that when President Theodore Roosevelt once visited the Mexico Point Club he told the proprietors that he was tearing down one of his Adirondack homes and if they wanted the big timber logs for free all they had to do was go up and get them," my guide told me.

When we stepped inside the front door it was as if we were stepping through a looking glass. The interior is like a Broadway set, similar to a small castle. Soft chamber music played from unseen speakers. A display of a full suit of armor welcomed us inside. Stained glass windows bathed the place in warm hues; shadows along the walls revealed carvings of people, animals, and objects. Latin writings are stenciled throughout the rooms. Canopied beds are tucked away in corners of the second floor. Large wooden doors are carved with family last names and coats of arms. Chandeliers add to the aura and intrigue. One wall features a large old-English inscription that reads: "Lay down your armor he at last within these walls."

A real head-turner is the second floor "chapel," which was built to honor Dr. Casey's mother. One doesn't have to imagine a couple ascending the stairs on their wedding night because it is all illustrated clearly in carvings on the wall. The bride, groom, and attendants are all featured going up the steps as if their shadows have been captured in wood that now lives on eighty years later.

"They loved this place and worked on it endlessly. They came here mostly on weekends and lived here at the park. We don't really know exactly why these two gentlemen undertook this. Perhaps it was because there was no TV back then," Scott laughed.

All of the walls, floors, and furniture were hand carved by the two men. A tall central stone fireplace features two large chains draped across the front of it, "to hook up the hounds," I was told. There are some personal possessions here as well, such as Dr. Casey's favorite old "fireside chair." There are also artifacts and displays showing the era when the whole park was busy with hundreds of guests each weekend.

"We are so lucky to still have this house after all that it has gone through. It was a lady named Grace Roop who formed a group in 1989 that prevented further deterioration and maintained the cottage for historical use in the future. After seeing the exterior of this house, most visitors just cannot believe what it looks like inside. And it has been put to good use over the years. We even had mini-Renaissance festivals in here. We could feed up to thirty or forty people at once. Everybody loved it," Scott said.

Be sure and put Casey's Cottage on your upstate bucket list. It is really a one-of-a-kind place.

Dr. William C. Casey was a renowned professor of sociology at Columbia University. He died in 1978 at the age of eighty-seven. His obituary appeared in the *New York Times*.

Severin Bischof, born in Germany in 1893, was a well-known master painter who learned at the knee of his father, an expert mason, working on some of Europe's most famous cathedrals. In 1928, while a student at Syracuse University, he met Dr. William Casey and they remained lifelong friends. Bischoff died in 1983 at the age of ninety. Several of his paintings can be found at Casey's Cottage.

Local boxing legend Carmen Basilio often trained near Casey's Cottage. A folk art statue of the champ stands near where his sparring ring once was.

Author's Notes

Casey's Cottage is about as far as you can get from the regal mansions found in New York's Hudson Valley, or the moneyed palaces found along such famous residential streets as Delaware Avenue in Buffalo or Union Avenue in Saratoga Springs or even James Street in Syracuse. Still, this small unassuming cottage holds as fascinating a story within its walls as any of the other houses in this book. It is the story of a quirky idea, a decades-long commitment to realize the creation of a dream, a lifelong friendship between two gentlemen from two different worlds, and the resulting rare medieval token that now rests in a 120-acre park in Mexico, New York.

Visit

Mexico Point State Park
120 Mexico Point Drive
Mexico, NY 13114
315-963-8216 (park)
Website: http://www.mexicopointpark.com

For Further Reference: Casey's Cottage is a favorite topic of paranormal adventurists. Many unusual "happenings" have been reported to have occurred here. For more information on this as well as interior photographs of the cottage visit https://hauntedhistorytrail.com/explore/caseys-cottage-at-mexico-point-state-park.

While Here: Mexico Point State Park is a nice place to enjoy a summer afternoon. There is a public swimming area, a sandy beach, some picnic tables, outdoor grills, and restroom facilities.

Tours: Casey's Cottage is open by appointment only. Contact Sandy Scott at sanscott@gmail.com. The exterior of Casey's Cottage can be explored without a guide. Tours are highly recommended, though, for the full interior experience. Around 2,000 people visit Casey's Cottage each year.

Admission: The park is free. It is open from sunup to sundown with full facilities, including restrooms, from Memorial Day to Labor Day. Donations are appreciated when taking a tour of the interior of the cottage.

26

Richardson-Bates House

Home of Maxwell Richardson
City of Oswego, Oswego County

One thing that I found almost constant in researching, writing, and visiting the thirty-five homes featured in this book is that most of them are situated on expansive plots of land. Most of them have rolling, manicured lawns, vast gardens, an array of historic outbuildings, or even distant mountain views.

This house is different.

The Richardson-Bates mansion is tucked into a crowded residential area of the city of Oswego. Homes, most of them on the smallish side, line the block directly across from the mansion and others come right up to the property on either side. Because of this, the massive pink and green Tuscan Italian villa, with multiple protruding balconies and a central tower topped with fancy seven-foot-tall finials, looks a bit out of place here.

"When this home was built in 1867, the location would have put it in a very populated area of a fast-growing port city on the Great Lakes," Justin White commented. He is an archivist and the Oswego County historian. "The house was designed with grandeur in mind by Andrew Jackson Warner, a prolific architect from Rochester. Many fine examples of his work still exist today, including the city halls of Corning, Buffalo, and Rochester. Originally, the residence was an eight-bedroom, six-bathroom structure encompassing three floors. This included a small apartment for the servants on the third floor with bedrooms, bath, and a parlor."

The home was built for Max Richardson, a wealthy investor, insurance broker, real estate attorney, and two-time mayor of the city of Oswego.

"As was the style of the day, the entranceway was designed to impress the first-time visitor. Max was a collector of rare artifacts, including Egyptian items. He made many trips abroad over the years, including to Egypt, buying items for his collections," White said. The front of the house is guarded by two large ebony Egyptian sphinxes on either side of the tall front doors. Each door features a carved lion's head in the center. Stepping into the house from here, you are confronted with a magnificent pageant of Victorian design, massive handsomely carved furniture, a glistening chandelier and a long, elegant staircase. "This is what a visitor would see for a first impression," White told me. "People didn't just drop in to a home like this, but rather they 'called' at the home. A tall brass card stand was placed by the front entranceway and a servant would take the visitors' calling cards, and place them in the tray for Mr. Richardson and his family to view. Later on, when they returned home, they would check to see who had called on them and then return the call at the visitor's address." The original card stand can be seen on display under protective glass.

"We are so fortunate in that ninety percent of all the art work, furnishings, furniture, and antiques are personal possessions belonging to the family. The rooms are spacious, both wide and nearly fourteen feet tall as well. This allows us to present the home exactly as it was from the earliest of days. In fact, Norman Bates, the son of Max's divorced sister, Harriet, had one of the earliest personal cameras in the area, and he took photographs of every room in the house in 1889. This has been a treasure trove for us as most of the items seen in those photos are still here today and have been placed where they are in the pictures. Of course, this wasn't the creepy, scary Norman Bates that we know from the movies," he added. During the tour, each room can be shown as it was in 1889 for comparison. There is also an 1889 photograph of the family gathered on the front porch between the two sphinx statues.

Perhaps the largest, most elaborate piece of furniture in the house is a large black walnut hallstand. It nearly reaches the ceiling and weighs more than any four men could lift. It is intricately carved and features two umbrella stands on each side, stands that cleverly contain water pans to catch the rain drops from umbrellas. Each stand is decorated with an image of a crying face. "Years ago we had to move this gigantic piece of furniture to repair the carpeting. It was quite an ordeal. It revealed the wall space behind it was still bare plaster that showed the outline of the hallstand. The original wall had never been painted. This leads us to believe that the house may have actually been built around this singular piece of furniture," White said.

The reception room and the formal dining room are connected and when needed can be separated by pocket doors. These rooms are filled with museum pieces. The furniture, accessories, antiques, and curiosity pieces rival any that this writer has seen in any upstate museum. The reception room is referred to as the Egyptian Revival Room and many of Max Richardson's acquisitions from his world travels are located here. There are more than seventy original oil paintings throughout the house, and many of them can be seen arranged on a wall in the drawing room, which is a Renaissance Revival room. "Notice that the paintings in this room are hung so as to evoke an Egyptian pyramid design," White said as he pointed to the collection over the square grand piano.

The family library is dark, ornate, and filled with items pertaining to Max's business ventures and world travels. We see the early stereopticon viewer he used to regale his visitors with pictures to accompany the tales of his far-flung journeys. There is also a large, white marble bust of Minerva, the goddess of wisdom, sandwiched in between the hand-carved bookcases filled with the family's 350-book collection. The coffered ceiling was done by a local craftsman, as were the elaborate chair rails. "The price paid to do the carvings on the chair rail was $1.80 a day, or $2.50 for two days' work according to family records," I was told.

The dining room is dominated by a towering oak sideboard topped with an elk's head. "Max was an expert hunter and he wanted to showcase a favorite prize elk head on a sideboard in it. Unfortunately, when the sideboard was finished the elk head was too large and they had to file down the antlers just a little bit to make it fit," White said. The dining room table, with carved lion's heads and clawed feet underneath, was set with family chinaware and silver service pieces. A butler's pantry held the other leaves of the table, ten in all, so as to seat thirty people comfortably for a large party.

Max Richardson was a wealthy businessman and civic leader. He was a lifelong bachelor. He lived in this home with his widowed mother, Naomi Richardson, his divorced sister, Harriet Bates, and her son, Norman. The family was one of the most prominent in the city of Oswego, and their civic contributions cannot be denied.

Naomi kept a meticulous diary of everyday events in Oswego and these memoirs have offered much insight in the day-to-day life of the growing city. On Saturday, December 27, 1884, Naomi wrote: "A pleasant day. I went to Mrs. Gordon to try on my dress, to the bakers for bread, to Mr. Harts for a peck of apples, to Long and Brothers for a peck of hickory nuts. Bell came and got a pattern at night."

Norman Bates managed his Uncle Max's vast real estate holdings and inherited the mansion in 1910. He and his wife Florence had four children and it was those children who made the decision to donate the mansion to the Oswego County Historical Society in 1946.

The Richardson-Bates mansion is "guarded" by two large ebony sphinx statues at the front door.

Author's Notes

This is a truly remarkable home. There are dozens of great stories about the people and the items in the house that are worth telling. Acknowledging the restraint of page space, I will just tell you my favorite.

There is a life-sized marble statue of a young boy in the drawing room. Richardson bought this statue, titled "Beggar Boy," on a trip to Florence, Italy, in 1889. Chauncey Ives is the sculptor of this young boy pictured with his hand out for some money from any passersby on the street.

As White told me, "The story goes that Mr. and Mrs. Bates often held soirees in this room. Their high society guests, enamored with this charming statue, would invariably leave small change in the open palm of the boy's hand. This was at the request of the Bates' children who would explain to them that the beggar boy needed their help. Later, after the party had ended, the children and their governess would sneak downstairs from their bedrooms and snatch up the small pieces of change to put in their little money banks."

Visit

Richardson-Bates Mansion
135 East Third Street
Oswego, NY 13126
315-343-1342
Website: http://www.richardsonbateshousemuseum.org

For Further Reference: Gelbert, Doug. *Look Up, Oswego: A Walking Tour of Oswego, N.Y.* Hendersonville, NC: Cruden Bay Books, 2001.

While Here: There are many interesting historic sites around Oswego. One of the most important is the Safe Haven Holocaust Refugee Shelter Museum. It is on the site of Fort Oswego, and this was the only place where Jewish refugees were allowed into the United States during World War II.

Tours:
Tuesday and Wednesday: by appointment
Thursday–Saturday 1:00 to 5:00 p.m.

Admission:
Adults: $8.00
Students and seniors: $5.00
Children (6 to 12): $3.00
Children under 6: Free
Children under 16 must be accompanied by an adult.

27

Hyde Hall

Home of George Clarke
Cooperstown, Otsego County

We all know the bucket list checkoffs for a visit to historic Cooperstown: National Baseball Hall of Fame and Museum (check), Farmers Museum (check), Fenimore Art Museum (check), Glimmerglass Opera House (check), and a few others. But one place that you might miss is the magnificent, sprawling mansion, Hyde Hall, located at the northern end of Lake Otsego.

You might miss it. But you shouldn't.

"We like to describe Hyde Hall as a British-American country house from the time of Jane Austen," Dr. Jonathan Maney said. He is the executive director and CEO of the home. When it was built (1817–1834), it was one of the largest private residences in America.

"The house has so many compartments to it. Certainly, it would have been a home of the highest standards, perhaps unparalleled," Maney told me. "It has grand rooms, high ceilings, magnificent architectural features, and all of the then-modern amenities that money could buy. But it also was a home that was filled with people. Real people. Wealthy landowners, high-society women, little children, servants, workers and field hands, long- and short-term guests, and visitors from every rung of society's ladder could be found here at any given time. And that is the story we like to tell. That of the house itself, for sure. But also of the people who lived here."

The home is filled with surprises. It is a stark, solid home built on an overlook above the lake. Four large Grecian columns grace the front of the edifice. Inside are six bedrooms upstairs and two down. The formal

dining room features an eighteen-foot ceiling and the room itself measures twenty-four by thirty-six feet. "This would have been one of the largest rooms built in America at the time, for a private residence," Maney said.

"The house is one of the most important existing neoclassic country mansions in the United States," John Bower, the publicity and promotions manager for Hyde Hall, told me. "Mr. Clarke was a visionary. An innovator. And he wanted the very best of everything that was available at the time. There are seven fireplaces in the mansion (not counting the one in the kitchen), and twenty-six woodstoves. Clarke designed a unique system of pipes and vents which spread the heat under the floors. The enormous woodstove was fed from the back, so the servants, who were never to be seen or heard from during social events, could place wood on the fire without being noticed," he said.

At every turn in this fascinating home you see another marvel of innovation and creativity. In the large dining room, we find two elaborate chandeliers that were lit with vapor light. The fuel for these lights is comprised of a mixture of five parts alcohol and one part turpentine. "We have had visitors from Great Britain tell us that these might be the only vapor light chandeliers in their actual location still in existence in the world," Maney said. The chandeliers can be lowered by hand to a level that made them easy to clean and refill with fuel.

There is a large kitchen, several servants' areas, a library, a china room, a chapel, and several large halls. Several of the rooms feature reproduction carpets and linens, as well as books, dinnerware, and furniture dating back to the founder, Clarke. "He was a fabulously wealthy landowner and his taste was impeccable. The public section of the house is exquisite and made to be shown off to visitors. However, the private family quarters, while beautiful, are rather plain in comparison. These would be rooms never to be seen by the public. The family lived in these sections, and Mr. Clarke had his business office here. Still, as you can see, he had an eye for beauty." With this, Maney opened a set of side doors directly off the office. The porch outside offers a stunning view of the lake and the village of Cooperstown some eight miles south. "This house was meant to see the lake, and to be seen from the lake.

"This home is typical of houses that were built by well-known, well-off, well-read, and well-traveled people with world visions. They were built with a sense of British dignity meant to impress the visitor with the power and authority of the owner. It was not meant to be simply a visual delight, not just a pretty home, but rather it was built to be a residence of importance. And you can see that in virtually every corner of the mansion. The house was styled so that when you drove up to it, the first impression was to see a simple limestone exterior. And then when you walked inside your eyes would open wide," Bower said.

A walled inner courtyard, with curving limestone walls, large planters, and an abundance of sunlight pouring in, is the finishing touch to this incredible Cooperstown mansion. The house was designed by George Clarke himself and the architectural plans were drawn up by Philip Hooker. Hooker was one of the most prominent New York architects of his era and was the architect for the original New York State Capitol building in Albany.

Brendan Gill, the famed architecture writer for the *New Yorker* magazine, once called Hyde Hall "one of the three or four greatest buildings in America from its time."

The view from the front steps of Hyde Hall offers a stunning glimpse of Otsego Lake, James Fenimore Cooper's famed "Glimmerglass."

This is the Cooperstown Clarke family with an *e*. The other Clark family is the clan who really turned Cooperstown into the place we know and love today. That Clark family gained their fortune as heirs to the millions of dollars that flowed from the Singer sewing machine company.

"The Clarkes of Hyde Hall were one of the most important families in the earliest beginnings of Cooperstown," the director told me. "They were wealthy landowners that could trace their lineage back to George Clarke, the colonial lieutenant governor of the province of New York. He was the great-grandfather of the George Clarke who built Hyde Hall. The Clarkes owned thousands of acres of land around this region and their home, Hyde Hall, was the center of their world. They were what is known as landed gentry. They were part of the British aristocracy. Many members of high society would have come to visit Hyde Hall. We do know that James Fenimore Cooper was a guest here, and, in fact, Clarke married the widow of James Fenimore Cooper's oldest brother, Richard, in 1814."

At any given time, many members of the Clarke extended family would reside at the mansion. The staff included around eleven full time servants, a figure that would swell to over two dozen when a social event was on the schedule.

"The house, of course, is magnificent. But there were always so many people milling about," Bower said. "And we tell about their connection to the mansion as well. The relationship between the generations, between the family and the servants, and so on. That is the real story. And we want our guests to feel that also. This is not a dead house. In the near future, we hope to use the old kitchen for cooking classes, to have people come in and utilize it. Smell the wood burning and the bread baking. Keep it alive."

"George Clarke enjoyed entertaining on a grand scale, loved to have music playing and people talking and laughing in his home. He built an impressive house in America that was a model of modern innovations. This house was completely thought out. It really is alive, and we want our guests to feel that energy," Maney said.

One of the most remarkable aspects of this house is the thorough documentation the organization has of virtually everything that ever took place here.

"We found over 150 boxes just brimming with original documents, deeds, legal forms, and personal papers in a stone-lined vault in the cellar. We relocated them to Cornell University where we are patiently researching them all. It is quite a treasure trove," the director told me.

Author's Notes

There are many aspects to Hyde Hall that are unique, surprising, and quite spectacular. Approaching the long drive up to the house you will pass the oldest existing covered bridge in the United States. Next, on your right, you will observe a mausoleum built into the hillside that holds the remains of distant members of the Hyde Hall family. Inside the home you will find curious little features that set this apart from a typical home of its stature. Notice that in George Clarke's office, a window, much shorter than normal, would turn into a door that acted as an entranceway for the tenant farmers to come and pay their rent and settle their bills. In entering they had to bend deeply to get through the short door. Was it bending? Or was it a not-so-subtle forced bow to the power of the owner?

One of the most outstanding features of the estate is the entranceway. Known as the Tin Top Gatehouse, this elaborate tin-domed entrance to the mansion's grounds has just recently been fully restored to its 1820s beauty.

And if the gleaming silverware, the fabulous oil paintings, the breathtaking view of the lake, the historic carpets, and the priceless antique furniture are still not quite enough to satisfy your historical thirst, be patient. Your moment will come during a tour of Hyde Hall when you turn a corner and the guide points to a tiny room tucked under a staircase. That room holds the first working flush toilet west of the Hudson River. And it still has instructions on how to use it.

Yes, this house has everything!

Visit

Hyde Hall
267 Glimmerglass State Park Road
Cooperstown, NY 13326
Landmark: Hyde Hall is located on the grounds of Glimmerglass State Park. Follow the park road to the end.
607-547-5098
Website: http://www.hydehall.org

For Further Reference: Logan, Anne Clarke and Karin Nelson. *The Ladies of Hyde Hall: History, Hospitality, Letters, and Recipes 1819–1963.* Cooperstown, NY: Hyde Hall, 2009.

While Here: There is so much to see in tiny Cooperstown, from baseball to history to opera to museums and more. I would suggest a lake cruise on Lake Otsego to really capture the beauty and scope of this unique American village. The Glimmerglass Queen Tour Boat has an active schedule of tours from Memorial Day to Labor Day.

Tours: House hourly tours given from the end of May through October (call ahead for exact dates and times or check the website).

First tour at 10:00 a.m.; final tour at 3:00 p.m.

Admission:

Adults: $15.00

Seniors, youth, and active military: $12.00

Children under 13: Free

28

Herman Melville House

Home of Herman Melville
Lansingburgh, Rensselaer County

Famed American writer Herman Melville had many ties to New York's Capital District.

"The Melvilles lived in two Albany homes, but this one in Lansingburgh is actually a house where the budding writer wrote *Typee* and *Omoo*, two of his most famous works, and really got his start," John Ward told me. Ward is the acting president of the Lansingburgh Historical Society, which now owns the home.

The house is of typical New England Dutch design and features a gambrel roof. It was built in 1786 for Stephen Gorham, a noted Troy shipbuilder and postmaster. The original structure was a two-and-a-half-story brick and wood structure with a two-story wing. Part of the wing is original, and the remainder was added later. The house underwent renovations into a more Victorian style in 1872. It had a living room with two marble fireplaces, a parlor, a kitchen, and an outhouse. Several bedrooms were upstairs, and the house was topped with a large attic. It has a long covered front porch and is located on a small plot of land overlooking the Hudson River.

"We love this old house for its history and its stories. But like so many houses similar to this, it is constantly in need of repair and sprucing up. Because of that, we had to allow renters to move into the upstairs bedrooms to help defray our costs. In fact, our current tenant is a literature major at a local university, and she occupies Herman Melville's former study. It is a room with a window overlooking the river. The student loves

that room and actually does her own writing there. She calls it 'Melville's Penthouse,'" he chuckled.

"You have to remember that the Hudson River and the Erie Canal were the New York State thruways of the past. The river just across the street from this house was always busy with large ships passing by. Melville could see all of this activity when he lived upstairs from about 1838 to 1847. We believe this sparked his interest in sailing, ships, and travel. He wrote extensively in that room," Ward said.

There are very few possessions of the family in the Melville house today. They do have a collection of books by and about the writer. Still, many of the furnishings are historic to the era. There are two large bookcases in the living area from some of Lansingburgh's leading families, including the Pines, who were cuff and collar makers, and the Judsons, who were coal importers. The large case in the hall came from the Westminster Presbyterian Church. There are also many objects relating to Lansingburgh's rich history as a major industrial center in the early 1800s.

By 1850, Troy was one of the richest cities in America per capita. And it was also the sixteenth largest city in population. Lansingburgh was a separate village and town until it was incorporated into the city of Troy in 1901.

The Troy and Lansingburgh area was recognized as a leading manufacturer of shirt collars, cast-iron bells, horseshoes, and bristle brushes. "Disposable collars were very important in the development of Troy's industrial base. They were invented here by a woman who was tired of washing her husband's whole shirt every day when really only the collar was dirty. Thousands of women worked in this industry all over the city, many of them right in their own homes. And, at one time seventy percent of all bristle brushes made in the United States came from here, with nearly forty-five active brush factories close by to this house," Ward said.

Herman Melville was born in New York City in 1819. His father died in 1832 and the family moved to the Albany area. By this time, the family was in dire financial straits. After the move, Herman's mother, Maria, at some point and for unknown reasons changed the spelling of her last name from the original Melvill to Melville with an *e*. Maria was the daughter of General Peter Gansevoort, a Revolutionary War hero who led the American defense at the Battle of Fort Stanwix. The general lived a life of wealth and comfort at his home northeast of Saratoga Springs. Still, Maria was ever reluctant to rely on his beneficence in dealing with her own financial problems.

"Faced with many problems, we do find that Maria was a proud, independent woman. Only in the most serious of times would Maria call upon her father for financial help. In fact, research revealed a note she wrote to General Gansevoort in which she tells her father that 'her family was down to its last half barrel of flour,'" I was told.

"Herman was a voracious reader. While attending school in Albany he was always borrowing books. The family as a whole was very well-read and kept up with the current issues of the day. Herman desired to be an engineer on the Erie Canal and applied for a job as such. He didn't get the position and was quite desperate for work. His brother told him about a ship leaving out of New York City that was looking for help on a voyage to Liverpool, England. Herman got hired and the beginnings of his global travels started. Later, he signed on with a whaler setting out from New Bedford, Massachusetts, to the Polynesian Islands. Melville was on board with his writer's journal and his sketch book. From these travels came his first two novels, both partially written in this house, *Omoo* and *Typee*," Ward said.

Melville was a great storyteller. His tales of the South Pacific were elaborate and exaggerated. The stories told of a primitive culture and of an exotic and sometimes violent locale. His books were peopled with naked women and cannibals. The American reading public responded overwhelmingly to these books and they were great successes.

Ward said, "Yes, it really all started right here for Herman Melville. His first two published books came from here. They were big hits, unlike *Moby Dick*, which came later and wouldn't reach classic stature for nearly a century."

There is a variety of iconic whale depictions through this house, like this fireplace mantel piece. Appropriate since the owner wrote the American classic *Moby Dick*.

Author's Notes

It is not hard to imagine a young Herman upstairs in the corner bedroom writing away while looking out over the Hudson just feet from the house. It is unfortunate that there is so little left of actual Melville belongings here, but the house tells an incredible story.

Along with the fact that they were actually in the house of one of my favorite writers, I found the articles that related to the history of the area extremely fascinating. John Ward took me on a tour of the expansive attic and showed off some of the Troy and Lansingburgh items on display up there.

While not a manufacturing city like Detroit with its cars or Pittsburgh with its steel, Lansingburgh was a key component to the Industrial Revolution by producing more ordinary yet much-needed items. "One of our greatest stories comes from the oilcloth industry. Oilcloth was a precursor to linoleum flooring and it was in great demand. The industry was the second largest employer in Troy of that time. Here at the Melville House we like to tell the story of Deborah Powers and we have many items on display that reflect her history. She and her husband owned the first and eventually the largest oilcloth manufacturer in the United States. She is a legend in the city. The factory suffered a major blow when a terrible explosion almost destroyed her business in 1829. Her husband was killed in the explosion and she was seriously injured. Still, she survived and recovered from her injuries and began to rebuild the business with her sons."

Powers was a pioneering woman in the local economy of Troy and her legacy continues on in the many acts of charity she bequeathed to the city. Powers Memorial Park was a popular green space in Lansingburgh before the village was incorporated into the city of Troy. It was given to the village by Deborah in memory of her late husband, William. There was a Powers Opera House, a Powers Bank, and a Deborah Powers Home for Aged Ladies. One of the original Powers and Sons Oil Cloth Factory buildings is still standing and has been converted into luxury apartments.

Although there isn't much to see here in the way of Melville family artifacts, this house holds some fascinating local stories in its walls. The story of Deborah Powers, who has been called America's first self-made millionairess, is one of the best. Oh, and she lived to be one hundred years old!

Visit

The Herman Melville House
Home of Lansingburgh Historical Society
2 114th Street
Lansingburgh, NY 12182
Landmark: The Melville House is located two blocks north of the 112th Street bridge over the Hudson River connecting Lansingburgh and Van Schaick Island, Cohoes; US RTE 4 and NY RTE 47.
518-235-3501
Website: https://lansingburghhistoricalsociety.org/

For Further Reference: Robertson-Lorant, Laurie. *Melville: A Biography*. Amherst, MA: University of Massachusetts Press, 1998.

While Here: Troy's Oakwood Cemetery is one of Upstate New York's most famous and beautiful final resting places (it is near the Melville House). Buried here are famous writers, poets, entertainers, politicians, and "Uncle Sam." Samuel Wilson was a Troy meat packer who became our country's symbol as "Uncle Sam," and his is the most visited grave in this cemetery.

Tours: The house is open the second Saturday of every month from March through November. Hours are 10:00 a.m. to 2:00 p.m.

Special arrangements for tours can be made by calling John and Mary Ellen Ward at 518-885-4292.

Admission: Donations are appreciated.

29

Mabee Farm Historic Site

Oldest Home in the Mohawk Valley
Rotterdam Junction, Schenectady County

You have heard the old saying, "Oh, if these walls could talk." How true that is here at the oldest home in the Mohawk Valley.

"There are so many great stories to be told about this home, and the many people who lived here for three centuries," Mike Diana told me. He is the program and education manager for the Schenectady County Historical Society.

The house is a classic Dutch Colonial cottage. It was built with thick stone walls, an H-frame structure, and a dramatic steeply pitched roof. Wood samples have been examined from the house and the best that anyone can come up with is that it was built around 1705. It originally had one large single room with fireplaces on either end. Eventually a wall was constructed midway, to fashion it into two smaller rooms. "The first room is the formal 'best' room and the second would have been the living room. The occupants did everything they needed in this one room, including sleeping and cooking. A second-floor bedroom was added later," the manager told me.

The first outbuilding at the farm site was erected in 1767. It has a fascinating story to it.

"The building, made of bricks, was referred to simply as the 'brick house.' It was used as a residence for older members of the founding family to live their final years in. Widows would come from the main house to live here, for example. Interestingly, the brick house also was the living quarters for the farm's slaves. So, they would all live together. The Mabee

family members who ended up here would live on the main floor and the slaves lived in a dark, smaller area in the cellar.

"We do know that the Mabees bought and owned slaves. In fact, in our records we have a bill of sale contracted by the Mabees for the purchase in Schenectady of 'a Negro wench and her child.' The cost was eighty British pounds. There was no formal slave market in Schenectady, so this was a person-to-person sale," Diana said.

The Mabee home is located about nine miles west of Schenectady. He explained, "This would have been deep in the wild woods back then. The family was really quite alone out here. They had to carve out their land and be on the lookout for wild animals like wolves, bears, and bobcats. They also had to worry about raiding parties from French Canada. However, Annetje Mabee was part Mohawk, so there was some goodwill between the family and the Mohawk Nation so the farm was never attacked. In reality, the Mohawks and the Schenectadians were relatively good friends up until the Revolution, and there are no recorded instances of warring between the two groups."

The house has a distinctive vernacular design with many interesting features inside. One such feature, in the living room, is a unique jambless fireplace. It is over seven feet long and has no walls so the heat would radiate throughout the room. The original floors are made of wide pine planks, and light pours into the room from an original tall twenty-four-pane window. In the "best room" there is an alcove bed for what little privacy could be garnered in this small space.

The house was built on a high bluff overlooking the Mohawk River. It is a stunning location and, because of its elevation, the house and grounds have never fallen victim to the periodic river flooding this region is known for. There are several old buildings on the grounds, including a 1760s-era barn.

"The first Mabee family members here were Jan and Annetje Mabee. Jan was born in New York City and moved north to Albany. By 1684, he was located in Schenectady and looking for a site to build a home and farm. Annetje was half Mohawk through her mother's side, and she received some property from the Mohawk Nation in Schoharie Crossing. Jan Mabee bought the land on which the farm was built from a friend of his named Daniel Van Antwerpen. Here the Mabees began raising a large family. It is quite astonishing for the day that ten of her children lived to adulthood," the manager said.

The extended Mabee family built the structures and tended the fields and crops and eventually became one of the wealthiest families in the Schenectady area. Their farm was over one hundred acres, which was very large for the time. They raised cattle, horses, and sheep and grew wheat in their fields.

"The Mabees lived here through many generations," Diana remarked. "The last Mabee descendant to own the property, George Franchere, deeded the property to the Schenectady County Historical Society in 1993, with the stipulation that it remain a museum and educational center.

"Believe it or not, there are hundreds of Mabees still around. In fact, every once in a while someone will come into the house and say they are a Mabee and we show them around. Recently we had a woman from Wisconsin do just that, and shortly after another Mabee descendant from Salt Lake City came here to research her family roots. Others live close by and some are even members of our historical society," the manager said.

Author's Notes

There is a Mabee family cemetery just a few yards from the brick house. Here we find the final resting place of many generations of the family. In fact, nineteen Mabees are buried here. The earliest burial is that of Peter Mabee, who died December 6, 1771, at the age of twenty-three. The most recent burial was in 2002 for Marion Mabee who died at the age of eighty-three. For those who love old cemeteries, that's over 200 years of a single family buried in the same spot. A low stone wall separates this beautiful country cemetery from the residence.

The house has many curious items positioned around the interior. One of my favorites was a branding iron that had three large iron initials on the impression end. "JPM" stands for the original Mabee owner and you can see places where he branded some of his own personal items in the house.

But the most interesting aspect of this historic home is the inn. Mike Diana told me the story.

> In 1794, the Mohawk River was quickly becoming the gateway to the West. River traffic was starting to increase and the Mabees took full advantage of their prominent riverside location to accommodate travelers. They built an inn, which once was freestanding but is now connected to the main residence, to house and feed weary travelers. Boaters would see the house high on a bluff and simply dock here for the night. The Mabees would feed the visitors and provide them with some hearty drink, either hard cider made from the apple orchard or homemade beer made from the Mabee wheat. We know that General Philip Schuyler visited here. He was traveling with a party that was surveying the Mohawk River and they stayed, ate, and drank here. They slept upstairs. The general's own records documented his overnight stay at the Mabee Farm in 1792.

Visit

The Mabee Farm Historic Site
1100 Main Street
Rotterdam Junction, NY 12150

518-887-5073
Website: http://schenectadyhistorical.org/

For Further Reference: Papp, J. Marvin and John P. Craig. *Rotterdam, N.Y.: A Pictorial History Commemorating Our Nation's Bicentennial.* Rotterdam, NY: Rotterdam Bicentennial Commission, 1976.

While Here: The Mohawk River flows through Rotterdam with several locks that are close by to view. Schenectady is just ten minutes to the east. Rotterdam was named by Dutch immigrants to honor the city of the same name in the Netherlands.

Tours: Tuesday through Saturday, 10:00 a.m. to 4:00 p.m.

Admission:
Adults: $8.00
Children: Free
Call ahead for group visit information.

30

Dr. Best House and Medical Exhibit

Home of Dr. Christopher S. Best
Middleburgh, Schoharie County

Except for a sign on the front lawn, you would probably never give this beautiful Victorian home a second look. There are lots of residences like this one in Middleburgh, a pretty little community of 3,500 nestled in the shadow of Vroman's Nose, an iconic Schoharie Valley natural landmark. The house is large and square and carries many of the features identifying it as of Italianate design. There is a long, curved front porch, tall windows with slat shutters on the second-floor exterior, and fancy geometric windows (including stained glass) on the first floor. There are two entranceways to the porch, including a porte cochere. Out back are two buildings, a small garage and a much larger barn. Although it sounds like an elaborate structure there are many homes like this in the valley, including several far more grandiose.

But the story that is told inside is without parallel.

"This house was built in 1884 by the village's doctor, Christopher Best. Over forty years later his son, Duncan, took over his father's practice. Between the two physicians, medicine had been practiced in this home for over a century. Certainly, few houses can claim that," Trish Bergan said. She is the director of operations of the house and medical exhibit.

The structure features three bedrooms, two full baths, a kitchen, and several extra rooms plus a medical exam room and patient waiting room. "The family side of the house is separated from the medical side of the house by two large oak pocket doors. Christopher's daughter, Emma,

would give piano lessons in the front parlor and the pocket doors would be closed tight so as not to interfere with the procedures going on in the examining room," Bergan told me.

The Bests, both father and son, were leaders in this small, rural community. Their home was a testament to their reputation and stature. "They had many fine features in this residence; some were one-of-a-kind and others were simply way ahead of their time. One parlor, for example, has walls that are covered in burlap. Much of the wood is tiger maple, there are exquisite stained glass windows, the two main rooms on the first floor are lit with beautiful chandeliers, and they even had a futuristic contraption that contained a series of white buttons which, when pushed, would direct heat to different sections of the house," Bergan said.

While the family side of the residence is a marvel in its own right, the medical side is extremely fascinating. The exam room and the doctor's office, where everything from delivering a baby to performing an amputation took place, offer a rare glimpse of early medical practices as well as the duties and responsibilities of a rural family doctor. "Both Dr. Bests did a full lineup of medical procedures here. We still have all of their original equipment, from the very large, such as an early X-ray machine, to the very small, like bottles of pills and elixirs that still contain medicine in them," she said.

One item that is sure to produce a grin from visitors is the doctor's original price guideline tacked up on the office wall. "Baby delivery, $5.00. Amputation of leg or arm, $30.00. Ordinary daytime visit, $1.00. Night time office visit, $2.00."

My favorite on this list was the last item: "Medical advice, 50-cents."

Although the caretakers of the house today do not call this a museum, the house has enough artifacts and historical provenance to more than qualify it as such. Homemade quilts, Victorian hair wreaths, a black blanket in the master bedroom that is made from buffalo hide, one of the first original telephones installed in Middleburgh, a collection of Dr. Best's

Dr. Best was the classic country doctor who performed almost any kind of medical service over a century ago. And all in his house/office. Here is his original surgical table in the back near the kitchen.

antique walking sticks and top hats, and a wonderful primitive kitchen hack—flour barrels that swing out from under the cupboard for easy usage.

As I said, the story that is told inside this residence is unlike any this writer has ever seen.

The Best family name is one of the great storied names in the village's history.

"Dr. Christopher Best and his wife, Ursula, were pillars of Middleburgh society. They were very well connected. They were beloved members of the community," Bergan said. "Dr. Best was an important participant in virtually every organization in town, from the school to the Red Cross, and he was a founder of the Middleburgh Telephone Company. He was president of the phone company when he died in 1934. He was also the last president of the Middleburgh and Schoharie Railroad. Ursula belonged to all the ladies' organizations and was a benefactor in her own right. Later, Dr. Duncan Best carried on in his father's philanthropic ways. The last resident in the house was Emma, she of the piano lessons. She was born here, never married, and died here at the age of eighty-three in 1983. After Duncan's death in 1991, the house was deeded to the village with the instructions that it remain open to the public."

One great trait shared by all of the Best generations was that they saved everything. "Yes, everything. They were the original pack rats," Bergan said. "There are hundreds of personal items, family papers and photographs, and all sorts of memorabilia in this house. If they bought a set of curtains in let's say 1902, you can bet we have the receipt for them."

You only have to look in the medical side of the residence to see the fruits of their collection. All of the doctors' equipment is still on display, as if the last patient just left. Incredibly, there are even sealed cans in the pantry that still contain food. "Yes, look at this," the director told me as she opened the old wooden pantry doors. Coffee tins, Hires root beer mix, Planters peanuts, breakfast cereal, and more are all sitting there in a pageant of food nostalgia. There is one interesting can containing something called Kulah-Ade. Maybe an early Kool-Aid? And also, a large can containing a fruitcake.

"Yes, that is a funny one. It is a can of Molly O'Rourke's Fruit Cake soaked in Irish whiskey. The doctor, however, would never have eaten that. Which is why it is still full. The Best women were upstanding members of the Christian Temperance Movement," she said.

Author's Notes

What a find this house is!

Situated on a side street, off the busy main road and behind a church, the Best house offers, well, the best of two worlds. It is an amazing showplace of family life in the late nineteenth century and into the early twentieth century, and it is a remarkable exhibit of early rural medical practices. As I mentioned earlier, there is a definite feel as if the family still lives here—that Ursula will come waltzing in at any minute from her gardening club meeting, or that Dr. Best will clip-clop in his carriage through the driveway returning home from treating a sick child down in the valley. All of the family possessions, or almost all of them, are still here in the same spot they were in one hundred years ago. It is a nice feeling, comforting actually, and it gives an extra quality of attachment to this wonderful home. A feeling that it is still lived in by the extended and multi-generational Best family.

Two things that I really enjoyed were on the exterior. Ursula was adamant that the family and medical sides of the house, although coexisting, were not comingled. On the front porch a visitor would see a small hole bored into the wall next to the front door. Patients would lean down and put their mouth near that opening and announce that they were there for an appointment. The sound of their voice would travel through a special tube all the way to the back of the house where the doctor or nurse would hear it and go let the patient in. This allowed family life, and piano lessons, to go on uninterrupted on the other side of the big pocket doors.

Another great treat can be found in the large barn in back of the house. Inside are several of Dr. Best's original horse carriages that he used for making house calls. You can imagine the country doctor harnessing his horse and hooking it up to his carriage on a cold winter night and then dashing off into the darkness to do his good deeds.

Yes, this house, though empty for decades, feels very much lived in by this benevolent and good-hearted family. The slogan the Dr. Best House uses on their social media platforms is: "You won't believe what's behind our doors."

How true.

Visit

The Dr. Best House and Medical Exhibit
1568 Clauverwie Road
Middleburgh, NY 12122
Landmark: The house is located directly behind the United Methodist Church, the tallest structure in Middleburgh.
518-827-7200
Website: http://www.drbesthouse.com

For Further Reference: Wilkinson, John P. D. *The Schoharie Valley.* Mount Pleasant, SC: Arcadia Publishing, 2012.

While Here: Vroman's Nose is the natural landmark that has become the icon of Schoharie County. The 600-feet hike to the top is relatively easy and the view from the pinnacle, on a long flat stone ledge called the "Dance Floor," offers a twenty-five-mile view of the gorgeous valley below.

Tours:
Memorial Day through Labor Day
Saturday and Sunday, noon to 4:00 p.m.
Tours at other times can be arranged by appointment.

Admission: Donations are accepted.

31

Lansing Manor

Home of John Lansing
North Blenheim, Schoharie County

This 200-year-old Federal-style mansion is a gracious, elegant gleaming white apparition located beneath a leafy tree-shaded spot overlooking the Schoharie River valley. This land was originally given to a John Weatherhead and thirty-nine other patentees in 1769 by King George III.

"The property originally consisted of over 40,000 acres," Linda Della Donna said. She is one of the tour guides at the manor. "We actually have the original indenture on display at the house. It is quite a remarkable piece of history and was from John Weatherhead to John Lansing dating back to 1803. A partition deed divvied the acreage among four men. Two thirds of that land was owned by John Lansing and Cornelius Ray."

Melanie Wood, another docent, added, "The house had nine fireplaces, four bedrooms, a parlor, and a working area in the cellar for cooking and food storage. A rudimentary aqueduct system was crafted out of hollowed logs which brought water from a spring atop a nearby hill down to the property. We have some remnant pieces of the old log piping system."

The manor house is a two-story picture of efficiency and early American beauty. It is a square house (forty-six feet to each side) and has a hipped roof and gracious sitting porches on three exposures. The front porch is magnificent, featuring a five-bay façade that goes the entire length of the home. Access is gained by a double staircase. The residence is of brick-lined, wood-frame construction on both floors. The bricks were sunbaked near the property and were used for both support and insulation purposes.

Also on the property are a well and its cover, a four-seat outhouse, ice house, milk house, barn and silos, servants quarters, and a possible office where the owners would conduct farming business and collect rent from the tenant farmers who worked the land.

"There are many wonderful attributes to this manor house which date back to the beginning, now 200 years ago," Della Donna said. "Since water was a scarce commodity, any water that came into this house was used many times over. You can see in the old sink where water, once it was used, was stored by a drain that was plugged with a rag and then reused for many other purposes. Absolutely nothing went to waste here."

One room, the library, is of special interest. "This would have been their version of a man cave," Wood told me. "Notice the artwork on the walls features outdoors and hunting scenes. This is where the men would retire after dinner and smoke pipes or cigars and talk politics." There are many items that are original to the home and several interesting pieces are in this room. One is a beautiful tall book closet with a folding table in the front. "The writing desk was an Irving family piece, and we like to imagine that Washington Irving himself wrote his tales of Sleepy Hollow on that very desk," she said.

Although the house seems quite large, there were many family members using every corner of it. This is highlighted in one of upstairs bedrooms. "You can imagine how crowded this room was. Two girls would sleep in the same bed, a baby would be in the crib alongside of the bed, and the governess, Grace Watson, would also sleep in this room. John Lansing Jr. was a famous and very busy man and he did not live here even though we refer to it as Lansing Manor. He built it for his daughter and son-in-law, Jacob Livingston Sutherland. All of the clothes in the children's closet belonged to the Sutherlands. On the bed is an 'autograph quilt' made by local women. They stitched their names and where they lived on the quilt patches," she said.

The Sutherlands' master bedroom is complete with period furniture and furnishings. Their tea service stands ready on a table and little steps lead up to the bed accommodating their small size.

The kitchen in the cellar was the hub of the house.

"This is where all the activity took place," the tour guides told me. "Just look at all of the old kitchen items we still have down here." These items included a large work table, one of the earliest meat rotisserie ovens, a "toe toaster," which toasted bread using the switch of the user's foot, a hanging pancake griddle, a brick oven, and a fully stocked pantry. "In the pantry we even have lunch boxes that were used by both the children and adults. They came from the Mattice family, the fourth family to inhabit this house. They were made from metal and the kids would put them in a stream during school to keep their lunch fresh and cool until they ate it."

The basement appeared like a comprehensive food market. There was a root cellar with original bins and tools, a dairy room where they made their cheese and churned their butter, a pickling room with a very early cabbage shredder, and a wine cellar with bottles lining the wall.

This house is a gorgeous, 200-year-old reflection of early life in the Schoharie valley, and the fact that there are so many original 150- to 200-year-old items makes this a truly historic place.

Although the house was originally deeded to John Lansing Jr., he was much too busy in other places to make this remote, rural location his

Lansing Manor was the first place where the author discovered guest signatures etched in the glass windows.

permanent home. Lansing was a prominent lawyer, politician, and businessman. His career was mainly seated in Albany, New York. In fact, he was mayor of Albany from 1786 to 1790. He was appointed chancellor of New York from 1801 to 1814. He served as an aide to General Philip Schuyler during the Revolutionary War and was a delegate to the Constitutional Convention of 1787.

John Lansing rose to the position of chief justice of the New York Supreme Court. Lansing's daughter, Frances, married Jacob Sutherland in 1811. They were the first of four families who called the manor home over the next century and a half. Sutherland and his family lived here until he too was appointed to the New York Supreme Court in 1828. The list of occupants that followed the Sutherlands carried the names of Van Rensselaer, Hogeboom, Rossiter, Spring, and Mattice. The final family lived here until it was sold to the New York Power Authority in 1971. They constructed a pumped storage facility on the land nearest the river from the house.

Author's Notes

This must be one of the largest 200-year-old collections of any house in Upstate New York. Despite the incredible array of vintage household and farming items, there are many rare one-of-a-kind items to see here that will leave you scratching your head.

My favorite was the "signed windows." Along the front of the house are large, hand-poured windows. On several panes of glass you can actually see where guests to Lansing Manor "signed" their names. Signed by etching the letters into the glass with a diamond! One is clearly dated 1842 and another 1847.

Another unique feature is the many windows that transformed themselves into doors. "In those days your property tax was arrived at by the number of exterior doors a home had. Naturally, they needed a front and back door to the house, but these other portals, made when a window opened up into a door, went unnoticed by the tax assessor. They were called jib windows and were quite common at the time. Also, notice that there are no closets in the house. The property was also taxed on the number of rooms it had. A closet was designated as a room. To avoid this expense the owners used armoires and chifforobes instead," Della Donna told me.

Along with the unique antique items found in the house, the interior of this residence tells many great stories of the many people who lived here. One of the most unusual ones is the story of the original builder, John Lansing himself. "John Lansing was in New York City in 1829. On December 12, he left his hotel to go and mail a letter. He was never seen again. He was seventy-six years old and the mystery surrounding his disappearance has been studied for years. Was he mugged or murdered? Did he get lost and fall into the river? Was he kidnapped? Nobody knows for sure what happened to the man who gave his name to Lansing Manor," the tour guides told me.

Visit

Lansing Manor
1378 NY Route 30
North Blenheim, NY 12131

Landmark: The home is located on the grounds of the Blenheim-Gilboa Power Authority Visitors Center.
800-724-0309
Website: https://www.nypa.gov/communities/visitors-centers/blenheim-gilboa-visitors-center

For Further Reference and While Here: The Lansing Manor home is located on property now owned by the New York Power Authority. There is a large visitor's center located in a nineteenth-century dairy barn that examines the history of the house and grounds, as well as informative plaques, exhibits, and displays about the Blenheim-Gilboa water power and electricity installation on the mountain across the valley.

Tours: The home is open for tours May through October from 10:00 a.m. to 5:00 p.m. Closed Tuesdays.

Admission: There is no admission charge.

32

Southworth Homestead

Home of Five Generations of the John Southworth Family
Dryden, Tompkins County

"This is all quite new and exciting to us," Gina Prentiss told me. She is the president of the Dryden Town Historical Society. "This house was built in 1836 by John Southworth and has been lived in by members of the family ever since until recently. But it is really because of Becky Southworth that we now have this wonderful home. She was born Sarah Rebecca Wood in 1918 in Ithaca, but within the week of her birth her mother died in the terrible influenza epidemic that was sweeping the world. John H. Southworth and his wife, Florence Montgomery, adopted the child, who was the daughter of Florence's sister, Fanny. She lived here until her death in 2011 at the age of ninety-two. So, it is an old house, with an old story, but relatively new to our historical society to whom she bequeathed its care."

The house is a combination of Greek Revival and Federal styles and combines an older wooden section in the rear and a newer tall brick part nearer the road. Family history relates that John Southworth intended to build a wood house on this site but while digging for the basement found hard clay that was suitable for the fabrication of bricks. "The clay is solid as a hard rock," Prentiss said. The brick exterior walls are two brick widths deep with solid wood beams embedded in the masonry walls. According to the story, the beams were added as a precaution in case the strength of the bricks was insufficient.

The original brick house had three bedrooms and two baths. The attached wooden structure originally held another eight rooms. Furnishings

and household items throughout the house date from the early nineteenth century through the twenty-first century. Many of the items are original to the several generations of the Southworth family members who lived here. The house also incorporates items from the Dwight, Montgomery, McGraw, Cady, and Wilson families that came to the Southworths through marriage and friendship. By local standards of the nineteenth century, the Southworths were already well off and well traveled, and some items in the home were acquired during these travels. Dryden was a small village, really a four-corners crossroads, but had great influence during the early to mid-nineteenth century. The Southworths' interconnectedness with other influential families through marriage, commerce, or acquaintance was evident in the beginnings of Cornell University, the Southworth Library, and the railroads.

The house, which is owned by the Dryden Town Historical Society, is a showplace of nostalgia. From the early 1800s and the original owners right up to Becky, the last family member to live here, you will see glimpses of the past around every corner.

We started our visit in the sitting room. "In this room we have early portraits of John Southworth and Nancy Ellis, some very early furniture pieces, and a handsome beaded petit point fireplace screen, which was made by family relative Miss Adelia Dwight, the daughter of a US congressman from Dryden, Jeremiah Dwight. But the real treasures in this room are the light sconces. And they have a fascinating story to them," Prentiss said.

The wall sconces, eight in all, came from a German luxury liner named the SS *Vaterland*. It was one of the most extravagant ships afloat. When World War I broke out, the ship was in New York and was seized by the US government on April 6, 1917. It underwent a total renovation operation and was transformed into the US troop transport ship the USS *Leviathan* for the duration of the war. In 1923, the ship again had a thorough overhaul and refit in Newport News, Virginia. At the time, John H. Southworth (the grandson of the house builder) was in the shipping business in Newport News, and managed to acquire the elegant art deco wall lamps from the *Leviathan*. They have been rewired for electricity and now add an air of old-world elegance to several rooms of the Southworth homestead.

As we entered the living room, my guide showed me the front entranceway and the unique doorbell arrangement. Arriving guests would pull on an outside doorknob and that would cause a coil of metal above the interior door to spring, thereby ringing the bell attached to it. It reminded me of something I saw once on *Downton Abbey*.

"As you can tell, this was a house that was well lived in. And that is how we intend to show it. After all, there were always children running around in here, so things were used, repaired, and moved around frequently. Becky kept the house up beautifully, and we keep it to high standards to show great respect to our benefactors. But, despite the long history of the house, it was after all a home to many people who lived here for over 175 years," Prentiss explained.

It is clear that the gem of any tour of this house is the formal parlor. "Yes, we keep the doors closed until we get to this room. And then when we open the door for guests, they are just amazed at what they see," Prentiss said as she opened the door and we walked into the parlor.

She was right.

The walls of this large, high-ceilinged room are covered with rare hand-blocked wallpaper imported from France. From floor to ceiling, every inch of this room is a pageant of colors and designs. The theme is a conjured European landscape with columns, fountains, strolling couples, animals, boats on a river, and children playing under cloud-filled skies. On all four walls. The delicate wallpaper is a bit fragile. In fact, every time a little piece would flake off the occupants would keep it in a drawer so conservators could match up the repairs with the original. The entire lower two feet of the four walls in this room are covered with wallpaper that looks like a palace balustrade. The trompe-l'oeil effect is stunning.

It is all sensory overload and quite beautiful. The fireplace (there are three in the house, all nonworking) has a rare Franklin cast-iron insert and an ornate mantel that holds three exquisite girandoles that have brass figures in the center holding up crystal prisms to reflect the candlelight. Another item, one that this writer has never seen before, is an elaborate hanging tea kettle on a stand. It is sitting on the floor next to a large wing-back chair. Under the little swinging brass tea kettle is an oil lamp used to heat the tea. I can only assume that five o'clock was tea time at the Southworth home because the words "5 o'clock" are written in iron script over the kettle.

On the stairway to the second floor is an ivory "point of perfection," which was traditionally installed at the completion of the house. The second floor contains three large bedrooms filled with family possessions. In a child's bedroom there is an assortment of toys and a large handmade doll house designed by architect and son-in-law John V. Van Pelt. "Again, everything has a little nick in it, which means it was played and loved by the children down through the years, and that is the way we intend to keep it."

Two items stood out for me in the upstairs. There are two old maple rope beds in one room. Each post of the bed is stamped by the local craftsman who made the beds: "Owen Westcott, Truxton, N.Y."

There are also two large coverlets. They are a brilliant indigo blue and bright white. They were made in the early 1800s by Scottish-born Archibald Davidson, famously known as the "Fancy Weaver."

A list of the Southworths who owned this home, going back five generations, include John (1836), William Harrison (1877), Ella Ward (1880), John Howard (1919), and Rebecca (1952–2011).

One of the most famous stories connected to a Southworth has to do with the village library, which was founded by Jennie McGraw, the granddaughter of John Southworth, in 1884. The library, which is a historic masonry building that features stone gargoyles and a tall Seth Thomas clock tower, is located in downtown Dryden.

On November 10, 1864, President Abraham Lincoln gave a speech to a large crowd at the White House. The speech ended up in the hands of Lincoln's son, Robert Todd Lincoln. Later, Lincoln gave the handwritten speech to John Dwight, a congressman from Dryden. In 1928, Dwight's widow donated the handwritten speech to the Southworth Library. It languished in a basement vault at the library for eighty years. Finally, facing much-needed improvements and repairs to the structure, plus with the hope of building a new wing for expansion, the board of trustees decided to sell the speech at Christie's auction house in New York City to raise funds for the library.

The handwritten Lincoln letter was sold on February 12, 2009, for $3.44 million. It was a record for any written American historical item.

Needless to say, the new wing at the Southworth Library is gorgeous.

Author's Notes

There is no question that this house has some pretty impressive bones to it, and some amazing features inside it. The hand-blocked French wallpapered parlor alone is worth a visit here.

But there was something else that really impressed me here. And that was the enthusiasm, or shall I say pure joy, exhibited by the volunteers who work here and act as guides for visitors. I think a lot of it has to do with the newness of it all. After Becky Southworth died in 2011, the house took a couple of years to work its way through the legal channels to transfer its care to the local historical society. As Gina Prentiss told me, "So we have only been in here for a short time. It is very exciting for all of us. We are always trying to solve puzzles about this house. People tell us things that we never knew. The research is fun and very interesting but there is much more to learn. Most of us knew Becky. She was a dear woman whom I loved and admired greatly. So, we do this in her memory. And it is a lot of fun."

I must say the guides, and all of the others I met during my visit, were extremely passionate and very committed to this house and its history. And their excitement was infectious, for me and the other guests I met that day.

When I walked in for my appointment to conduct an interview for this book, I met a large group of women leaving after the final tour. I asked them how it was. "The best! I wish I could go through it all again right now," one group leader told me. Others were asking to pose for pictures with Gina Prentiss and the other guides. Everybody was giddy with excitement over what they had just learned.

And that is exactly the way a visitor should feel after visiting this, or any of the other houses in this book.

Visit

Southworth Homestead
Home of the Dryden Town Historical Society
14 North Street
Dryden, NY 13053
607-844-9209
Website: http://drydennyhistory.org/

For Further Reference: Weldon, Harry Lawrence DuBreuil. *Around Dryden*. Mount Pleasant, SC: Arcadia Publishing, 2018.

While Here: Dryden is a suburb of Ithaca, just twenty minutes away. A visit to Ithaca's famous Commons pedestrian shopping plaza is always fun. And, of course, you could stop in to the Dryden library and ask them to tell you the fantastical story of the Lincoln letter!

Tours:

First Saturday of every month, May to October.
Tours are at 10:00 a.m., 11:00 a.m., and noon.
Tours can be arranged for any day and time by appointment.

Admission: Call ahead for admission prices. Special rates can be arranged for group tours.

33

Persen House

Home of Several Early Dutch Families
Kingston, Ulster County

This historic house, built in 1661, is located on one of the most serene urban intersections in Upstate New York. Situated in the Stockade National Historical District of Old Kingston, the Persen House anchors one of the four corners of a unique crossroads. "Yes, this house might just be the oldest house in the Stockade that is open to the public," Taylor Bruck told me. He is the Ulster County archivist. "Each of the four stone structures at this intersection of John and Crown streets dates to before the American Revolutionary War. We believe that no other location in America can make that claim. In fact, the entire intersection is itself listed on the National Historic Registry."

The Persen House was built for a barber-surgeon named Gysbert Van Imbroch. The house is of early Dutch Colonial design and features walls and foundations made of limestone. The original residence was basically one large room where everything took place. It had a sleeping area, a large fireplace for heating and cooking, a root cellar, and a grain loft. The house features wide pine plank floors.

"The house was built for Van Imbroch, but it was Matthewis Persen who lived here the longest. He was born in this house in 1739 and lived here all of his eighty years. Over time, the house grew with each generation that lived here. It was constructed in five different phases. In 1663, the house, then made of wood, was burned down by the Esopus Indians during the Second Esopus War of 1663. Later, in 1777, much of Kingston was burned down again, this time by the British. This house, and the other

houses around it, were damaged but stood strong because they were now constructed of stone. In fact, we can still see burn marks from 1777 over the Dutch door," Bruck said.

A tour of the Persen House is like walking through a timeline of the several families that lived here. Phase by phase. Phase one is the oldest room in the house. "Just one big room with five occupants," Bruck said. "Gysbert, his wife Rachael, and their three children all lived in these small, close quarters. Gysbert was one of the wealthiest men in the Stockade. He practiced both his barbering and medicine in this house. The oldest things in this room are the actual Dutch metal door hinges. They are over 300 years old."

The following four phases of the Persen House saw many changes, both in its occupants, its size, and its design, and as to what took place in the house itself. "So much of the history of this house and its occupants we know because of the interest by archeologists who conducted a dig in the home. In fact, the archeologists catalogued over 20,000 items found during the dig, which was conducted by Dr. Joseph Diamond, a professor at State University of New York at New Paltz. Many of these items are on exhibit in the house."

The house grew to several rooms over the years, including a tavern on the second floor. All of these rooms are open to the public, including the area where the archeological dig took place. Here the visitor can see the fresh dug-up dirt where so many items were found. Large photos on the wall of this room show the dig in progress and describe the process of how it was conducted. This area of the house was chosen for the dig because it was the only area of the house that did not have a basement. Therefore, the floor was soil that had never been disturbed.

A visit to this house offers a rare glimpse into what life would have been like inside the Stockade District back when it was known as Wiltwyck. After several centuries, the residence came into the ownership of the county. "Ulster County used this for office space for many years after they became owners of it in 1914. About twenty years ago, the roof was declared to be unsafe and the county offices had to move while repairs were made. It is now a wonderful place for people to come and visit, learn, and explore the history of early Dutch life here in the Hudson Valley," Bruck told me.

"The architect Kenneth Barricklo authored a historic structure report on the house in 2000. This aided us in the historic restoration and informed us greatly on what we know about the house," Bruck said.

Each of the families who inhabited the Persen House had a fascinating backstory. We know a lot of this because of the important finds uncovered during the painstaking archeological research. "So much can be learned about this historic house by just viewing the artifacts we uncovered," Bruck said. "For example, Matthewis Persen. We know that his father, Cornelius, and his uncle, Adam, were tailors while they lived in this house. Deep in the dirt here they discovered hundreds of pins, thimbles, and buttons from this shop."

Author's Notes

The first thing you may notice even before entering the Persen House is its surroundings. From the front entrance you can see the buildings around it are all beautiful stone structures of great elegance. Two are now offices, one is the Persen House, and another is an upscale bookstore and craft brewery. The area is quiet with the streets shaded by tall trees and the houses adorned with overflowing flower boxes. It gives you a sense that, without knowing more, this could be an intersection in say, old England, or even an ancient town in the Netherlands.

A Persen House tour is quite a revelation. Unlike many of the other venerable homes in this book, this house is spare and plain, like a blank palette upon which to draw your own conclusions. For me, this emptiness gave great insight into what it must have been like when so many people were crowded into such a small space to live. At one time, during phase four (1735), ten people would have all lived here at one time.

Still, the wow factor here is the incredible display of artifacts found during the famous 2000 archeological dig by Dr. Diamond. Countless items are on display with interesting signage describing each piece. Here you will find early pieces of china, glass items, some keys, a whistle, bricks, Dutch ceramic tiles, early toothbrushes, and hundreds more items, both commonplace and unusual. One oddity is a rare Dutch bodkin—a long needle used to hold hair in place. It had a jewel on the end of it, and the archivist told me it was only one of three known antique Dutch bodkins in New York State.

Also unearthed were hundreds of oyster shells. "Although shellfish are no longer harvested from the banks of the Hudson River, it wasn't always so. The river flows both ways. The salt line is near Kingston, and that is why so many ocean oyster shells ended up here," Bruck told me. Add to this the items that were discovered during the era when the residence housed a tavern. These other items include wine bottles, pipe stems, wine seals, cutlery, and more.

The original owner, Gysbert Van Imbroch, left a veritable treasure trove of information behind when he died in 1665. An inventory of his possessions was taken upon his death revealing an exhaustive list of all his belongings (written in Dutch) for his heirs (and history) to see. The list is amazing and quite reflective. A permanent display here shows the inventory, in the original Dutch, and lists the items in a more modern English translation alongside. Nothing went unmentioned in this remarkable twelve-page inventory that includes 1,400 entries: one large wash bucket, one oxen yoke, one copper shaving basin, one pair of ice skates, one cosmetic (red), one cosmetic (black), dozens of pieces of clothing (including a "child's coat made by savages"), livestock, personal possessions, and more. Van Imbroch also listed his book collection, which was considered to be the largest personal book collection in the New World.

Visit

The Matthewis Persen House Museum and Cultural Heritage Center
Managed by the Ulster County Clerk's Office—Nina Postupack, County Clerk
74 John Street
Kingston, NY 12401
845-340-3040
Website: https://ulstercountyny.gov/countyclerk/persenhouse.html

For Further Reference: Gelbert, Doug. *Look Up America: A Walking Tour of Kingston, N.Y.* Cruden Bay Books, 2010.

While Here: There are several different walking tours of historic Kingston available. The areas included are the Stockade and the Rondout area near the Hudson Riverfront. For information visit http://www.fohk.org/welcome/discover-kingston/walking-tours/.

Tours: The house is open Memorial Day weekend through Labor Day weekend, Tuesday through Friday 9 a.m. to 4:30 p.m. and Saturdays from 9 a.m. to 3 p.m. After Labor Day, the house is open Saturdays from 10 a.m. to 2 p.m. through the weekend prior to Thanksgiving. Phone ahead for large tour group appointments.

Admission: Free

34

Old Fort House Museum

Home of Patrick Smyth and Solomon Northup
Fort Edward, Washington County

Fort Edward was a frontier fort that existed during the French and Indian War (1754–1763). "After the fort was demolished in 1770, Patt Smyth salvaged the timbers and wood from it and used them to build this home. The dates of construction were 1772 to 1773. The home was used as headquarters for both the American and British generals during the Revolutionary War," Paul McCarty told me. He is the executive director of the Old Fort House Museum.

The house is a Georgian frame house. Over the years it has operated as a private residence, tavern, community meeting hall, county court, and a boardinghouse. The stately yellow house sits on Broadway, the main street of the town of about 10,000 residents. It is on a foundation consisting of a mixture of fieldstone and quarried bluestone. The home has around two dozen 6-over-6 pane windows, allowing maximum light into the residence. It has a slate gambrel roof and some flooring that dates to the home's construction.

"In doing research over the years, we have discovered that the house appears to be a smaller version of the famous Cherry Hill mansion in Albany and might even have been built by the same builder," McCarty said. (Note: Cherry Hill Mansion is the subject of a chapter in this book.)

While most of the house is original and intact, a smaller back part is a reconstruction. "We had an archeological analysis done here a few years ago and they discovered the original footprint of the foundation for us to build on. In this newer part we were able to expand our visitor's area and add a handicap bathroom."

Each room in the house displays artifacts of the various families that have lived here. Period furniture, antiques, oil portraits, archival photographs, pottery and chinaware, and local historic memorabilia fill the dozen rooms in the home.

"One piece that is of particular interest for us in Fort Edward is what we call the Jane McCrea mirror. Jane McCrea lived in Fort Edward, and her story has been retold in history books down through the generations. On July 27, 1777, while traveling to see her fiancé in Kingsbury, Jane and her friend, Sarah McNeil, were captured by a group of Native Americans marching with General Burgoyne's army. In short order, McCrea was murdered and McNeil was released. The death of Jane McCrea caused outrage throughout the colonies, and the incident caused many in the area to join the American army in her honor. She became known as 'The Bride of Fort Edward' and is buried in the town.

"When the two women were taken away, apparently one of them had a mirror with her. The Indians were fascinated with this mirror, believing that seeing their reflection in it was like seeing their own spirit or soul.

Eventually, this mirror was found in a field and was given to us by direct descendants of Sarah McNeil." The mirror is one of the first items a visitor sees when beginning a tour of this famous house.

Various rooms depict different eras of ownership of the home. The kitchen is a tableau of 1940s appliances, chinaware, ephemera, tables and chairs, and pantry items such as Sloan's Liniment, Postum cereal, and Puretest Epsom Salts. The threshold that carries you from the kitchen into the tavern room is an actual beam from the original Fort Edward.

The tavern room is set up as if a 1700s wandering traveler could stop in at any moment. There is a recreation of a bar and a grill area, vintage parlor games are set up on small tables, and clay pipes and cupboards filled with old cups and dishes can be seen throughout the large room. Tables are set for the serving of food and grog. A large 1780 Vermont highboy is filled with period items, and vintage maps and prints line the walls. One rare item that I have never seen before is a "stick-in tommy" candle holder. "This wrought-iron piece was used when a person wanted to read while sitting in a chair. You simply inserted the stick part in a hole in the armrest of a straight-backed chair and the attached candle would illuminate the book or newspaper for the reader," I was told. The room, dominated by a large brick fireplace, would have easily been converted into a meeting room, courtroom, and social gathering place on very short notice.

There are literally thousands of antiques and unusual items in this house. You will find artwork from famous painters, an entire room set up displaying two eras of furniture and accessories (one pre–Civil War and the other post–Civil War), vintage children's toys, an old gramophone, a pipe organ that arrived by canal packet boat, and rope beds with the wooden bed key used to tighten the ropes "so the bed bugs won't bite."

"Many places in our area boast that 'George Washington slept here,'" McCarty said. "Some are true, others probably not. But we actually have proof that General Washington visited here, not once but twice." With that he pointed to a framed document on the wall. It is a copy of George Washington's personal travel expense account. In this record of items, it clearly lists him having a midday meal at this home twice during the general's battlefield inspection tours during the Revolutionary War.

The grounds of the Old Fort House Museum contain several historic outbuildings that have been moved here over the years to fully illustrate the history of the area. These buildings (all open to the public) include an 1853 law office, a 1900s one-room schoolhouse, the 1848 Plank Road toll collector's house, and the Cronkhite Pavilion, a circa 1872 dining hall that is the oldest surviving building from the original Washington County Fair.

"Of course, many people come to our museum because it was once a boardinghouse of a now famous person who stayed here for several years. His name was Solomon Northup, who wrote the book *Twelve Years a Slave*. When the film of the same name first came out in 2013, a lot of people became interested in Northup's capture, years of enslavement, and his ultimate release. We had the busiest year at the museum we ever had," McCarty told me.

Patrick Smyth, the Irishman who built the original house, was one of the first settlers of Fort Edward. Over the years his family lived in the home as it took on many configurations, including that of a public house. During the Revolutionary War it became the headquarters for many famous military leaders, including generals John Burgoyne, Philip Schuyler, Benedict Arnold, and John Stark.

In the early 1800s, the building acted as a boardinghouse. In 1828, a charming young African American musician showed up and took a room. Later that year, this man married his wife, Anne Hampton, here on Christmas Day. His name was Solomon Northup, a free black man from Minerva, in Essex County. By 1834, the Northups were living in Saratoga Springs. It was from there that Solomon was kidnapped, drugged, beaten, and sold into slavery in Louisiana. There he suffered a grim captivity for a dozen years before he was found and returned to his home in Upstate New York.

Northup told his story in an important book, *Twelve Years a Slave*. "His book was a major success. Just after he was returned to this area he wrote it. He regained his freedom on January 4, 1853. By June a proof had been created. By August the book was printed. It sold over 30,000 copies in its first year," McCarty said. The book was made into an Academy Award–winning movie in 2013.

"We have one whole room dedicated to this house's most famous occupant," McCarty told me. "There was such an outpouring of public interest in his story after the movie came out. Solomon Northup spent more time living in Fort Edward than any other place in his life. In this room, a former boardinghouse bedroom, we display old Northup family photos, an 1853 copy of his book as well as examples of slave-era items like chains, shackles, and whips." In one corner stands the actual broken gravestone of Solomon's father, Mintus.

Author's Notes

While I had never heard of Patt Smyth before visiting here, I certainly had heard of Solomon Northup and that is what drew me here, and I suspect draws many of the visitors to the Old Fort House Museum.

The house, now owned by the Fort Edward Historical Association, is a rare treat for historians. It is a stately old historic residence that is overflowing with incredible historic pieces throughout. It is also the oldest wood-frame building in Washington County.

I was most impressed with the extended touring area of the outbuildings. With more than a dozen different buildings from one or two centuries ago, this campus truly reflects the history, culture, and people of this region of the state.

I must also acknowledge Paul McCarty, my tour guide for the day. He is a great storyteller and knows this house inside and out. Paul is a seventh-generation native of the Fort Edward area and his love for this home is evident. "I have lived here all my life," he told me. "In fact, in the early 1900s my family used to buy cabbage here when it was a truck farm. And to think that today I am here living and breathing its history. It is definitely a fun house to research and curate."

Visit

Old Fort House Museum
(Home of Fort Edward Historical Association)
29 Broadway
Fort Edward, NY 12828
518-747-9600
Website: http://www.oldforthousemuseum.com

For Further Reference: Brown, Clifford W. and Rachel Seligman. *Solomon Northup: The Complete Story of the Man Who Wrote Twelve Years a Slave.* Santa Barbara, CA: Praeger Publishing, 2013.

While Here: Jane McRae is buried in Union Cemetery located at 402 Lower Main Street. Her epitaph tells the story of The Bride of Fort Edward and a historical marker denotes her final resting place. She is buried next to her friend Sarah McNeil.

Tours:

Open June, July, and August every day from 1:00 p.m. to 5:00 p.m. (last tour begins at 4:00 p.m.)
September and October, open six days a week (closed Monday)
Closed on national holidays

Admission:

Adults: $7.50
Seniors: Discount available
Children under 12: Free
Group tours can be arranged

35

Skene Manor

Home of Judge Joseph Potter
Whitehall, Washington County

Of all the homes in this book, Skene Manor may just be the most photographed one of them all.

"Yes, she is a beauty, isn't she, a bit like the Addams family house," Richard Brewer commented. He is the president of Skene Manor Preservation, Inc. The mansion was built from 1872 to 1874 by Judge Joseph H. Potter for his wife, Catherine. It is of Victorian Gothic Revival design and the architectural firm was Isaac H. Hobbs and Son from Philadelphia. They were known for designing residences in a style known as "Victorian exuberance."

The mansion, which appears to literally hang off the side of Skene Mountain and offers a dazzling bird's-eye view of the landscape below, contains a total of fifteen rooms. "There are nine bedrooms and two bathrooms," Brewer told me. "Although it has three floors of living space in its 9,000 square feet, to our knowledge the third floor was never meant to be occupied. There were eight elaborate fireplaces throughout, and they were the only source of heat in each room (central heating was installed in 1902). Seven of them remain today." The ceilings soar to sixteen feet on the first floor, fourteen on the second and twelve feet on the third.

There is a tall tower rising over the main entrance. It did not have a clock in it originally, but the third family to occupy the home, the Sachs family, had one installed in 1922. It was the former clock of the local Presbyterian church and a large railroad bell was put in place to chime out the hours. The clock had two 100-pound weights that ran from the clock all

the way down to the cellar. It was reported that Dr. Sachs gave the weekly job of winding the clock to his two eldest daughters. The clock, not original to the house, has since been removed.

The exterior, which is dramatic and graceful at the same time, is constructed of gray sandstone that was quarried from the very site by Italian stone cutters. The slate for the fireplaces and the roof came from nearby Vermont. "The roof is extremely heavy with all the slate, which is why you will notice the deep thresholds which take you from room to room. They indicate where some interior walls of stone or brick were built which can bear the weight of the roof," I was told.

"Unfortunately, we have no personal furniture of the Potters. Over the years, the house has had many owners, as many as nine. So, furniture has come and gone through the years."

The large, grand foyer has a remarkable feature. "All along the top of the room we can see original wallpaper frieze which was printed in Europe using the old wood block technique. The wallpaper was installed around 1872 and was still available in the 1920s when it sold for $1.20 a roll," Brewer said.

This is one of only a few homes featured in this book that does not have a sweeping staircase that greets you at the front door. The staircase is located off the main entrance in the south hallway that leads to the south entrance, where guests would enter from a porte cochere. Although the staircase cannot be seen when first entering the front door, it is still quite lovely. It is made of mahogany, oak, walnut, and birch. A large stained glass window adds a colorful glow to the staircase landing.

Upon entering the house, a large formal parlor is located to the left. Here we can see photos of the judge, both as a young man and old. There is also a photograph of the room that was taken in 1874. "So, you can see, very little has changed," Brewer said. "If you look at the photograph you see how plain this room really was. Judge Potter and his wife were raised in Quaker households and there is no indication that the house was furnished and decorated in a luxurious manner. Despite the grandeur of the mansion, you will not see things like heavy, elaborate drapes or fancy furnishings. The wall-to-wall carpet, which was a new interior feature at the time, was made possible by the industrialization of the carpet production of the time. Any fanciness that can be found is in the architect's design, like the plaster crown moldings and chandelier medallions. The wood on the first floor is all mahogany and walnut."

The rooms are huge. Several are separated by enormous pocket doors, which would be opened or closed for heating purposes. "Yes, these doors are something. They are built into entrances that have arches to them and are extremely heavy. They do still work, but we have them anchored to the floors because if they ever come off the tracks, we would have to open up the walls just to fix them."

Other rooms on the main floor include a sitting room, the Judge's library (which also acted as a bar over the years) and a kitchen. The second floor has several bedrooms (one of which was occupied by a housekeeper), a former billiard room (which proved too small for its intended use), and a bathroom. The bathroom has a unique water supply system. "A copper cistern was installed on the third floor which collected water from the roof for personal use. This alleviated the problem of having to lug pails of water up from the ground level. Heated coals were used when hot water was needed. The coals would be placed in a canister attached to a pipe in the cistern. In a few minutes the water flowing from the tank would have been heated enough to take a tepid bath," Brewer explained.

Because of the mountaintop perch that the mansion occupies, all of the rooms on the second floor have tall windows so as to maximize light, and those facing west have a dramatic view of the village below.

Judge Joseph H. Potter was an esteemed jurist who served on the New York State Supreme Court for two seven-year terms beginning in 1874. Potter and his wife, Catherine, had four children. Their first-born died at the age of six. They had three other sons who grew to become famous in their own right. William Parker Potter rose to the rank of Rear Admiral in the US Navy and sailed with President Theodore Roosevelt's legendary Great White Fleet in 1907. Joel Sanford Potter was a lawyer for over four decades in the Whitehall area. In fact, he built a stone house near Skene Manor. Henry Whitbeck Potter graduated from Rensselaer Polytechnic Institute and went on to become a respected civil engineer who did much of his work in South and Central America and Mexico.

There have been as many as nine different owners of the mansion since the Potters built it. While the Potters built this home after their children were grown and gone, a subsequent owner lived here with nine children.

Author's Notes

"Judge Potter built this massive home for he and his wife as their 'empty nest,'" Brewer told me. "It is funny but the most common remark we get from visitors is 'All of this for just two people?'"

But all was almost lost.

"By the time of the 1990s, and after several owners and uses for the mansion, it was starting to slowly decline and it was up for sale for non-payment of taxes," Brewer explained. "Apparently the owner had two offers. Someone wanted to buy the property and tear down the house, and another wanted to dismantle the house and move it to another state. The thought of losing the last of the great Whitehall residences was just too much for the people of the village. They organized a not-for-profit Skene

Manor Preservation group and went to work trying to save this old house. They called their effort SOS (Save Our Skene) and they were successful in raising enough money to make a down payment on the house and keep it in Whitehall. The group still owns the house and keeps it open for public events. I, like so many others, just fell in love with this house the first time I saw it. I volunteered here for a few years and now am president of the group which owns it."

Despite all of the obvious wonders of this remarkable "castle on the hill," the one thing that really struck me about Skene Manor was the fact that the community saved it from destruction and continues to keep it alive for future generations to enjoy. On the day of my visit here the place was alive with activity. Sunday brunch was being served to a full dining room of happy guests, tours were being given, and there was an air of excitement throughout the house.

"This house is really quite unlike so many other famous old homes. It had a long life and when the end was near the community rallied together to save her. It is run completely by volunteers. Nobody, including me, ever receives a paycheck. The docents, the cooks, the servers, and the gardeners all do it with no compensation. Sometimes we can even convince a plumber or electrician that they are volunteers too! It is a labor of love for all of us. And we think that is what makes this place so special," Brewer said.

Visit

Skene Manor
8 Potter's Terrace
Whitehall, NY 12887
518-499-1906
Website: http://www.skenemanor.org

For Further Reference and While Here: There is an interesting museum dedicated to telling the story of Skenesborough (Whitehall). It is situated along a developed park area along the canal that runs through the village. The museum has a wide selection of history books concerning the area. The museum is located on Skenesborough Drive in the downtown business area.

Tours: Mid-April to mid-December: Friday through Sunday, noon to 4:00 p.m.

Note: The manor serves lunch during its open hours. It also serves dinner once a month on a Wednesday. Reservations are not needed. Call ahead for menu and details.

Admission: Free

Contents

for Josephine

Acknowledgements

The publication of this book leaves me with many debts of gratitude.

In particular I must mention Alan Hayes, the brave mastermind of Arlen House, who was an unfailing source of encouragement, and all the dedicated volunteers of Arlen House who have seen this book through to its completion.

This book has been published with the generous assistance of the Senate of the National University of Ireland.

I benefited enormously from the advice of colleagues and friends – I would especially like to mention David Isitt, who, some years ago, joined me in a search for ruined Byzantine churches in the back streets of Istanbul. As we climbed over walls and landed inadvertently in the garden of the Orthodox patriarch, our conversation led me to think seriously about writing this book.

I want to thank the Dean of Research at NUI, Galway for his very practical help and the Abbot and community of Glenstal for generous permission to reproduce the beautiful icon on the cover of this book.

Finally, I acknowledge especially the interest and enthusiasm of Josephine, who became my wife a year ago, and who has brought an unfailing radiance into my world

C.L., 25 August 2001

Exploring John's Gospel

Chapter One

A knighted and very senior British civil servant when confronted in court about the veracity of testimony given earlier by him conceded sportingly that he had been less than entirely candid, and he went on to remark insouciantly that he had been 'economical with the truth'. The elegance of that phrase took on at once the resonance of proverb even as the events giving rise to it faded quickly from the public mind. But if he touched a responsive chord it was in populations increasingly accustomed to the surrounding pressure of the salaried truth adjuster and of slickly packaged 'facts'. Indeed, such is the prevalence of managed information that only the most blatant distortion of events and only the most conspicuous indulgence in propaganda can nowadays provoke the active disquiet or even the passing indignation of observers.

The mistake, however, would be to imagine that the wish to make a sale or else to conceal something is the sole reason for picking and choosing among possible statements. A biographer, for example, knows that a recurring problem is the decision regarding what to leave out or to put in, and the point is made explicitly at the end of the fourth gospel:

> There were many other things that Jesus did, and if all were written down I do not think the world could hold the books that would have to be written (21.25)

This habit of being selective is an unmistakable and indeed necessary component of the human scene. Just as at the physical level the eye filters the blazing reality of sunlight, so in the profounder reaches of the self there are selective mechanisms, elaborated with age and with experience, which are deployed for better or worse whenever one deals with what comes into view. And because this is something long recognised for what it is, there have been, and there will continue to be, elaborate efforts to neutralise the consequent worry that, for one reason or another, human beings may somehow obscure the real, may disfigure it, may impose their own warm wish on the cold earth. To overcome this possibility and to safeguard the integrity of the real, systems of philosophy have come into being in the attempt to uncover and to secure what is actually the case, and if such systems are in regular disagreement among themselves this cannot obscure their shared commitment to something which has the clean, glowing lines of a longed-for goal, namely, truth.

The urge to deal in truth does not go away and it is also the ambience where *the act of reading* has to be located. For the engagement with reading is part of the wider life-long experience of trying to make sense of what one encounters. A text lies outside the self. Its words are there to be read. But what happens from the assembling of words by the writer to the registration by the reader of what they might mean has been the subject in recent years of much speculation and of lengthy, even passionate, discussion. Sometimes the focus has been on making the text speak for itself. More recently, attention has shifted to the reader. Irrespective of the starting point, however, analysis and argument continue on their way, with the prospect of unlocking further vistas and of generating new insights.

But whatever arises amid all of this scrutiny must inevitably have some bearing upon the specific celebrated text of the fourth gospel which, after all, is not a freak happening. It is a book like any other, an amalgam of chosen words, a shaped narrative. And if the evangelist has signalled that there is more to the reality of Jesus than has been written down he is implying that he himself has isolated only those episodes and utterances which fitted his own purpose as a writer. But if he has an agenda so, presumably, has the reader who is more than merely a passive recorder of what is on the page and who for many reasons will settle upon a conceptual framework by means of which a sense can be extracted from what lies in the text.

Consider, for instance, an episode in the gospel of John, where a Samaritan woman comes to the well of Jacob to draw water. The solitary figure of the Nazarene Jesus is sitting at the edge of the well. They talk, and at one moment in the conversation there is the following exchange:

> Call your husband, and come here
>
> I haven't got a husband
>
> 'I haven't got a husband'. Well said. You've had five and the one you have now is not your husband.

In making sense of what is set down here in the text readers have come from very different points of view and with very different aspirations. The great second-century Greek scholar Origen, claiming that the details of what happened must be understood to have a significance far beyond their frame of immediate reference, offers a set of meanings which includes the following. The well symbolises the Old Testament and the decision of Jesus to sit beside it is a sign of the abiding need to draw from its riches. The five husbands symbolise the five senses. The Samaritan woman in choosing to abandon these in favour of one man of unattached status evokes a life centred on the freedom and unpackaged reality of spirit. Augustine, by contrast, sees the well as the symbol of the filth and the turbid desires of sensuality. The woman, in typically human fashion, chooses to dip into it instead of looking upwards to the distant glories of heaven. A third reader, John Calvin, takes the term 'well' to signify, self-evidently, a place of refreshment. Regarding the five husbands it seems clear to him that none of them could eventually stand the Samaritan woman and the present man in her life is merely trying her out. And so it goes on with reading after reading offered by experts of every persuasion and status, until eventually the interested observer has to make some decision regarding the variant interpretations which are on offer or else must settle on a particular reading. This is certainly the case for Christian readers who, as such, have an important stake in words transmitted to them in texts like the gospel of John.

But words come always from a past which is two seconds or maybe two thousand years behind us. They come direct or mediated and, very often, the habits generated by linear time dissolve as we immerse ourselves in an endearment, a promise made, an old grief or an insight. And these may touch us if we are open to them, or, like travellers seeking shelter but left out in the night and the cold, they may pass us by because we are not really listening.

What we have here is a relationship, one between the self and those words which come our way. It has ever been so, for 'in the beginning was the word', something to encounter, something from an ambience older than any particular self and lined with the echoes of earlier times. Indeed it would be true to say that there is really no such thing as a truly dead language because in every inhabited corner there is pulsing, like a more or less distant star, the presence of earlier words. In modern European languages, for instance, the references to philosophy, to logic, to theology, to drama and to much else besides have the effect not merely of indicating the survival of updated terms from classical Greek but, more importantly, of pointing to the reality that the original use of such terms established the markers for enterprises which are still held to be important. And since one could multiply the examples of this phenomenon there would appear to be solid grounds for the suggestion that in any given time or culture there is some kind of carryover, some enduring substratum which influences, more or less significantly, the direction taken by current discourse. It is so with the many ideologies present or past which have put their sign on the human landscape. One need only think of Marxism, of the doctrines of colonialism and racism. There is the clear, long-term presence of Islam. There is the bond created for Jews by the constant plumbing of the depths of the Torah, and, nearly two millennia after the death of Jesus, the theologians of mainstream Christianity still resort to the intellectual scaffolding and the technical vocabulary created in the fourth and fifth centuries in reaction to questions about the nature of the triune God. In short, tens of millions of men and women regularly find themselves in the situation of having their lives and their choices directed by the structured terminologies at work around them.

Actually, Christians are what they are on the basis, ultimately, of hearsay. Or, more accurately, perhaps, Christians as individuals deploy their own personal resources to deal not only with memories reported long ago but with what others have made of such memories. Whether born or reared in communities avowedly dedicated to the man called Jesus or whether they are converts, they are united at least to the extent that the foundations of what they profess have come to them both in a selection of texts compiled in earlier times and also in the abiding commitment of some in each generation to speak insistently of what they have found, directly or indirectly, in such documents. Christians are inserted into a received discourse, with which, as individual selves, they have to forge some kind of relationship. In this they are no different from fellow human beings who must deal with what is other and, quite specifically, with what is brought in by the waves of continuing utterance.

It is important to remember here that only the naive imagine that language is something merely for use, like money in the daily exchanges of life. They forget that there is also a sense in which language may be said to use them, since theirs is a relationship with what they hear and read, and relationships work in at least two directions. Poets know this well. Boris Pasternak was writing from personal experience when he described the following moment in the life of Yury Zhivago:

> After two or three stanzas and several images by which he was himself astonished, his work took possession of him and he experienced the approach of what is called inspiration. At such moments the correlation of the forces controlling the artist is, as it were, stood on its head. The ascendancy is no longer with the artist or the state of mind which he is trying to express, but with language, his instrument of expression. Language, the home and dwelling of beauty and meaning itself, begins to think and speak for man and turns wholly into music, not in the sense of outward, audible sounds but by virtue of the power and momentum of its inward flow. Then, like the current of a mighty river polishing stones and turning wheels by its very movement, the flow of speech creates in passing, by the force of its own laws, rhyme and rhythm and countless other forms and formations, still more important and until now undiscovered, unconsidered and unnamed. At such moments Yury felt that the main part of

> his work was not being done by him but by something which was above him and controlling him.[1]

This feeling that one is mastered by currents of being which are opening up through the 'now' of one's language is marvellously suggested by Nadezda Mandelstam when she talks of her husband Osip in the throes of poetic composition, shaking his head as though plagued by a wasp, moving his lips, trying out the words which just might fit what he was striving to hear and what would soon be in existence as a finished poem.[2] This mutuality, in passion or subsidence, this give and take between self and language, language and self, is not peculiar to the great poet or indeed to the reader but is a defining condition of man, socially located and existing within the specifics of time and place.

Of course the ways of such a relationship are immensely complex, as will be obvious from a consideration of merely a couple of situations. For example, in the abundant record of those who became converts to communism in, say, the 1930s there is the recurring theme of how indoctrination included not just the exegesis of particular networks of ideas but also the deliberate exercise in the task of insinuating oneself into an acceptably redeployed language. Arthur Koestler described the process as it affected himself in his early days as party member:

> I now lived entirely in a mental world comparable to the self-contained universe of the mediaeval Schoolmen. All my feelings, my attitudes to art, literature and human relations, became reconditioned and moulded to the pattern. My vocabulary, grammar, syntax, gradually changed. I learnt to avoid any original form of expression, any individual turn of phrase. Euphony, gradations of emphasis, restraint, nuances of meaning, were suspect. Language, and with it thought, underwent a process of dehydration, and crystallised in the ready-made schemata of Marxist jargon.
>
> There were perhaps a dozen or two adjectives whose use was both safe and mandatory, such as: decadent, hypocritical, morbid (for the capitalist bourgeoisie); heroic, disciplined, class-conscious (for the revolutionary proletariat); *petit-bourgeois*, romantic, sentimental (for humanitarian scruples); opportunist and sectarian (for Right and Left deviations respectively); mechanistic, metaphysical,

mystical (for the wrong intellectual approach); dialectical, concrete (for the right approach); flaming (protests); fraternal (greetings); unswerving (loyalty to the Party).[3]

And it was Koestler who in his classic novel *Darkness at Noon* portrayed how, without being tortured or unduly oppressed, a loyal communist could be brought by an intense application of party logic to confess to a capital crime of which he was known to be innocent, and all for the common good of the cause. Although a work of fiction, the plausibility of what it portrayed was vindicated horribly in the first half of the 1950s during the show trials in such places as Czechoslovakia and Hungary.

But as Koestler came to speak of the time when he was taken over by the thought-world and, hence, by the language of communism it was from the point of view of someone who had once been faithful, in the full sense of that term, but who had moved on and out. Looking back he would say:

> I deplore the logical error that led me into the Communist Party; but I do not regret the spiritual discipline that it imposed. Purgatory is a painful experience; but no one who went through it is likely to wish that it should be erased from his past.[4]

But if he travelled on, there were many others who remained, their convictions shaped by the layered language of their party, their thought nurtured by an elaborate discourse which by constant repetition, as in a kind of liturgy, played often on their best feelings and on their deepest hopes.

What Koestler experienced is something familiar from numerous contexts. First, there are shared concerns of a more or less elaborate nature, and all this has a way of generating the use of words which try to give voice to the stirrings of aspiration and to the glimpses of better things. Such words eventually take on a life of their own, forming an available amalgam which assumes so much authority that lives are remade to accommodate it. Heart and mind seek to articulate a distant horizon; then by a process of reversal, which itself may be reversed by new perceptions and needs, that which has been articulated becomes the pilot for mind and heart.

So it goes for Christians as they live by received theological opinion or else turn anew to their scriptures. So it was for those in the early Church who, for instance, under the impetus of biblical utterance and exegesis took specific words for a master and withdrew from society in order to form alternative communities dedicated to the objective of making safe one's soul. A primary task was to restrict the body:

> One becomes stateless and homeless. One gives up possessions, friends, ownership of property, livelihood, business connections, social life and scholarship. The heart is made ready to receive the imprint of sacred teaching, and this making ready involves the unlearning of knowledge deriving from evil habits. To write on wax, one has first to erase the letters previously written there, and to bring sacred teaching to the soul one must begin by wiping out preoccupations rooted in ordinary habits.[5]

Envisaged here was a complete takeover of a humbled self by scripture. A monk, troubled by the intrusion of worldly thoughts, is advised to train himself so that day and night, awake or asleep his mind will be soaked, as it were, by the constantly piped words of the psalmist, 'God look to my help, Lord make haste to assist me'. Indeed all the psalms have a major role in the spirituality of early monasticism. They are songs with a power to direct belief and to promote particular forms of self-understanding. The practitioners of early monasticism were encouraged to realise, as St. Athanasius puts it, that:

> the one who hears the psalm is taught the emotions of the soul ... these words are like a mirror to the person singing them.

He becomes aware that each psalm:

> is about him, so that, convicted by the pang of conscience, he repents, or else, hearing of the hope that lies in God, of the help available to believers, of the grace that exists for him, he exults and begins to thank God.[6]

And one reason for exultation is the sense of not being alone, of being able to tune into words repeated by countless predecessors and contemporaries, all of whom are on the same journey, motivated by the same hopes and eager to live out the consequences of the same beliefs.

Christians, whether or not they withdraw from society, are consciously or unconsciously moulded to a greater or lesser extent by a received discourse which itself is, at any moment, founded upon the texts and the interpretations of the Old and New Testaments. Theirs is in each case a relationship between a self and a consecrated body of words. In this they are no different from the adherents of any '-ism', but in every instance the basic question to be asked concerns the present nature of that relationship and the extent to which it oscillates between the active and the passive, between the dynamic and the sclerotic.

In regard to the example offered by poetry, some people talk of the poet as the unceasing recipient of being. Oscar Milosz, on the other hand, declares the fundamental characteristic of a poet is to be in 'the passionate pursuit of the real'.[7] The former involves a stance of receptivity; the latter puts emphasis on activity marked by initiative and commitment. Neither is wrong. Both in fact are providing reminders of the nuanced complexity of what happens between poet and named reality. And in this they offer a paradigm which is useful in many respects, not least in its suggestion that just as the poet may, by virtue of talent, deepen the potentialities of received discourse, so too the ordinary adherent of an '-ism', conscious of being in some kind of comforting space, may enhance, even if only within the self, the potential for enlargement of vision at the heart of any group rhetoric.

The assumption here is that the glimpse of a promised land precedes the articulation of its precise geography and that with the passage of days such articulation, either as it develops or in its sanctified state, can become the source of endless inspiration and enrichment. But, of course, life being what it is, such discourse may also go dry:

We have forgotten that the word alone
Shone radiant over the troubled earth,
And that in the Gospel of St. John
It is written that the word is God.
But we have limited its range
To the paltry boundaries of this world,
And like the dead bees in an empty hive
Dead words emit a foul odour.[8]

If there is a shut-down of vitality in words and, most particularly, in the discourse of an established ideology the reasons can vary from the workings of inertia to a determination to maintain the status quo. Which is another way of saying that, since language does not exist independently of those dwelling within it and since human beings can soar as well as plod, any tendency to bloodlessness tells of what is happening in the human domain rather than in the intrinsic quality of his utterance.

For, of course, one is, sooner or later, back to the user and maker of discourse. And the experience of ideologies must be especially significant here since it suggests that at least three kinds of situation obtain between person and word. There is, first, the relationship where one turns to words as being the necessary instruments for the give and take of the common day. This is too evident to require elaboration and one need only imagine the quality of life of a monoglot speaker of Irish cast suddenly among the shepherds of Tibet. But there is, secondly, the relationship between creative impulse and language which he inhabits, and the example of good poets serves to illustrate what happens when words are so deployed as a consequence of human talent that they take on a hitherto unsuspected life, thereby making possible a marked heightening of communal perceptiveness. But, thirdly, there is the relationship between human impulses and an operative established group-discourse which over a given time impinges upon any scene ranging from social mores and politics to art and religion. What makes this third type of relationship so important and so interesting is that, more than any other, it brings to the forefront the issue of power.

Like language, which is regularly its instrument, power enmeshes all human beings. But its full presence can only be tracked in its effects. The most obvious measure of it is the extent to which it commands submission. However, when Mao Tse Tung claimed that power lay in the barrel of a gun he was engaging, as usual, in vast over-simplification, for the reality of power is to be found at every level of human life. Its presence is most easily marked when someone makes way for what is other or else is yielded to outside the boundaries of the self. One talks of the power of Church or party. One mentions submission to authority. Lover and terrorist, saint and sinner, benefactor and oppressor, deity and demon – all are exemplars of power. But it is only after the effects of power have been acknowledged and properly described that one may apply to them one's own determinants of what is good or bad. For power is neither benign nor evil. It is like the wind. It simply is. In every instance one submits to it or not, and its impact is measured and evaluated accordingly.

But words and power are close allies. Words can evoke submission or domination in inter-personal relations, while in the public arena gatherings of interlocking and self-perpetuating words can take over the space available for discourse. They can even work to exclude alternatives. And when multitudes go along with and direct their lives by the same discourse then indeed one may talk of this as truly powerful.

That is how it has been with Christianity. When the first disciples of Jesus began to spread news of him they brought into being not simply a catalogue of information about their founder, a checklist to be passed along some kind of proto-internet. They created a discourse which grew and was elaborated and which embodied the unfolding insights and the sense of excitement and purpose of the expanding legions of believers. In establishing the basic ingredients of such a discourse some prophetic voices were clearly more effective than others. Paul the apostle, for instance, with his urgent sense of the need to live on one or other side of the frontier between Christ and all else forged a language which has become classic and binding within the Christian scheme of things. Taking common words such as 'life' and 'death', the 'elect' and the 'holy ones', the 'world' and 'resurrection' he gave them meaning in a new context, stitching together a network of ideas and images which came to acquire a self-evident rightness to more and more Christians who directed their lives and hopes thereby. And looking to him and to the example he had set, others would, as Seamus Heaney put it, 'lie down in the word hoard', wishing to articulate the deepening and expansive ideas made possible by what Paul and the first Christian preachers and writers had proclaimed, and in the process a discourse would be created, one so distinctive that by the days of Augustine the simple Latin term *gratia* would signify in Roman law a corrupt influence on imperial and judicial processes, whereas for Christians it would point to the generous favour of God. Christians would be 'formed' within the ambience of such words, their lives, in consequence, acquiring meaning and validation, purpose and expectation. Words which had been reached for, in the effort to declare what was glimpsed, would now become themselves the warrant and authority for paths chosen in preference to others. By the Middle Ages they would be the very stuff of public opinion. But if the words of Paul, if the letters of this 'apostle of the gentiles' helped significantly to create the discourse and therefore the *milieu* in which Christians operated so too did the fourth gospel.

No observer of Christianity could miss it. It was active century after century since those days when it began first to circulate. To label it a seminal work would be to state the very obvious. To trace its influence among Christians would require energy and scholarship well beyond the capacities of any one person. But every time its pages are scanned there arises the issue as old as it is new, the question of what on each occasion goes into the reading of those celebrated words.

A case history might help here, that of André Malraux who wrote of moments in 1944 when, wounded, under guard in a convent, and believing himself destined for the firing squad, he asked one night for a bible and began to re-read the fourth gospel. His memory was filled already with Byzantine and Slav images of the evangelist, and he had once visited the tomb near Ephesus where John was said to be buried. Now in what he thought to be his own last hours he rediscovered words which had moved him deeply in other times, the declaration for instance of God's love for the world and the promise of rescue to those willing to put their trust in the Son. But the stumbling block was this invitation to trust:

> Faith means belief; I had a great respect for the Christian message which had pervaded this earth in which I would doubtless soon be lying, but I did not believe in it. The memory of St. John is more powerful against misfortune than his presence is against death.

For Malraux the reading of this admired book was ultimately a disappointment, because nothing within him would allow the requisite act of trust:

> All that remained in my memory was fraternity. In this convent silence, probably filled with prayers for me and broken by a distant clattering of a tank on the move, what lived as profoundly in my mind as the approach of death … was the despairing caress that closes the eyes of the dead.[9]

Malraux was looking from outside. He respected the discourse of Christianity and he was impressed by the fourth gospel:

> The genius of Christianity is to have proclaimed that the path to the deepest mystery is the path of love, a love which is not confined to men's feelings but transcends them like the soul of the world, more powerful than death and more powerful than justice. 'For God did not send his son into the world to judge the world but to save it'. Alone in face of death I encountered that immemorial compassion which had enveloped as many despairs as the Day of Judgement would roll back sepulchers.[10]

But he remained alone, for his convictions had left him beyond the frontiers of Christian discourse and 'cut off from the eternal', and his reading of the gospel changed nothing whatever of this.

Two events had occurred here. First was the act of reading. That is, there was the process of making sense of what was on the page. Then there was the interplay between self and what had been construed. The distinction between these two situations is more a matter of logical precision than an acknowledgement of how things actually work, since the making of sense is an act occurring within the self, and the self is at any given moment moulded by a particular past and moved by a particular present. On that night in 1944 when he appeared to be doomed Malraux had still the urge to find some point or purpose in all that was going on. He knew a great deal about religion, east and west, but this had not turned him towards belief in a realm beyond our own. Yet he admired the fourth gospel and he was willing to be surprised. That, however, did not happen, and so the text was returned to its owner in the convent, and a couple of decades later he would continue to carry the melancholy feeling of having been let down. He would have understood, and perhaps even accepted, the sentiment of his famous contemporary Jean-Paul Sartre, that God was like a beautiful woman. 'Fifty years ago there might have been something between us, but now it is too late'.

Malraux came with pre-conditions to the reading of the gospel. To an extent which he might not have admitted, his mind was already made up in regard to some of the most fundamental issues touching on the human scene and invoked by the evangelist. But in this he was really no different from believers, since it is unlikely that there is any such event as an unconditioned act of reading. Atheists and believers, historians and students of good writing are all at one, formally speaking, when they work through the pages of the fourth gospel. All are engaged with the process of making sense and of reacting accordingly. They are coping with the text. Yet the community among them breaks down as soon as each one has decided upon what the text must mean. Indeed it ends before that, since in each case the act of reading includes the deployment of what makes for the individuality of the reader, and that implies pre-conceptions and unexamined attitudes as well as all that has made a successful take-over from outside the self. The fact that many can find themselves in agreement over what they have construed does not alter the singularity of each act of reading. And if from all this there emerge groups of like-minded readers then and only then may one classify these groups under general headings such as believer and non-believer, Catholic and Protestant.

This matter of the individuality of the reader is central, especially since it would appear that the act of reading is one of construction or, indeed, of reconstruction, of putting together a sense of what has been set down by the writer. And in this case the evangelist is someone long dead and from a milieu significantly different from that of the modern reader. This being so, can any but the most pallid encounter ever take place between his text and the offspring of an era which comes over two millennia later? The question deserves to be raised since it must evoke at once the recognition of its inappropriateness. For it is not the respective psychologies of evangelist and reader which are of concern but, rather, the fact that each of these entered into a relationship with an object, this being the life and times of the man called Jesus. It is the tale which is important, and the reading of it is not, as it were, a procedure whereby, like a photocopier, one reproduces something written in the past. What happens, rather, is that a meaning for now is made within the self.

The reader enters into a relationship with what is on the page, and, even though the words may have been set down long ago and may refer to what is finished and done with, the understanding of those words occurs now, in the present moment when the resources of self are mobilised to lay hold of what has been written. Privately construed meaning arises now, for though the composition of the text may have happened in a more or less distant past the text itself has slipped anchor. It has left home, showing perhaps the signs of its origin but existing nevertheless as something independent. Like a human being it is there to be encountered. But while there is a potential responsiveness in a human being, there is in the text only the silence of the printed page. So the reader embarks upon what is a one-sided engagement which takes place in excitement or coldness or in the limited enthusiasm of a limited attention span.

Of course the neophyte may imagine that provided one is armed with the access code of basic literacy the quest to understand what is written is a routine of making words out of letters, paragraphs out of words and pages out of paragraphs. But it does not take long to discover that any such quest is always shadowed by the possibility of even the simplest kind of misunderstanding, as in the conversation of the three slightly deaf men:

> It's windy today
>
> No, it's Thursday.
>
> So am I. Let's go have a drink.

Such misunderstanding will compel the neophyte to realise quickly that in fact one is embarking on a course where the effort to make sense does not happen in a vacuum and that the wish to understand, as well as the conditions for its achievement, are determined by a multitude of different factors. Malraux, under sentence of death, read the fourth gospel with the curiosity and the urgency of a man seeking a new angle on his own situation. The immense bibliography of Johannine studies is itself an indication of the simple and evident truth that the reading of this gospel is undertaken from within a great variety of points of view. Interest, the exploration or validation of theological ideas, the search for norms, the quest for historical knowledge, for sociological data or for psychological insights – all this and much more will direct the venture into the text, so much so indeed that it is illusory to imagine that there will be a final and finished product at the end of what in churches is solemnly announced as 'a reading of the gospel according to St. John'.

To add a piquant complexity to the scene one needs also to bear in mind that the text – indeed any text – is itself a construction. Consequently, the work of scholars such as Bultmann is strongly influenced by the idea of this gospel as something more or less skilfully cobbled together from earlier writings and oral traditions, the traces of which can be uncovered like the strata in some archaeological site. As a result there is much debate centred on the question of whether one should talk here of a writer, an editor or both. Again, there are scholars who have set out to apply to the fourth gospel the results of recent general studies of literary texts. For example, there has been a proposal to look at the gospel from three angles, its characteristic existence as a narrative, the actual story it tells, and the way in which the story is told. The thrust of the suggestion is to take apart the gathered words on a page and, as it were, to make three reconstructions out of them, each time with a view to establishing a relationship with what is there. If, for instance, one takes a set of episodes from a sequence of chapters in order to find out if there is some underlying theme which, in turn, points towards a particular overall meaning, one omits whatever in the text has no bearing on the specific project of research and one puts together what one finds in order to study it. This is a construction, the making of which results from one's own procedures of selectivity such as they are. But if one is to have some confidence in one's construction, one will also seek to uncover the extent to which one is being manipulated and pushed in one direction rather than another by the composer of the text. For whether one is dealing with a writer or an editor, whose talents and skills have been long appreciated, the reader, conscious of not being some kind of recording machine, a seismograph registering external movements, will wish to construe not only what appears to be meant but what is actually meant. The impetus to do so in the case of the fourth gospel will be sharpened, for instance, by the knowledge that in early Christianity two distinctive schools of exegesis came into being, the one centred on Antioch, the other on Alexandria, the one focusing on literal meaning, the other on the figurative, both the products of an awareness of the complexity of what goes into the act of writing and therefore of reading.

So the neophyte will discover increasingly that the reading of the text is part of the wider process of coming to grips with what emerges out of life. One is into a relationship with what is other, but, given the propensities of human beings, relationships invariably come under scrutiny, rules are then laid down and, in particular instances, there is even the threat or else the decision to impose sanctions if particular means are not accepted. The reader seeking to make sense may come to find in fact that one's 'this is what it means' is tugged at by 'this is what it ought to mean'. And when 'ought' enters the picture one is into power situations, good or bad, obvious or covert. So, for example, following the interplay of discussion within a communal setting, the representatives of 'living traditions' would claim to have a more 'genuine understanding' than those readers who are outside such a tradition. Indeed, for their own reasons, established authorities take very seriously the act of reading, which is why there is censorship and the burning of books. The saying 'give me the child and I will give you the man' tells its own tale of a programme, with its own infra-structure, to bring the act of reading, among other areas of life, into the ambit of ground rules in which the reader is to be trained. In a non-pluralist society, that is pressure indeed. The decision in the Vatican to end the practice of informing the world of what titles were on the index of forbidden books was not the result of a change of basic attitudes but came, rather, from the recognition that in the reality of a pluralist world such a practice was a lost cause. For pluralism is a fact. It has been ever more so in the Europe of the west since the days of the Reformation, and indeed in the remainder of the world. Its consequent influence upon each reader calls up the matter of what happens when one tries to make sense of a book, and especially of a work with the consecrated status of the fourth gospel.

A Malraux turning away is not really an issue here. The question, rather, is what happens in the case of the reader in a pluralist world who happens to be a believer, that is, someone who believes in God and in the special significance of the historical Jesus.

A study of the approach to the gospel by Origen and Augustine, by Thomas Aquinas and Rudolf Bultmann, among many others, shows that they read the pages before them from points of view that were undeniably different. They also differed in what they chose to emphasise. They operated from cultural backgrounds and intellectual pre-suppositions which overlapped in some areas but were markedly distinct in others. Furthermore, Origen wrote in Greek about a work also composed in Greek, Augustine in Latin about a translated text. Bultmann, a polymath, wrote in his native German. And if, as is commonly supposed, there is, as it were, a distinctive genius or personality in each language one has to wonder about what is added to or subtracted from the original text, whose own words, at the time of writing, themselves emerged from within living patterns of particular image and intention.

It might be argued that whatever the difference – temperamental, historical, cultural, theological – between the commentators on the fourth gospel there are, nevertheless, parameters or boundaries within which all who speak of the text must operate. There are considerations to be excluded, such as, for example, that the fourth gospel is a brilliant novel or that the author was actually Origen. There are readings to be discarded, such as those which miss central details or episodes. There are interpretations which most, if not all, readers would agree to dismiss because they are plainly at variance with established historical facts or else with what the text itself supplies by way of refutation. Yet, having made due allowance for the highly improbable and the outlandish, it is still the case that agreement among readers has actually foundered on the rock of particulars, and this must inevitably prompt a question as to whether there can exist a criterion which for believers at least must ultimately guide and direct every act of reading the fourth gospel.

Thomas Aquinas and his colleagues would have no difficulty with this question. For him the sanctioned theology of the Church gives voice to that truth which will determine whether or not readings of a particular gospel passage fall within acceptable levels of exegetical variation. For him the heretic in fact is a bad reader precisely because he has failed to take for a guide what the Church proclaims to be the case. Such a heretic is also likely to have been simplistic, missing the subtleties made available by the interaction of literal, allegorical and anagogical interpretation.

In the world of Aquinas there is not much room for idiosyncrasy. The truth is there, and both doctrine and practice combine to affirm that the guarantor of such truth is the Church in council. This implies that within permissible limits of variation there has to be a 'correct' reading of what is contained in the fourth gospel. Otherwise one is into the scenario pithily articulated in the dictum about the devil and his quotations of scripture. One has therefore to read the gospel from within guidelines set by the Church, just as, in moral issues, one is expected to have a conscience so formed that one freely accepts the prescriptions of ecclesiastical authority. The reading of the fourth gospel is thus for Aquinas an exercise in channeled research. The goal is truth, but in so vital an enterprise there is no place at all for the unsubmissive assertiveness of the maverick.

But idiosyncrasy and truth are terms filled with difficulty. After all, to be idiosyncratic may often be a way of asserting that at the existential level where one speaks the word 'I', one is being true to one's deepest self. However much Thomas Aquinas and contemporary commentators like Bonaventure or Rupert of Deutz might wish to think that standing on one's own perception of the truth is something deplorable when it runs counter to what the Church proclaims, the historical reality is very much more complicated. When, for instance, John Calvin composes his own commentary on the fourth gospel it is from within the perspectives of a man convinced that while truth is indeed there to be contemplated, nevertheless the situation of Christianity in regard to this truth has been seriously compromised. In fact Christianity has been hi-jacked by the papacy. Corrupt tenants of the see of Rome have seriously and wilfully muddied essential truths, veiling them from the world as a consequence of overpowering depravity. The problem, then, is to get back to such truths, and one way of doing so is to read the fourth gospel properly.

But an immediate problem emerges, at least for the observer sitting in a pew and looking up to a pulpit. For he now has to choose between rivals. He hears, for instance, the words in the gospel where Jesus declares himself to be the 'true vine'. This is an image likely to have meaning for anyone with the experience of seeing things grow. And, since growth implies both dynamism and the obstacles to its realisation, the idea of trimming and pruning and boosting evoked by the reference in the text to the vine and the vine grower will make some kind of sense, even if only at the theoretical level. Furthermore, the image is likely to have meaning for a broader spread of people than would be the case if it has been drawn, say, from an abstruse relationship within the realm of higher mathematics. Indeed the fact that it was inspired by the practices of viticulture rather than of mathematics is itself indicative of the important circumstance that it was chosen to generate an immediacy of response and to convey an important insight into the relationship between Jesus and his followers.

When Calvin turns to these verses, he shares with Roman readers, 'the papists', the conviction that the words are those of God. And the observer can note the agreement. But discord immediately sets in. For having made the obvious remarks about cultivation and fruitfulness and about the death of branches separated from the vine, Calvin homes in on the declaration 'apart from me you can do nothing' and goes on to declare what this must mean:

> As long as we are outside of him we bear no fruit that is good or pleasing to God for we are completely unfit to do anything good.

He adds however that this meaning, discerned in the text and to him so very clear, is not acknowledged by others:

> The papists do not merely weaken the statement. They exhaust it utterly. Indeed they skip it altogether. Although paying lip-service to the idea that we can do nothing without Christ they have a fantasy about some faculty within us which is not self-sufficient but which, with the help of God, co-operates with grace. They cannot accept that man should be so empty as to be devoid of the capacity to contribute anything from himself. Yet the words of Christ are too obvious to permit so easy an evasion. The papist fabrication is that although we can do nothing without Christ, we have something of ourselves besides his grace when his help becomes available to us. Christ says, on the contrary, that we can do nothing of ourselves (15:5).

For the believer, sitting in his pew during the sixteenth century, this is not an argument among *litterateurs*. There can be no civilised agreement to disagree, because key issues of doctrine are at centre stage and, in this instance, while both sides are reading the same words of the same text, each is imperiously demanding allegiance. Rome and Calvin proclaim the existence of God's truth, and together they assert their commitment to this truth, which they see as independent of any person and also as something to be discovered and articulated. Yet what is one to do when they manifestly disagree on the meaning of crucial sections of scripture? If they are at odds regarding one text or many, the same issue remains of the choice to be made between them. The issue itself is complicated by the circumstances in which it arises, for the observer may well be deafened, enraptured, intimidated or even turned off by the thunder and the clamour of conflicting hieratic voices.

Uproar was a palpable feature of the conflict between Rome and the Reformers, the 'truth' of one side being the manifest wickedness or folly of the other. But when one leaves aside either the barrage of mutual abuse marking this conflict or else the arrival much later of the attempt at good manners which came under the heading of ecumenism, the central and abiding theme continued to be relatively uncomplicated and it has remained so, namely, the extent to which idiosyncrasy is tolerable for Christians. Of all the questions summoned by the Reformers it is difficult to envisage any as significant or, eventually, as pervasive as this matter of the relationship of the self to proffered truth, and especially to the truth both of texts and the interpretation of texts such as the fourth gospel.

The spread and increase in the number of Christian denominations from the sixteenth to the twenty first centuries only makes this issue more obvious. If one adds that the majority of Christians nowadays acquire their beliefs as a consequence of where they are born the claim of any one group to an exclusive inside track has no longer the same compelling power as might have obtained in the days of Aquinas. The recognition that this is so may explain why, despite the momentum of past habits and rhetorics, the strident and impassioned denunciations of one another, characteristic of say, the sixteenth century, have largely disappeared, so that it may even be possible to envisage a time to come when the word 'church' in its large and singular sense will apply to all believers in God and Jesus, regardless of whether or not they belong to a particular denomination with its particular ideology.

Be that as it may, the central reality continues to be that of the relationship of the self to what is on offer both in the texts and the textual interpretations which have been at the heart of Christianity. The methods which have grown out of a subject/object metaphysics, the power of generalisations such as 'Church and individual', 'tradition and private judgement', 'authority and the person', 'community of interpreters' may largely disguise but cannot wholly conceal the prime existential situation which is that a specific self, engaging with words, is the arena where meaning of sorts continues to be made. Education, constant preaching, the regular performance of a liturgy and much else besides are among the influences brought to bear on that arena. But when the last persuasive and forming gestures have been made it still remains the case that one makes meaning, such as it is, within one's aloneness.

So, after two thousand years, why do committed Christians continue to make meaning out of their texts? The reasons must be very numerous indeed. But, at the risk of great over-simplification, at least one may be proposed, namely, that they are *Christ*-ians, that, in some way which is not peripheral to their being, they have become caught up with this figure who walked and talked in a corner of the old Roman Empire. If pressed to explain, many might falter and grow silent, while staying fully within their involvement. Others might resort to analogy, pointing to the existence for a particular person of someone gradually, steadily and profoundly loved. One would have managed to get by, perhaps even in comfort, without that someone; but, once encountered, life would be felt to be uniquely impoverished in the absence of that other discovered being.

Whatever the reasons, Christians take their cue from their texts, one of which is the fourth gospel. To read this gospel is to construe meaning which may be refined, changed, enlarged or deepened as a result of what others have made of it as they entered into the same process. The reading is itself merely one aspect of the larger, lifelong activity of making sense of otherness. And since at the heart of such dealing there may be insecurity or the workings of doubt it could be that one will seek reassurance by looking over one's shoulder to someone else, to a group, to an institution. This may especially be so in regard to a text with the reputation of being sacred, one which, moreover, does not blink or blush, change countenance or try to be helpful if one plainly misconstrues what is there. The famous example of Freud proclaiming the significance of a dream of Leonardo da Vinci on the basis of his own mistranslation of a crucial word in the notebooks of the artist is a warning among a multitude of what can go badly wrong.[11] And so only the supremely arrogant will be entirely innocent of the temptation to turn in the direction of some useful though not necessarily authoritative voice. Of course to yield to the assertion that someone or some group is an authority is no proof that such is actually the case, and the realisation that this is so will in all likelihood grow with the awareness that this someone else is also a reader, like oneself.

Yet again one is back to the self and to the spectacle of what makes each human being distinctive. Part of that distinctiveness lies precisely in the relationship between private judgement and whatever may be external to it. Entire epistemologies have grown up around this problem, yet, paradoxically, the conviction as to the rightness or otherwise of any one of them must continue to rest within the privacy of countless individual selves.

So, if reading is an act whereby one construes what is at hand in a text, then this act has to occur within the stream of a particular life, such as it is. Which implies that today, as in the future, as in the past, the construction occurs amid the changes, the losses, the mood of the stream. But this is another way of acknowledging that instead of bringing to the act of reading merely the skills, say, of a trained and practiced secretary in front of a keyboard one carries to the text one's self such as one is.

But this suggests that one should take to heart the implications of the episode in the fourth gospel centred upon Nicodemus. In its own way this is a warning, with the force of a parable, of what may happen in the process of reading. For the episode is a classic example of two people talking past each other and of two points of view which never meet, so that Nicodemus, baffled by what he has heard, elicits the sad and surprised reaction of Jesus, '… and you a teacher do not know these things?' Nicodemus speaks from within settled and not necessarily foolish convictions, Jesus from within wider horizons. Nicodemus, not understanding what he hears, refuses to admit something outside of his own mindset, and the simple but masterly presentation of his reaction to Jesus becomes a warning of what may happen in any age confronted by the words of Jesus. There is, as it were, a Nicodemus syndrome waiting to afflict everyone. It is the urge to take control not just in regard to Jesus but actually in the entire arena where a self attempts to make sense of what is other.

So one must therefore look to oneself, to one's limitations, to the often unacknowledged or unrecognised wish to make otherness conform to what one expects of it. One must look to one's responsiveness and to the influence of one's attitude to life. It may be, for instance, that one has reached the stage of seeing oneself merely whiling away the time in the shadow of death:

> Come the night
> come the hour
> the days pass by
> but I
> endure.[12]

It may be that one has energy abundant or else doled out by a miserly hand, that one has courage and no sense of humour, that despair is one's twin and the past a burden.

It may be that one lives more or less programmed by the institution to which birth or passing circumstances have consigned one.

It may be that, regardless of age or condition, one lives each day, like the Greek poet, waiting in excitement at the shore to see what the tide brings in:

I drink water, cut fruit
Plunge my hands through the wind's foliage
Lemon trees quicken the pollen of summer days
Green birds cut through my dreams
And I leave, my eyes filled
With a boundless gaze where the world becomes
Beautiful again from the beginning, according to the heart's measure.[13]

But one is as one is, and when one has mastered the letters which convey one's language one enters into a relationship with a text as with the events of one's own life, and the extent to which one is taken up by it or else is kept at arms length depends upon the complexity of what is within the self.

And so the reader circles around the text and from the sidelines come the voices of those claiming the authority to declare what the words there must mean. It falls upon the reader to decide at any given moment the extent of one's deference to these voices. One may drift along with what one is told. Or, out of respect for one's own perceptions of how things are, one may state honestly and as best one can a meaning discerned in the cherished pages of this gospel.

And having settled responsibly upon a meaning for now, one may do something about it. Or not. But whatever happens is a tale told not by an idiot but by someone who at any point may properly say 'I have lived'.

CHAPTER TWO

If it is true that reading is, ultimately, the private engagement of a person with a text and if it is also the case that no two readers can be exactly alike in what they bring of themselves to their task, it would be valuable, nevertheless, to have a sense of the many routes along which the endeavour has proceeded since the fourth gospel first began to circulate. It can be no surprise to discover that the vast majority of those who have written about the gospel are themselves believers in God and in the significance of Christ. Nor is it unexpected that within the general category of believing readers there are many distinctions to be observed from the point of view of such matters as attitude, agenda, education and scholarship.

So, for instance, whatever the degree of their fellowship with others, Origen and John Calvin are clearly driven by the power of personality and by the strength of convictions which took shape within the specific confines of the world as they each experienced it. Others, seeing themselves as primarily within the Church, deploy their abundant talents accordingly. The obvious examples are Augustine and Thomas Aquinas. Again, there are some for whom dedicated scholarship, which may or may not be fuelled by belief, is the means of dealing with the text. Rudolf Bultmann and John Ashton are exemplary here. So too is Diarmaid McGann. And the listing could go on.

But something more than a catalogue is needed. Nor is it sufficient to rest on a broad general account of how numerous readers, famous or obscure, have responded to the text. Precisely because reading is a private enterprise it is important and illuminating to get glimpses, whenever possible, of what is actually going on. This is one reason why interpreters and commentators matter greatly, because by allowing themselves to be observed to some limited extent as they go about their business they create opportunities for insight into the responsiveness which has greeted the words of the evangelist. And this responsiveness can be an inspiration and encouragement to other readers.

What follows below, therefore, is an overview of the differing perspectives of a small group of readers who turned again and again to the pages of the fourth gospel.

ORIGEN

There is a great potential for caricature or indeed for plain misrepresentation in any attempt to convey something of what Origen, in the third century, put into the composition of his *Commentary* on the fourth gospel[14] It is not enough to remark on his evident scholarship or on his intellectual energy or on the astuteness with which he ponders the words of the evangelist. All of these qualities are quickly obvious and easily illustrated. More difficult but much more important, however, is the task of conveying the perspectives within which he goes about his chosen work. For without a sense of these perspectives one runs the danger of missing the reality that for Origen the act of reading a gospel is quite different from the encounter with a text, such as the *Annals* of Tacitus or a work of Plutarch. In his point of view the encounter with the fourth gospel is part of a general engagement with all of the scriptures, and this in the lifetime of a special kind of reader. What he actually envisages may be summed up as a transformation of the self brought about not so much by the dispersal of ignorance or by the encounter with profoundly aesthetic and moral experience as by the fact that personal horizons are dramatically enlarged through a learning process which in essence is a series of contemplative acts.

This notion of the reader as contemplator is clearly enhanced for Origen by the language in which he functions. For there is a certain type of mainstream Greek which suits and indeed largely shapes a particular and notable temperament. It is a temperament manifest in figures such as Plato and Plotinus and it operates with an enduring conviction that there is actually a world beyond our own and that there are realities – the ultimate and most important realities – to be discerned behind the visible and the palpable. Such a perspective draws reassurance from the Greek in which it is so regularly expressed, and this is a Greek which, as it were, is untroubled by the concern that one may be putting oneself, ones' idiosyncrasies and one's aspirations, acknowledged or otherwise, into the declaration of truth. It is unworried by the possibility that truth may as much be made as found. It trusts without too much question that the truth of things, the reality of things can surely be brought into the contemplating gaze of that human attribute called *nous*, 'mind', that faculty so characteristic of human beings.

This act of trust has for a foundation the subtlety and the flexibility of the term *logos* which designates singly or in combination, mind, the structure producing the modalities of being or, thirdly, the language which arises out of mind to proclaim whatever is held to be true. And *logos* is something alive since it is at once questing intellect, the words embodying at a given moment the search, and the reality which is eventually found. *Logos* produces *logoi* which, in turn uncover the *logos* underlying all that is.

To put the matter this way may help clarification but it is also in some fashion to oversimplify. Origen knows this well since part of his task is to deal with the problems caused by scriptural commentators who have gone down the byways of inadequacy or error. In these instances *logos* has given utterance to *logoi* but truth has not been served because the generating *logos* and the *logoi* which have been spoken or written are themselves variously flawed. Origen does not offer any systematic analysis of the sources of these flaws as, say, Aristotle, in earlier days and in a different context, examined the rules for making correct *logoi*. Instead, he makes the point that a successful reading of scripture requires the help of Christ the Logos who is the illuminating source of true perceptions of being.

Now this theme of Christ the Logos signals a crucial moment in any attempt to envisage the nature of the act of reading which, in the view of Origen, is required for a gospel. In fact, only one sort of person can qualify as a successful reader at all, and this, obviously, is the believing Christian, actual or potential. Origen makes this clear at the start of his commentary when he directs his attention to the term usually translated as *evangelium* or 'gospel' and meaning in its Greek form 'news which is good'. The defining adjective is very important since a gospel is something 'good' by virtue both of its intrinsic character and also of the attitude of the hearer:

> The gospel is either a discourse which contains the presence of a good for the believer or is a discourse which announces that an awaited good is present (1:27).

The point about an awaited good complements the notion of a believing attitude touched upon in another definition where a gospel is described as 'a composition of announcements beneficial to those who believe in them' (1:28). Indeed Origen goes further and posits the idea that one has actually to be ready for a gospel, to be in a condition or state charecterised by the two verbs *pisteuein* and *prosdokan*. That is, a value free term such as 'text' or 'book' will not catch the point that so far as a gospel is concerned a reader or listener is not engaged in a passive submission of self to crafted words but, on the contrary, is coming trustingly and expectantly to what the evangelist has set down. Indeed:

> it may even be the case that some injunction lays it down that no one receives a gift from God except the person who asks for it (13:5).

Hence the 'good' of the written news will in some measure be co-extensive in its effect with the trust and expectation of which the reader is capable, and where there is such a capability the self will be opening up to a power of the kind described by Simon and Kleopas after their experience on the road to Emmaus when 'as he explained the scriptures to us did not our hearts take fire?' (1:47–50)

But hearts will only take fire under the aegis of Christ. Yet the idea that the *Logos* of God is the source of any adequate grasp of being has in languages other than Greek a certain banality about it, a vagueness, even if it is unimpeachably rooted in fact. Greek, however, reacts against any hint of vagueness and it encourages a flow which creates a marked vitality in the various overlapping meanings of the term *logos*. So, for instance, when the God of *Genesis* looks with approval at his handiwork it is the *logos* in each being which he finds to be good (13:282). Or, again, in a comment on the injunction 'raise up your eyes to see the fields, for already they are white for the harvest', Origen suggests that:

> it may be that all perceptible things up to the very sky itself with all that it contains are white for the harvest to those who raise up their eyes to see clearly the *logos* in each thing (13:280).

That is to say, there is a potential meeting between the *logos* in things and the searching *logos* of the contemplator. Such a meeting is potential, not guaranteed, because there has to be a 'perfecting of concepts which occurs in everyone who has gone beyond childhood' (1:273) and each person, depending on capacity, has both to grow and to be led into the truths of reality. This process has no assurance of success except under the guidance of the illuminating *Logos* of God, and so central is this requirement that Origen is moved to remark:

> If we think of the Logos who is in the beginning, the Logos who is with God, the Logos who is God, it may be that we should say that someone can only be described as 'rational' to the extent that he participates in this Logos. We could also say, in consequence, that only the saint is rational (2:114).

An attunement to the *Logos* of God is therefore the condition of real knowledge, for:

> by participating in him we arise and are enlightened ... we become rational in a divine manner when he destroys in us all that is irrational and dead in so far as he is *Logos* and resurrection (1:268).

'He illumines the minds of those deemed by him to be worthy of his light' (13:136). Indeed:

> those who have contemplated the bodiless realities, called 'invisible' and 'unseen' by Paul, those who exist by reason and apart from everything that is perceptible by sense, are ruled by that permanent nature of the only-begotten (1:200).

That is, the believing reader is in direct relationship with the transcendent *Logos*, and the character of this association is the very opposite of all that is static:

> No evening of God is possible and, I think, no morning, but, if I may so put it, the time which is co-extensive with his unoriginated and eternal life is today for him the day in which the Son has been begotten. Hence, neither the beginning nor the day of his generation is to be found (1:204).

Nor, as a result, is there an end to the ongoing character of the subsequent relationship between this *Logo*s of God and the questing logos operating in each self, but especially in the self of the believing Christian.

But there is a further consequence to this potential living relationship, involving God, the *Logos* of God, the logos in things, and the outward-looking *logos* of the Christian. The believer, as exemplified by Origen, has the deepest wish to rise into ever expanding horizons of being whose marvel is such that the corporeality in which at present he is himself enveloped becomes a burden and a sorrow. 'He who is in a body does bodily things unwillingly', (1:93) all the more so as he grows in awareness of realities beyond the ordinary and is seized by the conviction that the world that we observe around us, a world with its own undeniable truths, is only a pallid likeness (1:67) of a greater, transcendent realm into which we can enter.

This is not a realm made known and unmasked by the procedures of philosophy but is one which was adumbrated by the writers of the Old Testament and finally revealed by the Nazarene Jesus. It is a domain whose sheer lustre has the effect on those properly made aware of it that they come to regard the world which they now inhabit, with its materiality and its passage from sunrise to evening, as a limiting imprisoning *cul de sac* in the foothills of being. Yet such is the deadening power of the body that the passage upward to truths beyond all telling can only begin on historical clay and with that figure hailed as *Logos* and Saviour and as source of any true guidance out of the morass of the ephemeral:

> … the beginning of learning is 'the *Logos* made flesh', that he might dwell among us who are able to receive him (1:107).

That Jesus revealed truths of a world beyond our own is, of course, the central message of Christianity and not, therefore, peculiar to Origen. But it is what Origen makes of the message as set out in the gospels that require a glance, especially if one is to appreciate the point of view which directs his reading of the fourth evangelist. And what is particularly characteristic of him is the vivid sense he has of the transcendent world as a living, pulsing presence, dim perhaps to those who must walk the byways of earth, but vibrantly there in an unceasing now where the taint and the ravages of time do not prevail. Indeed past and future, dogged companions of the world of man, are nowhere around this Now, with all its inexhaustible being and richness and mystery. Origen has no doubts about the fact that as a consequence of the revelation of Jesus one may proceed in the certainty that over and above this world, indeed thrusting into it, there is the transcendent domain where one may learn to travel despite all the disadvantages and distractions of being a self in the visible cosmos. To Origen that domain is excitingly present, a summoning tide, and one of the ways of reaching it is through the words on offer in the text of the fourth gospel. In fact, to read a gospel is actually to enter into this living mystery, not in the sense of absorbing information about it nor of reconstituting it within oneself in a rationally ordered structure. What happens, rather, is that by turning properly towards what the evangelist has written one encounters not the read-about Jesus, for example, but Jesus himself. If one reads that Jesus is the 'way' and the 'resurrection', these are not abstract concepts drawn from the daily criss-cross of being. They are words pointing to a dynamic reality and if we open ourselves to this Jesus-centred reality then Jesus is neither reportedly nor metaphorically 'the way' but is actually so:

> ... the way itself is sufficient in place of any provisions; no traveller on this way has any need since he is adorned with a garment befitting one invited to a wedding (1:184).

Or, again, to describe Jesus as 'the resurrection' is to focus on the present and not on some future moment such as the aftermath of death:

> ... he is called 'the resurrection' from the fact that he effects the putting away of all that is dead and implants the life which is properly called life, since those who have genuinely received him are risen from the dead (1:187).

And if he is declared to be Logos this is:

> because he removes everything irrational from us and makes us truly rational beings who do all things for the glory of God, even to eating and drinking, so that we perform both the more common and more perfect works of life to the glory of God and because of reason (1:180).

In short, the reader is at best a contemplator and, as such, passes through the written words flat and linear though these may be into an ongoing living dialogue with what he contemplates.

This needs to be expressed somewhat more precisely, for the process of journeying through written words into the presence of truths which are there to be contemplated is one requiring more than just the open receptive disposition of the believing Christian. There are proper techniques of reading to be availed of, or, rather, there are some understandings which need always to be kept to the fore if one is to read a gospel correctly. For instance, if, like Origen, one has a constant sense of a world beyond our own this will need to be reinforced by the knowledge of how *logoi* may bring us there. Words on a page, words created in the human domain do not of themselves guarantee an automatic passage out of the cosmos and into transcendence because there are modes of reading which are a positive obstacle to the Christian who seeks to push beyond the lineaments of the day. He will be doomed to impoverishment for instance if he allows himself to be confined to a literal interpretation of words, and, most especially, of the words of a gospel, for he denies himself access to the 'mystical meaning stored up like a treasure in the words' (1:189).

> The letter kills and procures death, not as in the case of the separation of the soul from the body but with the separation of the soul from God ... (13:140).

Therefore, beyond the immediate and the obvious there are meanings lying in wait for the discerning reader who proceeds amid the signs that a divine agency, a spiritual power, has shaped the perspectives which led each of the evangelists to write as he did (10:10). That same reader will know also that since a literal understanding of the gospels will raise the spectre of the evident discrepancies between the various narratives the solution to any consequent difficulties will lie in the realization that such discrepancies will vanish only when the words giving rise to them are construed at levels above the material and the ordinary. Indeed, so far as the evangelists were concerned:

> it was their intention wherever possible to give voice to truth in a spiritual way and, at the same time, in a material fashion. Where this could not be done in the two ways they preferred the spiritual over the material. Often the spiritual truth is preserved so to speak in an untrue material mode (10:20).

Hence the requirement on the reader to approach the text unblinkered and free and with only his own human limitations to get in the way of a prospect summed up by the Origen in words which he imagines coming from the mouth of Jesus and which themselves have to be understood at a level beyond the literal:

> I have a *logos* of such a kind that it turns into a source of life-giving drink for anyone accepting what I have to tell. Whoever takes the water which I give shall benefit so much that there shall well up within him a fountain of waters bearing him upward to find all that he seeks. His mind will swirl up and fly with the speed of these waters as they carry him springing and jumping to what is higher up, to life without end (13:16).

But how does one go about the task of uncovering the hidden meaning of the gospel? No guiding precepts are suggested by Origen. Nor does he offer any clear directives regarding the question of how to distinguish between correct and inappropriate formulations of what lies beyond words. He simply declares what he himself has found, and this – along with the terms of his disagreement with fellow exegetes offers the only clue, however imprecise, to the criteria he employs for the accurate location of concealed meaning.

A good example of his method is provided by what he has to say about the episode of Jesus and the Samaritan woman. Not all of his exegesis has survived, since the twelfth book has disappeared, but there is enough to show how he set about the job of reading this part of the gospel text. And what becomes rapidly clear is that the incidents of the historical event are taken to refer to realities beyond the time and place of their occurrence. The Samaritan woman fades as an individual person and takes on the character of exemplar. She is an image of all the seekers of truth who have returned again and again to scripture but who have ultimately remained unsatisfied (13:6). The scripture itself is symbolised by the well of Jacob from which 'it is a good thing to drink first' (13:23). Jesus sitting beside the well is a sign that it is right and good to seek in scripture a satisfaction of the desire for truth. Even the bucket dropped beside the well by the Samaritan woman is a token of something else, the abandonment of worldly concerns in favour of the search for what is profoundly more important. Indeed, all the details have implications far beyond themselves.

And so they should. For if *logoi* have to do with the real then in their layered meanings they must show some correspondence to the ever more complex and exalted strata of being. Our journey towards the real, and especially towards what is supremely so, has to be made by way of *logoi*. Yet *logoi* may themselves fall short of the truth of things, a fact which makes sense if one reflects that since the farthest reaches of being are approachable only by the believer and since the Christian is in a minority within the world then only the *logoi* of the minority have the prospect of rising beyond the more commonly grasped ingredients of what is true and what is real. For Origen, being is hierarchically structured and this conviction forms both a central motif in the delineation by him of the objects of human belief and at the same time offers a basis for marking the difference between the Christian and all others:

> Some, therefore, have the God of the universe as God. Second are those who take their stand on the Son of God, his anointed. Thirdly are those who settle for the sun and the moon and the heavenly universe. These have wandered from God, but their error is much different from and better than that of those who give the name of god to the works of human hands, to gold and silver and the products of art. Last are those who turn to so-called gods which are not gods at all (2:27 = PG.14:112–113).

In other words, all who share a common humanity have to deal in *logoi*. Where they differ among themselves is in the reach of these *logoi*.

But from all this it does not follow that by virtue of belief in the real God the Christian reader of the gospel – his *logos* engaged with the *logoi* of the text – will automatically arrive at the summit of being. In fact he may not even correctly grasp the scope as well as the limitations of the *logoi* set down by the evangelist. So, for instance, regarding the remark of Jesus to the Samaritan woman that God is a spirit (*pneuma*) who must be worshipped in spirit and in truth Origen makes clear his awareness of the extremely demanding conditions attendant upon the journey of the zealous Christian through *logoi*. For to describe God as *pneuma* or, indeed, as light or fire is to resort to words reflecting the realities of the physical universe and because this is so there have been interpreters who, according to Origen, have misread the text and have done so by failing to go beyond the literal interpretation of what is set down. Although acknowledging that God must somehow be different from all else they have nevertheless conjured him up as a being with more or less attenuated corporeality, and this because they have remained stuck in their failure to read properly. That one should look to scripture to discover the nature of God is entirely appropriate (13:123) but the corporeal terms applied to him must all be seen as allegorical (13:131) if an absurd theology is to be avoided. Hence *pneuma* and light and fire have to be taken in this way, so that *pneuma*, for instance, the word for 'breath' can be seen to refer not to the breath which gives life to the body but, rather, to that giving life to what in each of us is 'more divine'.

Origen fully recognises that the act of reading which enables the believing Christian to rise beyond the literal interpretation of the scriptural text is not something easy. It requires great effort. Indeed many disciples actually give up:

> Most followers of the *Logos* understand how difficult it is for human nature to arrive at the truth. They see the distinction between life of a different sort and life as it actually is. So they postpone for the present the goal which they have been seeking and they consider that they will attain truth only after they have gone beyond their kinship with the four basic ingredients (of corporeality) (13:262).

On the other hand those who persist must work constantly to do so:

> We need more exercise to become perfect at this so that, as the apostle says, sharpened in perception and distinguishing between good and bad, true and false, we may gaze upon what only the mind can contemplate. Then to the extent that human nature may do so and also in a manner more precise and more appropriate to God we will be able to see how God is light and fire and *pneuma* (13:44).

But here an important clarification is required, for the emphasis upon the difficulty of correctly reading the *logoi* of a gospel could encourage the notion that belief when combined with sheer effort will ensure that the Christian will truly arrive in the presence of his God. This, however, is not necessarily the case. There are *logoi* which exist far beyond the capacity of human beings either to discover or to express. There are *logoi* which only the angels can grasp (13:28) and some are out of the reach even of these. There are *logoi* which are sighted by a few privileged human beings not because of their talent or discernment but because of a divinely granted gift and for those few the granted vision often eludes all possibility of description. The writer of the *Apocalypse* could find no way to record the speech of the thunder and since there are things which 'eye has not seen nor ear heard' it would appear that all of the scriptures however fully grasped, are only the lowliest elements of and the humblest introduction to the totality of knowledge (13:30). In short, 'no text contains the most sovereign and the most potent of God's mysteries' (13:27). Hence scripture is but a way of approach to realities beyond all that is written, and from 'the well of Jacob', from accurately grasped texts:

> the journey must be made to Jesus so that he may give us as his gift a fountain of water surging into everlasting life (13:37).

These, then, are the horizons of being and of knowledge which are glimpsed by Origen in his reading of the pages which describe the encounter between Jesus and the Samaritan woman. There is no apology, no attempted defence for proceeding in this manner. And so it is throughout the entire commentary, which turns into the spectacle of a man straining to call upon every insight of his vast erudition to assemble *logoi* concerning this fourth gospel, *logoi* which are not, as it were, packets of information or cold propositions but are elucidations in the primary sense of that term, light coaxed out of the myriad aspects of that 'house of the *Logos*' (6:7) towards which all God-centred people feel the urge to travel. Origen is a man passionately immersed in texts, astonishing in the power of his memory, unfaltering in his concern to uncover meaning. There is about him a supreme confidence which is the outcome not only of his Greek-shaped conviction that the world makes sense, that there is a *logos* to give substance to all things, but that this *logos* is actually the *Logos* of God whose loving human face was manifested in the person of Jesus. And so, assessing, probing, comparing, he becomes himself a dealer in the *logoi* which open the way to a living relationship with that *Logos* of God, and because he has so vivid an assurance of the fact that limitless truths are waiting to be uncovered in the pages of the fourth gospel he has the freedom to operate with the zeal not of the dogmatist but of the explorer, ever willing to venture a 'perhaps' and an 'I think' and a 'maybe', never suggesting that the last *logos* has yet been uttered.

AUGUSTINE

In the second decade of the fifth century A.D. when Augustine begins a lengthy series of homilies on the gospel of John it is against a background where a complicated personal history has been yoked to the status and the obligations of his role as a bishop. The homilies show him to be a man with an active sense both of distant heights where divine glory shines and of low nearby places where the human worm crawls. So, for instance, when seeking to describe the fourth evangelist he looks to the great multitude of biblical descriptions available to him but draws upon the image of a mountain:[15]

> This John was clearly one of those mountains of which it is written 'let the mountains receive peace for thy people and the hills righteousness'. The mountains are elevated souls, the hills little souls. John was of these mountains ... How exalted! He had ascended beyond all the mountain tops of the earth, beyond all the fields of the sky, beyond the heights of the stars, beyond all the choirs and legions of the angels. And if he had not gone beyond all created things he would not have reached the presence of him by whom all things are made. And you can have no idea of all that he passed beyond unless you catch sight of where it was he arrived (Homily 1: 21–4ff)

But if one thinks of where the evangelist arrived it becomes clear to Augustine that in some way he must have ceased to be a man, that he had 'begun to be an angel' (l: 4,13), one of those beings existing in a domain beyond the reach of any physical sense (cf. 1: 9, 24). By contrast there are the many, even among those gathering to hear the words of John, who are so unquestionably the creatures of the flesh that what they know is confined to the realm of the corporeal, and, in consequence, they are not yet able 'to raise themselves up' to a level of understanding which is 'spiritual' (1.1:4–5).

The rare few climb the heights, while the multitudes must remain below, and although the fourth gospel speaks of the light available to all, Augustine talks of 'stolid hearts' unable to receive this light because they are 'weighed down' by their sins. Yet if there are people who actually reach the stage of being able 'to raise themselves up' this must be in the right away, in appropriate conditions and certainly not in that raising of self 'up' which is the consequence of pride. Indeed if God created the mosquito, that 'least and lowliest' of creatures (1: 15.18) it was for the purpose of tormenting the proud so as to bring them 'down' (1.15.12).

This melancholy perspective of far off heights and of familiar low places inevitably ensures a reading of the fourth gospel which is quite different from that of Origen. In the Latin from which he reads and in which he writes there is not for Augustine the antidote to distance available to Origen in that fluid term *logos*. Indeed the potential comfort of being able to think of one's own logos as able to engage with and be illuminated by the Logos of God gives way, and a kind of fragmentation occurs with the translation of *Logos* into *Verbum*. The support which a cultural infrastructure gave to the term logos, a support bringing the commoner, the professional and the sage on to the same wavelength – all this goes away, and almost from the first mention of *verbum* Augustine is obliged to become technical, to adumbrate a theory of knowledge if he is to have any hope of reaching his audience:

> We also uttered words when we spoke. Was the Word which was with God like one of these? Did not the words which we uttered sound and then pass away? In that case, did the Word of God sound and pass away? How was it then that all things were made by that Word and that nothing was made without it? ... But what sort of Word must that be which is both spoken but does not pass away? ... By being spoken day after day words have become cheap to us. They sound and pass away and have thereby become commonplace [1:8, 3–11]

Yet to say 'God' is to voice a word:

> What a little word it is! Three letters and one syllable. Is this all that God is, three letters and one syllable? (1:8, 16)

The question is itself sufficient to indicate the absurdity of any affirmative answer. But why? Because the idea one has of God is of a being too exalted to be enclosed by three evanescent letters. And just as a major work of art is a testimony to the power of the idea which engendered it, so the splendour of creation is a testimony to the uniquely exalted nature of the idea (*consilium*) which is the Word of God:

> Look at this fabric of the world. See what has been made by the Word and then you will understand what the Word is like. Look at those two bodies of the world, heaven and earth. Who can find words for the glory of the sky? Who can speak of the fruitfulness of the earth? Who can duly praise the passage of the seasons or the life in seed? You can note what I pass over without mention, in case my list would fall short of what occurs to you. So from the fabric of this world think what kind the Word is which made it, and not only this world. There are all things seen because they come within the range of our physical sense. But angels were made through that Word. Archangels were made through that Word, as were Powers, Thrones, Dominions, Principalities. All were made through this Word. From all this just think what the Word must be! [1:9, 15–27]

A formidable thought indeed, and one to be addressed. by man. But what is 'man'?

> Man is first called *rottenness*, and afterwards the *son of man* is called a *worm*. For since worms are produced from rottenness, hence 'man is rottenness and the son of man is a worm' (1.13. 28–30)

But also a worm to whom rescue was offered by the Word of God, who 'stooped' for our sake 'that you might be fed with milk since you were not able to masticate solid food' (1.13, 33). That is, there is a possibility of escape. And this thought, indeed the hope that one can get away, is a recurring note throughout the homilies. So for example, when Augustine turns to consider the words 'I give you a new commandment, that you love one another as I have loved you' (John 13:34) he starts with the consideration that the commandment to love one another is described as new. Yet in Leviticus 19:18 there is the injunction 'you shall love your neighbour as yourself'. So what then is new about this commandment? Evidently it is the phrase 'as I have loved you', words which have now to be interpreted, and the details of the interpretation reveal more of the perspective of Augustine than they necessarily do of the evangelist.

Augustine is immediately exercised by the determination to establish the nature of that love declared by Jesus. He speaks of Jesus as Lord and thus he sets up an immediate distinction between what is to be attributed to the divine figure and what, on the other hand, is grounded in these human realities which Augustine characteristically labels carnal (65.1.9). This use of the term carnal unleashes its own momentum. The carnal is the arena of trouble (cf. 98:5, 1–5). But it is where human beings are found, and if love (*dilectio*) occurs among them this is not something commendable in all circumstances. Tolerable love has to confine itself to sanctioned relationships:

> For husbands and wives love one another, parents and children, and whatever other tie of human relationships bind men to one another (65.1.10–11).

Relationships of this sort are a 'tie' and the Latin word used by Augustine *necessitudo* carries its own hints of bonds and obligations and of constricted freedom, so that love, where it has to exist, is directed, reined in, controlled. Not so with:

> adulterers and adulteresses, with fornicators and whores and indeed with any others bound together not by human obligation (*necessitudo*) but by the disgusting poison of human life (65.1.12–16).

The love which exists here is 'culpable and damnable' (65.1.130).

Hence the relief with which Augustine turns to the 'new' kind of love. It is a relief not unlike that of Plato many centuries earlier in *Phaedo* when with a supreme consciousness of the soul as contaminated and infected by the body, troubled and enslaved by it, he directs the spirit away from the follies of corporeality towards the purity of what the undistracted mind may happily contemplate (cf. *Phaedo* 65–67). This too is the relief of Plotinus who in his shame of being in a body seeks asylum in the untarnished realms of intelligibility. And for Augustine, who was once a disciple of such men, the relief lies in the possibility of facing away from the mess of the physical to the unsullied milieu where Christ is present and in command.

So when Jesus instructs his followers to love one another in the way he loved them that love is indeed utterly new in the experience of the world:

> This is a love which makes something new of us so that we become new men, heirs of the New Testament, singers of the new song (65.1.17–19).

This is a love which now renews the nations, which makes and collects a new people from the entire race scattered over all the earth. It makes the body of a new spouse the bride of the only begotten Son of God spoken of in the *Song of Songs* 'who is this that comes up all in white'. She is surely white because she is made new (65.1.22–26).

What is emerging here is the fact that the interpretation of verse 34 in this thirteenth chapter of John is an occasion for Augustine to give expression to a set of passionate convictions about the nature of the world in which humanity finds itself. Such convictions derive from a heightened sense of a person as an amalgam of body and spirit, with body as the disabling addendum. It is this awareness of being hobbled by the body and by the world which underlies that celebrated passage in the *Confessions*, the vision of Ostia, when Augustine and his mother try to imagine what it might be like to break free of corporeality, to have:

> the tumult of the flesh grow silent, the images of earth, of water, of air and of the skies cease to resound (*Conf.* 9, 10, 25).

And from that way of seeing things he takes here the gospel phrase 'as I have loved you' to point blessedly to a love utterly different from anything on offer in the world and, hence, a way of escape from the world:

> By this love it comes to pass that while yet in this corruptible body we die to this world and our life goes to hide with Christ in God. Indeed this love is our death to this world, and our life with God. For if it be death when the soul goes out from the body how is it not a death when our love goes forth from the world? Love, then, is strong, like death. What could be stronger than that by which the world is defeated? (65.1.44–50).

Yet Augustine cannot shake off a grim conviction that the obstacles to be defeated are enormous and that the greatest obstacle is human nature itself:

> Just as a house is bad, not because of its walls but because of the people who live in it, so the world is bad because its inhabitants are bad (3:5, 31–32).

The remark in the gospel – 'men loved darkness rather than light, for their works were evil' (3.19) – seems to touch a particularly responsive chord in Augustine, for while he is conscious of the great offences, murder, for instance, and theft, he also has a sharp perception of man as caught up in a continuous round of misdeeds 'of tongue or thought or lack of moderation' (12: 14, 11–12) which can bring death:

> Small are the drops which fill rivers, small the grains of sand. But if sand is piled in abundance it bears down and it crushes. Bilge water allowed to accumulate in a ship turns into an overwhelming wave. It comes little by little into the hold and when it is not pumped out it sinks the ship. This pumping out, what is it except the doing of good works – mourning, fasting, giving, pardoning – so that sins may not pull us down. Indeed the journey through this life of ours is rough (12: 14, 15–24).

Hence the admiration for the author of the fourth gospel:

> John the evangelist rose beyond the flesh, beyond the earth where he walked, beyond the seas upon which he gazed, beyond the air in which the birds fly. He rose beyond the sun, moon and stars, beyond all unseen spirits. By the power of his mind he rose beyond his own mind and rising beyond all, pouring forth his spirit above himself where did he arrive? What did he see? 'In the beginning was the Word and the Word was with God' (20: 13, 2–16).

But John is not unique. In the eyes of Augustine he is one among several, a member of a special group of writers, privileged as few have been and with extraordinary access to truths which otherwise would rank as beyond telling. But if this is so, it would then appear that the reader of the fourth gospel ought not to act as a free and idiosyncratic interpreter of what is found in the pages of this or, indeed, of any scriptural text. In fact heresy in more or less deadly form has come into being precisely because of the insistence upon reading these texts in ways that are deemed to be inappropriate or perverse, a situation to which Augustine returns in many of the homilies (cf. 18:1, 29–29). He does so not only because of the character of his own personal beliefs but also because of the concerns which arise from his obligations as bishop. The homilies themselves are not so much the fruit of dispassionate research as part of an exercise whose aim is to renew and to preserve in the members of the congregation an allegiance to a whole package of ideas and beliefs which Augustine, in common with his episcopal colleagues, is committed to uphold. A homily, in other words, serves to reinforce the buoyancy of a believing milieu and it is a device born of the recognition that life, at all levels, is never still, that there can be a faltering and fading, seasons of growth and enlargement, or else a marking of time. At a minimum the homily aims to prevent a slide into the abandonment of belief or even into indifference. But since a minimum is not enough there is the hope that each member of the congregation, standing and listening, will be led to a richer more active mode of Christian life. And so a paedagogical, missionary intent underlies every engagement in homily. But it is also an exercise in power. The congregation is being worked upon. The homily, therefore, is the means to a well-understood end, and the presence of the members of the congregation is a token of consent to being involved in that end and in fact to being worked upon.

The means to that end deserve a closer scrutiny since, after all, the interpretation of the fourth gospel is not, for Augustine, something apart, something unto itself. The means themselves arise among other factors from the historical circumstances of the society which produced Augustine himself, so that, for example, when he launches upon the one hundred and twenty four homilies on John he can operate on the assumption that his listeners will be impressed by the abundant scriptural quotation employed by him to interpret specific verses of the gospel. In Homily 22 where the focus of attention is the fifth chapter of John, verses 24 to 30, Augustine draws upon lines in six psalms, in Matthew, in 1 Timothy, 2 Corinthians, Romans, Ephesians and Galatians, in Genesis and Habacuc. That is to say, the constant deployment of biblical allusions becomes a way to establish the validity of the particular interpretation of the verses read to the congregation. Such a deployment helps to secure an interpretation which is itself not disinterested but which accords with the terms of that theological orientation described elsewhere by Augustine as the *regula sana catholica* (18: 2, 16). And if this mosaic of quotations can be counted upon to be effective it is because the general culture of the fifth century, unlike that of the twenty-first supports a reliance upon words as respected and meaningful coinage. Besides, forging the receptive attitude of the congregation will be that dynamic called *fides*:

> For the way of piety is faith and the outcome of faith is understanding so that we may come to everlasting life where no gospel is read to us, where all the pages of the reading, where the voice of the reader and of the preacher will be left behind, and where the one who gave the gospel may stand before those of his own who wait with hearts made pure (22: 2, 8–13. cf. 40: 9, 10).

However, such purity must be won not only in the quality of a mode of living but also in the soundness of belief. Which is why the text of John is slotted into larger perspectives throughout the homilies. The reference by Augustine to the *regula sana catholica* is a useful reminder that for him there are doctrinal parameters within which believers are expected to function. Those who are 'well instructed' (9: 2, 9), those for whom 'the correct faith of the Catholic Church' (34: 2, 10) is guide and norm will turn from the errors which it is the obligation of bishops like Augustine to point out to them. Just as there are doctrines which are well or poorly conceived so too are the many interpretations of what is found in the pages of the fourth gospel. Hence, the exegesis of the verses read day by day to the congregation must draw its character from within the wider ambience of theological affirmation. That is to say, there is, in fact, a 'correct' reading to be achieved.

The persistence of Donatism can be attributed to misreading. Here is a controversy which had sundered North African Christianity for a century. Augustine is profoundly exercised by the Donatists, by the disunity caused by these men whom he considers to be arrogant deceivers with their claims to a spurious authority. And so in the thirteenth homily he turns to the words in the gospel where John the Baptist acknowledges Jesus and compares himself to the friend who must step aside in favour of the bride and groom (3:22–29). These scriptural words provide Augustine with the opportunity to shore up a doctrinal and disciplinary scenario, to protect his congregation from points of view which are at odds with what he takes to be the truth. With an eye to current disputes he looks to the statement – 'Jesus baptised. And John was also baptising' – and he uses this to give a foundation to the argument that since John had set an example of humility by asserting his own inferiority to Jesus and since Jesus was the source of true baptism then whoever outside of the Church was now arrogating to himself the right to baptise was clearly flying in the face of the implications of what the evangelist had set down (13.13, 30–31).

Or again, there was the continuing presence of Arianism where the application of a humanly grounded logic to scriptural terms such as 'unbegotten Father' and 'only begotten Son' had resulted in the assertion that the Son is inferior to the Father, that he is the most perfect of created beings but is a creature nevertheless and that, hence, any Trinitarian theology which seeks to put him on a level with the Father is fundamentally mistaken. Arianism had a certain simplicity about it and was, consequently, a continuing challenge to mainstream Christianity. One result of this is that Augustine, faced by the task of interpreting verse 19 in chapter five of John takes care to close off a possible Arian interpretation since there is an obvious challenge in the statement:

> the Son cannot of himself do anything but what he sees the Father doing; what He does the Son also does likewise.

Augustine hastens to remind the congregation of the doctrine that, whereas the Father is greater than the Son in the context of the Son's humanity, he and the Son are equal with respect to divinity. Since this is the doctrine, the interpretation of verse 19 must proceed accordingly. That is, the correct grasp of the verse must start from something which has been laid down and defined, a 'rule':

> Let us direct our understanding to that sound Catholic rule, which you ought especially to know. Hold on to it, those of you with knowledge of it. Your faith must not slip away from it. It must not be torn from your hearts by any human argument. And if there are things we happen not to understand let us put them aside as something to be referred to this rule when we are ready for them (18:2, 16–22).

In other words, the correct understanding of verse 19 will take place not against the background of competing doctrines but as a consequence of accepting one such doctrine, that which is Catholic.

But there are some topics not directly covered by Catholic doctrine, which entails that there are some sections of the fourth gospel whose meaning will depend on Augustine the interpreter as well as upon the guidance of solemn theological affirmations. There is, for example, the troublesome pair of sentences in the account of the wedding feast of Cana when Jesus says 'woman, why look to me? My hour is not yet come' (Jn. 2:4). The attempt to deal with these lines is played out in the knowledge of two kinds of interpretation which Augustine considers to be wholly repugnant. There is the view of those he calls heretics who seemingly read into the words a tone so inappropriate to an exchange between a son and his mother that the inference was drawn that this could not really have been his mother at all, and this despite the explicit gospel statement that Mary was actually present. A second interpretation, in this case by astrologers, seemingly took the reference to 'my hour' as referring somehow to what was fated by the stars. But it is the first which really upsets Augustine. Sensibly, he insists on the fact that the text declares the presence of Mary. If, then, there is a problem it must lie in the words used by Jesus, yet when Augustine sets out to explain these words there is unmistakeable evidence of strain. Distinctions are drawn between that part of Jesus not born of Mary, namely, his divinity and that part which when suffering on the cross had its undeniable kinship with her. The 'hour' is interpreted as the hour of his death, though how this could be so in the context of the failure of the wine supply is nowhere clarified. Actually, Greek interpreters took this 'hour' to refer to the proper time for miracle working. But what the uneasy exegesis of Augustine brings really to the foreground is that the terms of reference of such interpretation lie outside of the text and, as many of his listeners doubtless knew, there was currently a pressing and urgent debate going on in regard to how to understand the relationship between the divinity and the humanity in Jesus, an issue eventually to be set in the theological framework provided by the council of Chalcedon. Knowing the controversy, Augustine has to proceed here with some wariness even if he is not commenting directly on the wider theological issues.

But the interpretation of other verses leaves Augustine with more freedom as can be seen in the way he deals with the declaration:

> upon whom you shall see the spirit descending and abiding upon him as a dove, the same is he who baptizes with the Holy Ghost (1.33).

He considers these words in the course of a long and tedious homily which displays among other elements a willingness to explain what is on the mind of God, an explanation which can in any case proceed in the secure knowledge that God is unlikely to issue a contradiction! He takes the scriptural words detail by detail. If the Holy Spirit was manifested under the form of a dove why was this so? Why not some other bird? It is a question which seemingly offers no difficulty to Augustine, given that what characterises a dove is that it moans (6:1,15) and that in *Romans* 8.26 the Holy Spirit is described as making 'intercessions for us with moanings which cannot be uttered'. But, since the connections may not be immediately clear, Augustine goes on to say the following:

> What, then, my brethren? Shall we assert that the Spirit moans in that place where he enjoys perfect and eternal blessedness with the Father and the Son? For the Holy Spirit is God, as the Son of God is God and the Father is God. I have said God three times not three Gods, because the Father, Son and Holy Ghost are one God as you well know. Do not think, therefore, that the Holy Spirit in himself, with himself, in that trinity, in that blessedness, in that eternity of his substance, gives way to moans. It is in us that he moans because he causes us to moan. Nor is it a trivial matter that the Holy Spirit causes us to moan for he shows us that we are on pilgrimage and teaches us to sigh after our native land so that it is out of longing that we moan (6:2, 6–17).

What has happened here is worthy of note. There is nothing in the fourth gospel to suggest what significance is to be attached to the fact that the Holy Spirit descended as a dove nor are any of the characteristics of this bird described or named. But because Paul speaks of moans this suffices to give Augustine the authority for his own speculation. The sounds of a dove are contrasted with those of a raven, and since Augustine has an evident bias against ravens he moves on to draw a comparison between two types of human beings. There is the one:

> with whom it goes well in this world, or rather who thinks it goes well with him, who in the joyousness of carnal things and the abundance of temporal things and in empty felicity leaps for gladness and has the note of the raven, a note of clamour and not of moaning.

On the other hand there is the one who knowing himself to be on pilgrimage and absent from the Lord moans:

> and does well to moan. It was the Spirit that taught him to do so and it was from the dove that he learned thus (6:2, 17–26).

Parallel with speculation of this sort is the occasional resort to allegory. While Augustine himself was to speak famously of the distinction between the letter and the spirit there is no obvious sign in these homilies that he always felt comfortable with the pursuit of allegory in the pages of John. However, since the objective in reading the gospel is to seek an understanding of the text [9:91] and since meaning is occasionally wrapped up in figurative language there is seemingly no way to avoid the dimension underlying the surface significance of words. But there is also no acknowledged principle for the divining of such significance and, as a result, there is a certain arbitrary character to the process of uncovering what the evangelist is really conveying in various parts of his work. That this is the case may quickly be seen by comparing the approach of Origen and Augustine to the episode of Jesus and the Samaritan woman. One detail will suffice. Whereas Origen sees the well of Jacob as a symbol of the riches of scripture and the bucket as the device for seeking refreshment there, Augustine has no such notion. Instead, his bleak vision of people and of the world impels him to the following:

> The water in the well is the pleasure of this world in its shadowy depth. Men draw from it, using the water container of lusts. Bent over, they let down the lust that they may reach the pleasure drawn from the depth below. With lust going freely they enjoy their pleasure. Whoever does not send his lust cannot arrive at pleasure. Therefore, assume the bucket to be lust and the water from the depths to be pleasure. But will there not be renewed thirst for the one who arrives at the pleasure of this world – food, drink, the baths, the theatre, love-making? (15:16, 5–14).

The same arbitrariness may also be observed in the actual choice of episodes regarded as allegorical. For example, drawing the attention of his listeners to that moment in the narrative of the crucifixion when the garments of Jesus are divided into four, whereas the destiny of the cloak is determined by lot, Augustine remarks that:

> the fourfold division of the clothes of our Lord Jesus Christ was a sign of the fourfold division of his Church, scattered throughout the four parts of the world (118:4, 2–6).

But the cloak which went by lot was a token of the unity underlying those divisions, a unity ensured by 'the bond of love' (118:4, 10), while the lot itself points to the act of submission to the secret judgement of God (118:4, 34).

Again, in the same narrative a sponge is dipped into a vessel full of vinegar then put upon hyssop and lifted to the mouth of Jesus (19.28). The meaning of this seems immediately evident to Augustine:

> The Jews themselves were the vinegar in their degeneracy from the wine of the patriarchs and the prophets. Theirs was a heart like sponge – deceptive, so to speak, with its hollows and tortuous hiding places – and drawn from 'a full vessel', filled with the iniquity of this world. But the hyssop on which they put the sponge with vinegar is a lowly herb. It purges the breast and it is right for us to take this to mean the lowliness of Christ which the Jews had surrounded and which they imagined themselves to have circumvented (119: 4, 19, 26).

If these episodes are deemed to have an allegorical intent there is no evident reason why many others were not subjected to the same process of scrutiny. But there is no obvious principle of selection. And in some instances Augustine has to go through such manifest contortions that a member of the congregation might well be tempted to wonder why he had chosen this route at all (cf. Homily 17). Yet, in fairness to Augustine, it must be said that he never strays too far from the major purpose of the homilies, which is to talk his audience into continuing orthodoxy. It is a task which he approaches with high seriousness, with passion and with undeniable eloquence. Nor has he forgotten all that he learned during his years as a teacher of rhetoric, the skillful use of language, the counterpointed arguments, even the moments reserved for displays of verbal pirouettes such as when he seeks to comment on an episode where Jesus faces down a crowd (7, 19–24). To Jesus' question, 'why do you seek to kill me?', the response is 'you have a devil'. The drama of this confrontation is irresistible to Augustine as he measures the accusation against the character and the significance of the accused, and the Latin term for 'crowd', provides him with his point of departure:

> 'The *turba* answered him'. Its answer was, as it were, a disturbance that had nothing to do with order but with perturbation. Look at it – this turbulent *turba*, look at its answer 'you have a devil! Who is trying to kill you?' As

> though to say 'you have a devil' were not worse than killing him. He to whom it was said that he had a devil was the very one who was casting out devils. But what else could a turbid *turba* say? What else can stirred-up mud do except stink? The *turba* was perturbed. By what? By the truth. The brilliance of light has disturbed the blurred *turba* (30: 2, 6–24).

All this points inevitably to the conclusion that there can be a very thin line between commentary and the appropriation of the text of John. If in Origen there is the excited pursuit of unfolding panoramas of truth, the goal for Augustine is determined by the circumstances in which he finds himself, forced by the obligation not only to reach the members of his congregation but also to save them. Like Origen he has a clear reverence for the fourth gospel, and the great Alexandrian would doubtless agree with the principle laid down by Augustine himself in one of the homilies:

> That which is briefly said in the holy gospel should not be expounded briefly. This is in order to ensure that sense is made of what is heard. Great but few are the words of the Lord, to be reckoned not by their number but by their weight. They should not be despised because they are few but sought out because they are mighty (37:1, 1–5).

Yet for Augustine, at least, this process of making sense has to take place within the boundaries of sanctioned doctrine. Otherwise, the road to heresy lies open. In other words, sanctioned doctrine which draws its own authority from scriptural utterance becomes, in the eyes of Augustine, the measure by which to evaluate specific readings of scripture in general and, in particular, of the fourth gospel. The text underwrites the doctrine and the doctrine underwrites the interpretation of the text in a process intelligible, in all likelihood, only to those in whom the dynamic of faith has found a home.

THOMAS AQUINAS

When Greeks devised the word *cosmos* to convey the notion of a world that is patterned and arranged, intelligible and therefore capable of being adequately described, they unloosed a formidably influential motif in the life of the West. They inaugurated an avalanche of explanations. They gave apparent substance to the idea that for every why there is somewhere a reachable answer, that increasingly sophisticated models can be constructed of all the manifestations of being, that mind, matching, if not mastering, the complexity of how things are, can in some funadmental manner become that which it contemplates. And from this unshackled confidence in the capacity of proffered explanation to mesh with the real it was only a short and seemingly inevitable step to the assured proclamation of increasingly sophisticated doctrine. In so comfortable an arena no place could be found for a character such as that in Chekov who ridicules those in pursuit of the meaning of rain when the only evident reality is that it is there and that it falls.

From the start of the Middle Ages in the West this confidence in the capacity of the mind to know began to take on a new quality of vigour, since those who wrote or spoke about ultimate issues were believing Christians in whom faith and intellect operated as a dynamic unity.

This can be seen abundantly in one of the outstanding commentaries of the Middle Ages, that of Thomas Aquinas. The commentary is actually the version, subsequently corrected by Thomas himself, of lectures given in Paris at the beginning of the seventies of the thirteenth century, and, because it is so comprehensive and because it incidentally raises so many issues of importance in relation to the act of reading the text of the fourth gospel, its programme and its methodology require some attention.[16]

Perhaps the best approach would be to look at how he deals with some of the incidents related by the evangelist, such as the moment when Jesus goes on a rampage against the merchants and the money lenders in the Temple at Jerusalem.

This episode thrusts itself upon the reader. There is the drama of it, the image of an outraged man laying about him in the crowded precincts of the holiest place of Judaism. There is the hint of a personality strong enough to overawe the pusillanimous, the hot-tempered and the self-righteous. There is the violence of it, the flailing whip, the tables kicked over. And there is the aggressive, hurled response to those bystanders who are demanding a warrant for what he is doing. 'Destroy this temple and in three days I will rebuild it' (2.19). It is so absurdly far-fetched an answer that the evangelist interrupts the sparse unelaborated narrative to explain that Jesus was actually referring not to the Temple but to himself in the aftermath of his own execution. The explanation might itself seem odd were it not for the further remark that long after it was over the immediate followers of Jesus would remember what had happened on that day in the Temple and in the memory of it they would find cause for a deepened belief in him and in the words he had uttered. For them this was an incident filled with a significance far beyond its own emphatic self.

Thomas, therefore, like other readers before and after him seeks to uncover that significance. He suggests that the episode in the Temple may be understood in three ways. The Temple may be taken to exemplify the soul of a man:

> A man sells oxen, sheep and doves in the temple when he gives sanctuary to bestial movements in his soul ... For oxen, which are used for the cultivation of the earth, signify earthly desires, sheep, which are stupid animals, signify man's instability. These things are driven out of the hearts of men by God.

But this way of understanding the incident in the Temple has a blandly general character. However, the other two modes of understanding arise quite evidently from a concern which was particularly strong in the period from the eleventh to the thirteenth century and had to do with the widespread practice of simony. So, for Thomas, the oxen, the sheep and the doves put up for sale may be taken to signify the spiritual goods of the Church, namely, the teachings of the apostles, the blood of the martyrs, and the gifts of the Holy Spirit. The merchants, then, are bishops or indeed any clerics who, out of naked avarice, engage in the open traffic of such goods, and it is against these that the fury of Jesus is so openly directed. But not all simoniacs do their commerce openly. Thus, ten years before the birth of Thomas, the Fourth Lateran Council entered a vigorous complaint against the covert forms of simony. Arising from this kind of situation Thomas is moved to note:

> It happens, secondly, that there are certain bishops or heads of churches who sell these oxen, sheep and doves not overtly by simony but covertly by negligence when in their eagerness for and preoccupation with temporal gain they neglect the spiritual welfare of their subjects.

In this context, those under the authority of church leaders form three classes. These are the contemplatives, signified by the doves. There are the teachers and the wise, symbolised by the oxen. And since Isaiah (32:20) has proclaimed 'happy are you who sow beside all the streams letting the ox and the donkey range free' it only remains to declare in a mild unfaithfulness to the words of the text, that the simple and the uneducated are assuredly the donkeys (9:380–383).

The narrative of what happened in the Temple provides Thomas with an opportunity to comment on problems of his own day. But this method of reading the text is not exclusive to that one episode, as is obvious in what Thomas makes of the feeding of the five thousand. On the one hand there is the unornamented directness of what the evangelist chooses to write, but on the other, there is deployed by Thomas a range of quotations, ideas and considerations which ensure that every word and every phrase in this part of the gospel emerge to suggest a virtually limitless panorama of meaning. First, there is the text:

> Now the Passover was near, a festival day for the Jews. Then as Jesus lifted his eyes and saw that a great crowd had come to him he said to Philip, 'Where shall we buy bread so that these may eat?' However, he said this to test him, for he knew what he would do. Philip answered, 'Two hundred denarii worth of bread would not be enough for each to have a little bit'. Andrew, one of the disciples and brother of Simon Peter, said to him 'There is a boy here who has five barley

> loaves and two fishes, but what are these for so many?' Jesus then said, 'Make the people sit down'. There was much grass in the place. Therefore the men sat down, about five thousand of them. Jesus took the bread and when he had given thanks he distributed it to those reclining. He did the same with the fish, as much as they wanted (6: 4–12).

On the face of it each detail is part of the unfolding narrative and one accepts or rejects them as such. But for Thomas it is not enough merely to assent to their historicity. They have to be read in accordance with his abiding conviction that meta-historical realities are lying behind their particularity, and the believing, medieval Christian culture which supports him and of which he is himself a famed exemplar prompts him to a form of discourse where chanelled personal reflection and the impact of systematised ideas lift these words of the text out of the confines of the narrated historical moment. To say, as the evangelist does, that the events occurred at Passover is no longer sufficient. One must add that:

> this time was well suited for their refreshment ... (since) anyone who desires to be refreshed by the bread of the Divine Word and by the body and blood of the Lord must pass from vices to virtue (846).

When Jesus 'lifted his eyes' this is a reminder that:

> the eyes of our Lord are his spiritual gifts and he lifts his eyes to his chosen ones, that is, he looks at them with compassion, when he mercifully grants these gifts to them (848).

And if one were tempted to imagine that the remarks of Philip and Andrew reflect no more than understandable helplessness at the prospect of feeding so many, Thomas is quick to insist upon the intended discriminations and nuances of the evangelist. Philip 'was slower in learning than the others', a fact demonstrated by his continuing need to ask questions of the Lord, and here he:

> does not seem to have any understanding or anticipation of the coming miracle. And so he suggests that money is the way by which they could feed all the people (852).

Andrew, by contrast, in referring to the five barley loaves, may be assumed to have been thinking of the miracle performed by Elisha who fed a hundred men with twenty barley loaves (2 Kings 4:42).

But even this does not exhaust the significance of the remarks by either Philip or Andrew, for since the context of what they say has to do with feeding and refreshment there is for Thomas an especially natural progression to the idea of the nourishment of the spirit. And because Philip is the less bright of the two apostles it is he who cannot look beyond the ordinary confines within which human beings operate. Thomas is therefore moved to comment:

> The number one hundred implies perfection. Two hundred, consequently, the twofold perfection necessary for this wisdom, for there are two ways by which one attains the perfection of human wisdom, by experience and by contemplation. So he says 'Two hundred denarii of bread would not suffice', because regardless of what human reason can experience and contemplate of the truth it is not enough to satisfy completely our desire for wisdom.

By contrast, Andrew has a surer sense of where wisdom must be sought, for his statement 'There is a boy here who has five loaves' shows him to be conscious of the law of Moses and of what it has to teach:

> He does not want to buy other bread, but to feed the crowd with the loaves of bread they already had, that is, those contained in the law ... The boy had five loaves, that is, the teaching of the law, either because this teaching was contained in the five books of Moses ... or because it was given to men absorbed in sensible things which are made known through the five senses ...

And the additional detail about the two fishes must not be lost for 'the two fishes, which gave a pleasing flavour to the bread indicate the teachings of the psalms and the prophets' (854).

When the crowd is made to sit down by the disciples, on the instructions of the Lord, this is a token of the fact that it is 'through the disciples that the knowledge of the truth has come to us' (856). And if the crowd sits on the abundant grass this is because grass is a sign of the flesh and there is, therefore, an intended twofold reference to:

> the teachings of the Old Testament which were given to a people resting on things of the flesh and wise according to the flesh …

or else to 'the one who perceives true wisdom, which cannot be attained without first abandoning the things of the flesh' (857). Furthermore, the fact that all those who sat down were men has also its lesson to give, for as mentioned in *Numbers* 1.3:

> Moses counted the people who were twenty years and older, without including the women. The evangelist does the same because only men can be completely instructed (858).

And so, presumably, in this interpretation, only men can fully be brought to grasp the significance of the miraculous occurrence.

Throughout all of this the recurring methodological motif is the dilution of immediacy for the sake of a presumed lesson intended by the evangelist. The wish to know takes precedence over the wish to be. One enters into a relationship with Christ in his capacity as teacher rather than as a beloved being, and the talk is of wisdom, of contemplation, of ultimate truths made known by the divine, supremely authoritative pedagogue. If there are meanings behind even the most banal detail in the pages of the fourth evangelist such meanings lie there as truths to be learned, as guidance to be absorbed.

There is no let-up in this insistence upon the withdrawal from immediacy in favour of wider horizons. The wedding feast at Cana recedes to make way for reflections both on the symbolism on marriage (338) and on the doctrines of Jesus which are taken to be a fulfilment rather than a rejection of old ideas (358). The weariness which led Jesus to rest by the well of Jacob, the thirst which proves to be the occasion for a dialogue with the Samaritan woman, even the hour at which Jesus chose to sit down become carriers of moral and theological meaning (561–565). And so it goes with incident after incident. The evangelist establishes his spare record. But the gaze of the commentator shifts elsewhere. As a final example of this way of reading the text one might consider the comments of Thomas on some of the details of what is, after all, the most violent section of the narrative, the sequence of events forming the Passion.

The violence begins early, when Peter strikes off the ear of the servant with his sword. It is an episode which has caused some difficulty to those who would speak of it. That Peter should be carrying a sword at all is plainly a cause of embarrassment. Some argue, as Thomas reports, that it was on account of his knowledge that a conspiracy against Jesus was afoot and that he wanted to defend him. Others claim that it was not a sword but a knife which Peter had happened to carry with him from the table of the Last Supper. But if so there is still the problem of how to understand that Peter should strike the servant, given the explicit injunction (Mt. 5) not to resist what is evil. Thomas faces two possible explanations, that the injunction applied not to defence of oneself but to defence of someone else, in this case the Lord, or else that Peter, like his fellow apostles, was not yet perfect in the virtue required of him. And so the ear was severed, but the Lord moved to heal the servant, and, here, Thomas is clearly more at ease:

> For the servant is a token of the Jewish people who were oppressed by their priests ... Peter, prince of the apostles, cut off the hearing of this servant because he was wrongly hearing the words of the law, in a worldly manner probably, but the Lord restored him to a new hearing, 'In the hearing of his ear he has obeyed me' (Ps. 17.45). This being so, he was rightly called Malchus, that is, king. Because through Christ in a renewed life we are made to be kings. 'You have made us a kingdom and a priesthood for our God and we shall reign over the earth' (Apoc. 5.10).

So Peter on the Lord's instructions puts his sword in its scabbard, an act which draws from Thomas a somewhat laboured comment:

> The mystical significance of this is that the sword of God's word must be put into the belief of the gentiles.

And the question to Peter 'Do you not wish me to drink the chalice which my Father has given me?' is a token not only of the fact that the will of God must not be resisted but that the bitterness of the chalice is actually tempered by the will of God to do what is good.

Yet the truth of the day is that a man is arrested. So the text declares. Nor is there anything new in the fact that a human being is taken into custody. But the prisoner is Jesus, and that is what makes for almost unbearable paradox, since in the eyes of Thomas this is not just another historical figure but is the incarnate Son of God, the object of complex discourse, the focus of daily prayer, the proclaimed saviour. Yet here he is, imprisoned omnipotence, and the occasion has somehow to be coped with and, typically, the strategy for dealing with it is by recourse to the resolutions which the verbal patterns of the Latin version of scripture can provide. Jesus is 'grasped' by the arresting mob, yet he is someone actually impossible to 'grasp', for as Jeremias proclaims (32.19) he is 'great in his plans and in his thinking impossible to grasp'. There are too the supporting words of the psalmist (70.11) 'God abandoned him, so pursue him and grasp him since there is none to seize him'. And these words serve as a reminder of the declaration in *Lamentations* 4.20 'The Lord God, the spirit of *our mouth* has been seized in our sins', that is, as Thomas adds, 'on account of our sins so that he might indeed set us free'. There is, finally, the declaration in Isaias (49.25) 'captivity has been lifted by the brave one'. The prisoner is actually the liberator.

A harsh reality, narrated in the text, is somehow made tractable. The bitter, painful and ultimately lethal sequence of events almost becomes tolerable in a distancing process through resort to scriptural quotation. There is a stepping-back from and a dissolution of the palpable events for the sake of something else, for an overview in which the engulfing horror of a set of moments is manoeuvred to take its place within a divinely centred, intelligible and, therefore, expressible scheme. Jesus suffers. But fortunately it makes sense. And making sense matters greatly to Thomas.

This need to find meaning shows up plainly when Thomas, continuing his study of the passion narrative, is confronted by the episode where Peter denies Christ. The servant girl asks 'are you not one of his disciples?' and Peter says 'No' and Thomas feels obliged to find some acceptable interpretation of this moment in the life of the premier apostle. He offers three reasons for the denial. First, there was the status of the person who asked him. It was not 'an armed soldier nor a high priest who has to be respected'. It was a woman, and a servant woman besides, and, hence, apparently, no more need be said. Second, she asked in a friendly way, and not as someone with an entitlement to interrogate him. Seemingly, the status of the questioner is sufficient to take some of the seriousness out of the denial since:

> he who denied Christ in response to the servant girl, later professed and proclaimed the name of Christ before the high priests.

Yet the lie cannot really be evaded and so a third reason is proffered:

> The Lord permitted the denial of Peter since he wished that he who was to take charge of the whole Church would be more compassionate to the weak and to sinners once he had experienced in himself the weakness of sin (463).

Nor, by implication, ought the denial come entirely as a shock, given the preliminaries to the episode. For while John managed to get into where Jesus was held Peter had to remain outside. Thomas, more relaxed here, is able to discern meaning behind the words of the text:

> These two disciples may be understood to represent two ways of life in the following of Christ. There is the active mode, signified by Peter, and the contemplative, signified by John. The active follows Christ by way of obedience ... the contemplative by way of seeing and beholding ... John enters with Jesus because the way of contemplation is known to him ... Just as lower reason is guided by what is higher, so is the active life directed by the contemplative.

And so in the context of 'lower' and 'active' the reader is in some way cushioned against the inescapable datum of the denial.

The process is continued at other moments in the tragic saga. Details such as the crown of thorns, the ironic dressing up in royal robes and the jeering at the prisoner are all moved by Thomas into a mosaic of scriptural quotations and moralising comment, so that the thorns pressed into the flesh serve as reminders of how the pricking of conscience becomes a way out of sin and the royal robe becomes a token of that 'passion of the martyr by which the whole body of Christ, that is the Church is made red'. Even the jeers are significant, symbolising those who pay lip service to Christ but deny him in their deeds.

The brutal course of the crucifixion is itself swathed in the lineaments of pedagogical discourse:

> Christ carried his cross like a king bearing a sceptre, a sign of the glory which is in the universal domination of all things. 'The Lord shall reign from a tree' (Psalm XCV9). 'And power is laid on his shoulder and he shall be called admirable, counsellor, a mighty God, father of the era to come, prince of peace' (Is. 9.6). He carries it like a winner bearing the trophy of his victory. 'Devastating principalities and powers he has paraded them in public behind him in his triumphal procession' (Col. 2.15). He carries it like a doctor with a candelabrum in which there has to be placed the light of his doctrine, because the word of the cross is the virtue of God among the faithful. 'No one lights a candle and places it under a bushel but on a lampstand so that those who enter may see the light'.

The place of execution is Calvary, outside the city walls, a fact with a twofold explanation:

> first, to show that the virtue of his passion must not be confined within the frontiers of the Jewish people, and, secondly, to show that those who wish to enjoy the fruit of the passion must leave the world, at least in sentiment.

And the arrangement whereby Jesus was in death between two thieves is itself a sign:

> It is right for a judge to be in the middle. As the Philosopher (Aristotle) says, to go to a judge is to go to what is in the middle. So he is placed in the middle, with one on his right and one on his left because in a process of judgement someone renders a verdict upon the sheep on the right and the goats on the left. Thus, the thief on the right who had faith is freed and the other on the left, the one who offered insults, is condemned.

The final moments of the death are similarly treated. When Jesus declares himself to be thirsty this is immediately pressed into the service of a teaching:

> Because he says 'thirst' he shows his death to be real and not imaginary. At the same time he shows his ardent longing for the salvation of the human race. 'He wishes all men to be saved' (1 Tim. 2:4). 'The Son of Man came to seek out and make safe that which had perished' (Luke 19.10). Furthermore, we are accustomed to express vehement longing by 'thirst'. 'My soul has thirsted for the living God' (Psalm XLI3).

When he dies it is in the terms set down by the evangelist. 'And having bowed his head he gave up his spirit'. Thomas moves in to comment:

> This is not to be understood as saying that because he gave up his spirit he therefore bowed his head. On the contrary, for the bowing of the head shows the obedience through which he endured death. He was made obedient until death (Phil. 2.8).

Also, the power of the dying man is posted in the words 'he gave up his spirit', ... For as Augustine says 'no one can sleep at will, but Christ can die when he chooses'.

What emerges in all of this is a determination to take the literal meaning of scriptural words and to move through and beyond this particular meaning to orders of reality which are independent of time and of contingency. So Jesus on the cross cannot simply be thirsty, which is a passing characteristic of a passing moment. His thirst must foreshadow something permanent, because where there is permanence there is God-created intelligibility and, in consequence, a lesson valid for every era and every circumstance. The thirst of Jesus is therefore not a detail to be noticed for its own sake but is one of the several items of evidence which point irrefutably to his humanity. And this humanity cannot be invoked in isolation from his divinity and, hence, from that unique conjunction of essential attributes summarised in the Chalcedonain formula of two natures in that one special person. The thirst of Jesus is not primarily a throat-drying, body-wracking medical phenomenon exhibited by a suffering individual, but is, in this case, a piece of evidence to be contemplated within the wider context of enduring transcendent truth.

This wish to move constantly into a great panorama of abiding and stratified truth is the dynamic which sets the commentary on its course, and the process of interpretation adopted by Thomas is not an attempt to offer a view of the evangelist but is a confident search for the layers of reality indicated by the pages of the text. The conceptual framework underlying this search is set down not in the commentary itself but in the *Summa Theologica.* Although well known it deserves to be quoted in full:

> God is the author of sacred scripture. It is in the power of God not only to use words, as men do, to signify something but also to use things themselves to convey meaning. Whereas in every other science things are signified by words it is characteristic of this science that the things signified by words have themselves also a signification. Hence, that first signification, whereby words signify things, belongs to the first sense, namely the historical or literal. That signification whereby things signified by words have themselves also a signification is called the spiritual sense. This is founded on the literal sense, and it presupposes it.
>
> The spiritual sense has a threefold division. As the Apostle says, the Old Law is a figure of the New Law, and, as Dionysius says, the New Law is itself a figure of the glory to come. Furthermore, in the New Law whatever the Head has done is a sign of what we should do. So, where the things of the Old Law signify the things of the New Law one has the allegorical sense. Where the things done in Christ or in that which stands for Christ are a token of what we should do, one has the moral sense. But where these same things signify what

relates to eternal glory, one has the anagogical sense. Since the literal sense is that which the author intends and since the author of Holy Scripture is God, who comprehends all things by one act of His intellect, it is not unfitting, as Augustine says, that one word in the literal sense in Holy Scripture should have several senses.[17]

But on what basis can such several senses be determined? And, in view of the fact of heresy, what are the criteria which must be employed in order to ensure that a particular and proclaimed sense is the correct one? If Origen and Augustine can propose contradictory interpretations of the significance of Jacob's well, if Thomas can detect in the episode of Jesus and the moneylenders a warning against medieval simony, what, if any, is the decisive argument to refute the suspicion that interpretation is ultimately no more than arbitrary assertion, more or less disguised and with a greater or lesser degree of apparent authority?

It is this matter of authority which is crucial in the milieu to which Thomas belongs, for unlike Origen and unlike Augustine he thinks and prays and works in a non-pluralist world and if some details of his interpretations are different from those, say, of his contemporary, Bonaventure, they both are at one on what would be deemed to be the essentials, for they both are the faithful sons of a larger and visible ever-present system. So, for example, when dealing with the account of the wedding feast at Cana Thomas notes that on the subject of the information that the wedding took place 'on the third day' at least two interpretations have been put into currency, one being that the wedding took place in the same year as the baptism of Christ. But Thomas will not allow this since the matter has been authoritatively settled:

> Both the teaching and the practice of the Church are opposed to this, since three miracles are commemorated on the feast of Epiphany, the adoration of the magi in the first year of the Lord's birth, the baptism of Christ, which implies he was baptised on the same day thirty years later, and this marriage, which took place on the same day one year later. It follows from this that at least one year elapsed between his baptism and this marriage (337).

In other words, because of an officially determined stance the detail in the gospel may not be interpreted in any but one way. This act of reading cannot therefore be idiosyncratic.

And this same perspective is applied throughout the commentary. So, for instance, when considering the words 'I will raise him up on the last day' Thomas takes this to refer not only to a renewed natural life but even to one of glory:

> For the Catholic faith teaches that the world will be made new ... and that among the changes accompanying this renewal we believe that the motion of the heavens will stop and, consequently, time ... Since at the resurrection time will stop so also will night and day, in accordance with 'there will be one day known to the Lord, not Day and night' (Zec. 14:7). This is why he says 'And I will raise him up on the last day'.

This is then elaborated by an assertion which should be quoted:

> As to why the motions of the heavens and time itself will continue until then and not before or after, we should observe that whatever exists for something else is differently arranged in accordance with the different states of that for which it exists. But since all physical things have been made for man they should, in consequence, be arranged in accordance with the different states of man.

Now, in *Corinthians* 15.54 it is said that:

> 'what is mortal will put on incorruption'. So, where men are resurrected they will put on the condition of incorruptibility, which means that the corruption of things will also then stop. Therefore, the motion of the heavens, which is the cause of the generation and corruption of material things will cease [940].

It is a seamless garment woven of appropriate scriptural quotation, the particulars of the fourth gospel, the teachings of 'the Catholic Faith', the acceptable assertions of Aristotle and, one must assume, prevailing opinion. The ingredients run in and across each other in an assured grid where nothing is amiss. Thought travels in a universe so ordered and patterned that the intelligence can move through it to articulate the innermost laws of its constitution and then discover, as a consequence of God-given grace, a divine realm where the purest of arrangements may be glimpsed.

Indeed, a recurring and particularly striking move throughout the commentary is the willingness to declare the mind of God. Thus, regarding the words 'No one can come to me unless the Father who sent me draws him', Thomas hones in on 'unless the Father draws him' and offers theological arguments to indicate how the words of Jesus must be interpreted. Such arguments, seeking to maintain fidelity to the text, are concentrated upon elaborating the notion that belief is not possible without the activating agency of the Father. And yet the world is made up of those who believe and those who do not, a fact which prompts the question as to why God should choose to draw some to himself, but not others. In the answer given by Thomas one may glimpse the spectacle of a mind so dominated by a notion and expectation of order in the universe that he can confidently discern the actual intentions of his God:

> A general reason can be given why God does not draw all who are turned away from him but only some ... The reason is so that the order of divine justice may appear and shine out in those not drawn, while the greatness of divine mercy may appear and shine in those who are drawn ... One can give as the reason why a builder places some stones at the bottom and other at the top and sides that it is the arrangement of the house whose completion requires this. But why he puts these particular stones here and those over there depends on his will. Thus it is that the main reason for the arrangement is referred to the will of the builder. So God, to complete the universe draws certain ones so that his mercy may appear in them and there are others whom he does not draw so that his justice may be shown in them. That he draws these and not those depends on the pleasure of his will. Similarly, the reason why in his Church he made some apostles, some confessors and others martyrs is for the beauty and the completion of the Church [938].

These are the words of a consciousness fundamentally at ease in the conviction that the truth of even the most profound things is accessible. One need only reach out for it, and one may do so with the special confidence induced by the sense of being part of and protected by a comprehensive network of acknowledged and unfailing authority. The interpretation of the fourth gospel is therefore not an enterprise in the dark. The comfort of it lies in the awareness that one is re-articulating what is already there and that correction will swiftly come if one stumbles or goes astray. Nowhere is this clearer than in the comments of Thomas on the opening words of the prologue.

Speaking with the majestic self-assurance which in the Homeric poems would have earned for a champion warrior the title of 'god-like' Thomas, addressing the question of how the term 'Word' in the prologue is to be understood, in the prologue, proceeds, in the company of Aristotle and Augustine, to delineate the workings of the realm where God, angels and man are to be found. Operating on the basis of what for him is a self-evidently correct theory of knowledge he makes of intellect the key consideration. It is a mode of being and it is also a manifestation of power. Intellect generates understanding, and understanding, the product of discriminations and distinctions, may properly be called a word. But a word is primarily something formed within. It is the offspring of cogitation and, in the human arena, it is then enclosed in speech.

But since there are three kinds of intellect, human, angelic and divine, and since angel and human being are the creatures of God and therefore subsequent to him it follows that the Word mentioned in the first affirmation of the gospel must indeed be the Word of God. Hence the requirement to establish the difference between this Word of God and the human word. But the task is made feasible for Thomas not only by his theory of knowledge but also by what one might describe as the category of appropriateness. Thus, a person must take a series of rational steps in order to arrive at a particular and specific understanding, one which, when formed, will be a word and, therefore, capable of being spoken. However, this journey to understanding implies a change from a lack of a particular understanding to its eventual possession. But to speak in this way of God, to posit any kind of change in him would be inappropriate. Hence, using the classic Aristotelian distinction, one should speak of a person as having understanding potentially, whereas God must have it actually. For the same reasons of appropriateness one should mark the difference between the imperfection of human understanding and the perfection of what is in God. Furthermore and in accordance with the same principle one must affirm that the possession of understanding is not included in the essence of a person, that, indeed, a person must work to gain possession of such understanding, but by contrast:

> in God to understand and to be are the same, and so the Word is no accident of the divine intellect but is of its essence. It must therefore be subsistent because whatever is in the nature of God is God (1.28).

Like a logical sequence, clean of line and summoning its own inevitable resolution, the interaction of Thomas and his text then moves towards what must seem to be the only possible interpretation of what has been set down at the start of the gospel. Such an interpretation has the simple directness of a law of nature and, once stated, it takes on its own secure charisma. With a bow to Aristotle and a quotation from the admired Augustine, with a disapproving flick at Anselm for having at one point spoken 'improperly' Thomas turns to the problem of why the evangelist chose to speak of the 'Word' instead of the 'Word of God' and, secondly, why he used 'Word' instead of 'Son'. Both questions were originally posed by John Chrysostom, as Thomas acknowledges, but it is Thomas himself who provides the answers. He does so with the serene assurance that he knows precisely what the evangelist had intended, namely, to focus on the Son instead of upon the Father and to draw from the term 'Word' the advantage of wider horizons of meaning than would be possible with the designation 'Son' which, after all, has the potential of being so misunderstood that:

> someone might imagine that this generation is something he can comprehend, that is, a material and changeable generation (1.31).

To avoid any such misunderstanding and 'to signify the separation and elevation of the Word above all things' the evangelist uses what is available in Greek but is denied by the absence of the definite article in Latin and he talks of *the* Word, thereby pointing to 'the supereminence of the divine word' (1.33).

And the reality of this supereminence is emphasised with the phrase 'in the beginning', an immensely fruitful choice of terms, given that 'beginning' implies order, 'a certain order of one thing to another'. This being so, the way for Thomas is open to three profound theological truths.

First, since the Son is 'the power and the wisdom of God' (1.Cor. 1.24) it follows that in him is the creative programme which makes of him the cause of all things. He is the beginning of things and, in consequence, one might paraphrase the initial statement of the prologue by saying 'the Word as cause was in the Son'. Second, 'beginning' may also be taken as signifying the Father, and to declare that 'in the beginning was the Word' would be to proclaim, like the Council of Nicaea, the consubstantiality of the Word with the Father. Third, 'beginning' can be understood as that which precedes any duration. But because the Son is the cause of everything and since everything is measurable within duration, that is, within time, the consequence is that the Son, insofar as he precedes time, must be eternal and, hence, must be co-eternal with the Father. Thus, the phrase 'in the beginning' manages to encapsulate three inter-related truths, and, therefore, the three explanations of the opening words of the gospel are not in any way to be taken as either mutually exclusive or merely parallel. In fact, they come together to confirm the presence of the enormous vistas opened up by what the evangelist has written (1.34–38).

Such vistas are fundamentally intelligible. That is to say, the deployment of human words can encompass them, provided such deployment is conducted in an orderly fashion and also in accordance with the category of appropriateness. Thus, to the reasonable question of how the begotten Word can be co-eternal with the Father, given that a human son is subsequent to his progenitor, Thomas replies that whereas under the horizons of time and duration an originative principle must precede that which it originates this is not the case in the realm of the supratemporal and the divine:

> God did not first exist and then proceed to the generation of the Word, for since the generation of the Word is nothing other than something formed in the intelligence it follows that God would understand potentially before understanding in actuality. But that is impossible. Again, it is impossible that the generation of the Word could involve succession, for in that case the divine Word would be unformed before being formed ... which is false. Also, it cannot be said that the Father pre-established a beginning of duration for his Son by his own will, because God the Father does not generate the Son by his will, as the Arians asserted, but naturally, since God the Father, in the act of self-understanding conceives the Word. Hence, God the Father did not exist prior to the Son (1.41)

All of this serves to emphasise the perfection of the Son, which is something incapable of being expressed by a single name:

> We call him 'Son' to show that he is of the same nature as the Father. We call him 'image' to show that he is in no way unlike the Father. We call him 'brightness' to show that he is co-eternal. He is called 'Word' to show the immaterial mode of his begetting (1.42).

The initial affirmation of the gospel is therefore a harbinger of the innermost reality of the triune God, as are the next three declarations, namely, that 'the Word was with God' and 'the Word was God' and that this Word was 'in the beginning with God'. Not only do these provide a glimpse of the divine realm but they offer an irrefutable challenge to errors which have come from past thinkers. To say 'in the beginning was the Word' is to cut the ground from under the followers of Ebion and Cerinthus, of Photinus and Paul of Samosota who had joined in asserting that *Christ* took the beginning of his being from the Virgin Mary. To declare 'and the word was with God' is to posit the distinction in being between the Father and the Son, and, therefore, to condemn Sabellianism, with its claim that fatherhood and sonship were but two faces, two aspects of the one God. To assert 'and the Word was God' is to repel the notion, promulgated by Eunomius, that the Son is entirely unlike the Father. Finally, to say 'he was in the beginning with God' is to deny the doctrine of Arianism that the Son, for all his perfection, is subsequent to and, therefore, of lesser status than the Father.

But even here the richness of the first sentences of the prologue is not exhausted for Thomas. There are also eminent philosophers who, like heretical theologians, have gone astray, and the evangelist, in the opening words of his prologue has shown up the errors and the inadequacies of their thought. Those, like Democritus, who posited a primordial material cause for all things are rebuked by the proposition that 'in the beginning was the Word' from whom – 'and not by chance – all things derive their origin'. There are the Platonists with the notion that eternal Forms, each separate and each one distinct, exist as the cause of material things. It is a notion which fades before the pronouncement that 'the Word was with God'. Neo-Platonism, describing the downward passage of increasingly inferior emanations gave voice to the concept of one such emanation as the cause of everything and as a being which, for all its splendour, is yet inferior to its source. Such a perspective, however, is ruled out by the declaration that the Word was God. And the fourth assertion, that the Word was in the beginning with God, is a denial of the claim by Aristotle that the matter of the universe is eternal. In short, so far as Thomas is concerned, theologians and philosophers must look to the gospel of John for the truth of things, and it is especially fitting that they do so in the light of the fact that whereas the other three gospels focus on the historical Christ the fourth evangelist operates upon a loftier plane in the arena of the eternal relationship between God and his Son.

What is happening here deserves the closest scrutiny. There is the self-assurance of a brilliant and believing man who engages in his task with a methodic unhectoring demeanour. But this confidence is not merely due to the ease with which he can employ his abundant talents. It is something which rests upon, indeed draws continuing strength from, a confluence of intellectual, cultural and social currents which encourages in him the sense of being right, not arrogantly so but undoubtedly so. To examine such currents would be a project too immense to undertake here, but some are immediately evident in his treatment of the statement that 'in the beginning was the Word'. There is the particular theory of knowledge by which he operates, one which for him is not so much a theory as a permanent and secure explanation of how we know, one which has acquired the further confirmation, if such is needed, that it has the support of Aristotle. There is the particular conception of God as not merely possessing intellect but as actually being intellect. There is the conviction that this theory of knowledge and this conception of God – exciting, exalted, imperious in demanding recognition – must yield the criteria by which to decide what may or may not be said of the Word. That is to say, a particular theory and a particular concept have generated what has been referred to above as the category of appropriateness, a measure which will not only mark what may be said about God but which carries with it the implication that anything said under its aegis must actually be the case. Hence the notes by Thomas on what is 'impossible' and 'false' or the comment such as that 'the Word, properly speaking, is always understood as a Person in the Divinity' (1.29). This category of appropriateness has doubtless many sources, including the attempt of apophatic theology to create a presentiment of what God is by way of asserting what he is not. But in the hands of Thomas the criterion of what may be right and properly said becomes an important exegetical instrument in his dealings with the gospel of John.

It must be stressed, however, that this criterion of appropriateness is not simply the invention of Thomas. In fact Thomas is bringing to the reading of this text not only the workings of his own immense talents but the complexity of a prayerful, God-centred lifestyle which is embedded in, and supported by a pervasive and rarely challenged cultural infrastructure. Thomas belongs to a society characterised especially by a corporate Christian presence, one, moveover which has been styled 'the papal monarchy',[18] and one to which no real alternative is on offer. He is both heir to and transmitter of a richly articulated overview of how things are, of how person relates both to person and to the unignorable

God, and all this in a society organised over many centuries around the motif of 'true doctrine'. The overview, the particular explanatory order imposed upon an inter-related heaven and earth becomes the source of the intelligibility of individual manifestations of being. There exists, as it were, a kind of supra-text, offspring of doctrine and communal experience, of gospel and private prayer, of theology and public worship, and this supra-text provides the certainty, the confidence as well as the reference point which will open the way to the understanding of particulars and especially to the correct reading of such words as those available in the fourth gospel. The interpreter of the evangelist has no need to fear. The supra-text guarantees a safe journey through the words of the gospel. It allows some measure of intellectual latitude but it is also the haven where one may rest assured that one is within the boundaries of authorised truth. So when the interpreter reads the gospel, indeed any sacred text, it will be with the confidence of finding true explanation, for every Thomas can turn and turn again to the supra-text:

> their lives a tome of meaning holding all this for its fief.[19]

CALVIN

John Calvin is an impassioned reader and meticulous scholar. But, unlike Origen, he broods sulphurously over the wickedness he sees around him. He is fierce in his anger and blunt in his speech.

He writes his commentary[20] on the fourth gospel in a western Europe which is becoming pluralist and where the great central issues of religious belief and practice no longer depend solely on the approval of papal authority. If in some of his pages there is nothing much to distinguish him from an Augustine or a Thomas Aquinas the drama of what has happened is nevertheless unmistakable. For Calvin is an apostle of the Reformation and the words he sets down in response to the gospel have, as it were, raised anchor and require no longer the sanction, actual or presumed, of any ecclesiastical bureaucracy surrounding the bishop of Rome. In a way that could never be the case for a loyal medieval commentator Calvin is on is own, fierce in his determination and looking within himself for whatever assurance he can bring to bear on his reading of the evangelist. He has few references to the opinions of other writers. He does not compare and contrast the ideas of Origen and Chrysostom. Theoretical questions hold no interest for him. His engagement is with the actuality of the text, and the confidence with which he speaks, from within a moral and theological framework, is powerfully his own.

However, some precision is called for here if his reading of the gospel is to be properly understood. For the ultimate aloneness of every self is not an issue for him. Calvin is firmly on his own in the sense that he is unwilling to allow any mediator between him and what he takes to be the word of God. Commenting, for instance, on the declaration of Jesus at the last supper to the effect that the apostles will be unable to arrive at full truth until they are led by the spirit, Calvin says:

> The spirit led them into all truth when they committed to writing the substance of their teaching. Whoever thinks that anything should be added to their doctrine, as though it were imperfect and incomplete, not only accuses the apostles of dishonesty but blasphemes against the spirit ... Their writings may be regarded as enduring records of the revelation promised and given to them. And so nothing can be added to them without terrible injustice to the spirit ... If we do not wish to be ungrateful to God let us rest in that teaching of which the apostles' writings declare themselves to be the authors (16.12)

These remarks follow an earlier, ringing assertion:

> Let us remember that what he said then to the disciples is also spoken to us ... We should allow [his words] to sink in ... (16.1).

Taken by themselves these declarations are neither startling nor unprecedented. But they arise in fact from a point of view which is stern, uncompromising and regularly outraged. For in the eyes of Calvin there is an enemy to be reckoned with. Human beings:

> have the virtually innate vice of being clever at building obstacles that will keep them from arriving at the knowledge of the truth ... Even on a plain and smooth road everyone would make a stumbling block for himself (7.27).

And they will continue to do so as long as they look for earthly props on that journey which should be taking them to their God. Yet they insist on fashioning such props and, in the process, they go on to 'mangle the scriptures' (7.27). So when Jesus appears on the waters during the crossing to Capernaum he:

> gives a small example of his divinity. But at once we indulge in imaginings. And in place of Christ every man constructs for himself an idol (6.17).

The insistence upon fashioning idols is a mark of sinful, tarnished human nature. Because of the corruption rampant within them human beings lack any purity of attentiveness, and although the divine realities are at hand, available in the sacred texts, nevertheless:

> we foolishly and perversely wander into byways. Life is put in front of us, and still it is rejected by most. For who does not invent for himself a life outside of Christ? And how many are satisfied with Christ alone? (6.5).

'There is nothing to stop us from making right judgement' (7.17).

We could have a clear-eyed view of the things of God. But we are largely unteachable. We are self-willed, stubborn creatures, hypocritical in our doings. Even when we give public expression to doubt or uncertainty regarding divine matters this is nothing more than a mask for a decision to engage in wickedness:

> One person will declare that he prays for the dead out of distrust of his own judgement and he will not speak out against the perverse inventions concerning purgatory, and still he will plunge readily into fornication. Another will say he lacks the ability to distinguish between Christ's pure doctrine and the fabrications of man, yet he will have brains

> enough to steal or else to perjure himself. In brief, those who go through public hesitation are actually hiding behind a veil of doubt regarding our current controversies and are in open contempt of God regarding matters that are not obscure (7.17).

This last phrase deserves to be highlighted, for it encapsulates a recurrent view, one which, moreover, significantly directs the way for Calvin in reading the gospel. For while on the one hand there is revelation, a reality plainly on view in the text, there is also the insistent human refusal to take it on board. Or else, if human beings deal with it, then, in all likelihood they deform and disfigure what divine generosity has made available to them. Nor is this the consequence of ordinary frailty of mind stumbling in its task but is the token of something deeper. Human beings are not simply incompetent students of revelation. They are irremediably corrupt. As Calvin puts it, commenting on the Nicodemus episode and on the phrase 'see the kingdom of God':

> We bring nothing from the womb except our carnal nature. It follows, then, that our nature also precludes us from the kingdom of God. We are deprived of the life of heaven. We are slaves to death ... Since flesh is contrasted to spirit as something corrupt to what is sound, the crooked to what is straight, the defiled to the holy, the polluted to the pure, we may conclude, therefore, that the whole of man's nature is condemned (3.6).

Any inklings we might have of God and of righteousness are polluted inevitably:

> Just as wine which has been completely spoilt and tainted by the stink of its leather bottle loses its good flavour and has a bitter and horrible taste ... So, in the whole of our nature there lingers not a speck of goodness (3.6).

And this means that when the prologue of the gospel speaks of the true light enlightening every one the interpretative emphasis must be on the coming of the light and not on the receptive capacity of human beings. For these have a 'dullness' which is not intellectual but moral. Such retardation, such 'pitiable perversity and vice' had in earlier times the effect of keeping at bay the knowledge of Christ before he was manifest in the flesh. But, worse still, it continues to be the case even now. Human beings draw water 'from a running stream and never think of the spring from which it flows' (1.9). Sunk in guilt, their gift of reason blocked, they do their wicked deeds and fabricate their monstrous idols.

Calvin is not dealing simply in generalities here nor in the common stock of dyspeptic preaching. Specific instances of human perversity come regularly to his mind and none more so than what appears in the arena of what he castigates as papism:

> Those who today are the most ferocious enemies of the gospel and the most vigorous defenders of the papacy have nothing more praiseworthy about them than a burning zeal. But if one looks at their lives they will be seen to hide ugly shame, so that they are actually in open mockery of God. Who does not know that gross hedonism rules the court of the popes? Do bishops and abbots possess enough modesty to conceal their filthiness so that at least there may be a semblance of religion? Are not monks and thugs of this type given up to every wickedness, to lust and avarice, to every sort of unnatural crime, so that their lives cry out their forgetfulness of God? (7.19)

Papism, in other words, is for Calvin the most obvious example of the tendency to construct idols, a tendency which itself springs not so much from intellectual failure as from sheer moral depravity of the kind exhibited above all by Rome and its evil minions. And so when he begins to comment on the narrative of the wedding feast of Cana and, especially, on the seemingly brusque put-down of Mary by Jesus ('woman, why turn to me?') he looks first at the particular moment and then at its implications:

> Though neither ambition nor any other carnal affection motivated her, yet she sinned by going beyond appropriate bounds. Her concern for the inconvenience of others, her wish to remedy it in some way came out of kind-heartedness and ought to be given its credit. Still, by putting herself forward she could have obscured the glory of Christ. But we should also note that Christ spoke thus for others (2.3).

Calvin, of course, is saying this with an outraged awareness of the status given to Mary by the Church of Rome:

> It is certain that this statement by Christ gives direct warning to men not to transfer to Mary what belongs to God through the superstitious exaltation of her name as mother ... The need for this warning is clear enough, given the subsequent gross and abominable superstitions. Mary has been made Queen of Heaven, the Hope, Life and Salvation of the World. Such indeed have been their lunatic babblings that they have just about stripped Christ and adorned her with the spoils (2.4).

The lesson of the text is clear. 'Extravagant honour' must not be paid to Mary, in case the glory of Christ is obscured. And none are so guilty of this as the deluded followers of Rome, which is hardly surprising since:

> we see in the papacy today that everything said to belong to the worship of God is arranged for pure display ...

and also for the worst excesses of idolatry. Small wonder, then, that there have even been papist crooks laying claim to possession of the very water pots used at the wedding feast and offering them for sale to the gullible public. What, then, is the remedy? If the followers of Rome 'pollute the worship of God with their inventions' (6.15) how should one break free of the conditions which produce this? In particular, how should one read the word of God and, especially, the fourth gospel? The answers of Calvin may be summed up in one remark. 'I refuse to philosophise beyond the grasp of my faith' (1.1). Here is the central theme, faith and its presence, faith as a determinant, faith as the road out of idolatry and into a true understanding of the words, the historical words, recorded by the evangelist. Faith is a field of energy in every human being. It is stripped of all supports and of all self-validation. The possessor of it has to renounce their own point of view (7.17), and has also to despise the world:

> Christ warns that the heavenly life must be put before the earthly, since the only reason for the godly to be living here at all is that as pilgrims in the world they may hurry to their heavenly homeland (6.27)

And yet human beings have no talent for it, and, hence, no reason ever for a sense of achievement.

> Faith brings nothing to God – rather it places man before God, empty and poor, so that he may be filled with Christ and his grace. This is in consequence, a passive work, as it were, and is one to which no reward can be paid. And it gives man no righteousness other than what he receives from Christ (6.29).

Calvin returns again and again throughout the commentary to makes this latter point. It determines, for instance, his reading of the words 'but as many as received him to them he gave the power to become the sons of God' (1.12). The term 'power' is for him, clearly, open to wilful misinterpretation or indeed to 'papist fiction', for there is a Roman reading which, engaging in 'trivial quibbling', insists that corresponding to divine grace there is a human capacity either to make use of or to reject what is on offer by way of God's gift. In this perspective faith owes at least something to self. But this view unleashes the indignation of Calvin since it gives an undeserved status to sinful humanity. The word 'power' as employed here by the evangelist must be taken to refer not to a natural attribute but to an honour bestowed by God. To read otherwise is 'like getting fire out of water'.

Faith, then is the only guarantee of safety open to a humanity destined otherwise for extinction by reason of its vileness and of its immersion in everything corrupt. Even so there are limitations to be acknowledged, for although the prospect of salvation appears on the horizon of all the faith which is the lifeline of the rescued is available not to everyone but only to those nominated by the Father:

> Christ is available to all and is displayed to all, but God opens the eyes only of the elect that they may look for him by faith ... It is through faith that Christ is given to us by the Father (3.16).

The believer is plucked from destruction, not because of any initiative of his own, since he is too mired to be able to turn of his own accord to God. He believes in Christ only because he has been given a chance to do so, and the chance has been offered only to a lucky few.

This perspective, shaper of reading for Calvin, is constantly at work, as for example when he comes to the following:

> Jesus said these things, and raising up his eyes to heaven he said: 'Father, the time has come. Glorify your son, that your son may glorify you. And through the authority you gave him over all the world, let him give eternal life to all those you have entrusted to him. And eternal life is this, to know you the only true God and Jesus Christ whom you have sent' (17.13).

The key phrase here for Calvin is 'those you have entrusted to him'. This marks an exclusion:

> Christ does not say that he has been placed in command of the whole world to grant life indiscriminately. He restricts this grace to those given to him ... The kingdom of Christ extends to all men, but it is saving only to the chosen who follow the shepherd's voice with willing obedience. He forcibly obliges others to obey him until he finally destroys them with his iron rod (17.2).

It is 'not the function of Christ to give life to all, but only to the chosen'. And, for Calvin, there are other words in the prayer of Jesus which carry the same message:

> I manifested your name to the men whom you gave, men out of the cosmos. They were yours and you gave them to me (17.6).

Or again, 'I do not pray for the world but for those whom you have given me' (17.9), all of which points in only one direction:

> ... from these words we gather that God chooses out of the world those whom he sees fit to be the inheritors of life. Such choice is made not according to human merit but is dependent upon his good pleasure (17.9).

And if this restriction of salvation might seem in any way unfair, Calvin is quick to assert that man is so utterly corrupt that the offer of salvation to even a few must be reckoned to be an act of outstanding mercy and generosity on the part of the Father.

Clearly, such views are not only encouraged by a particular way of reading the fourth gospel but they are also the product of a special temperament constantly at work, a temperament that is harsh, gloomy and quick to see fault. An example of this is what he has to say about the raising of Lazarus, the details of which are taken to be historical fact. When Jesus declares that 'Lazarus is fallen asleep' (11.11) the disciples fail to understand him. Calvin, convinced of their stupidity, is moved to comment:

> But their ignorance is amazing when they take Christ's word as meaning sleep. For although this is a metaphor it is so frequent and common in scripture that it should have been well-known to all Jews (11.11).

But he does not reserve his disgust for the disciples alone. When he comes to the words which place Bethany close to Jerusalem he sees the choice of location and the readiness of access to it for numerous Jews as a token of divine foresight:

> that Lazarus' resurrection might not be obscure or that witnesses might not be only his own family. And this convicts the malignant ingratitude of the nation, that this shining demonstration of divine power at a well-known place, before a vast crowd and near the city gates – as if it were performed in a theatre – instantly vanishes from everyone's eyes. More, the Jews maliciously shut their eyes and refuse to see what is before them. Nor is it new or uncommon that men who too incessantly gape after miracles are quite dull and stupid in thinking about them (11.18).

When Martha cries 'Lord if you had been here my brother would not have died', Calvin is stern in his assessment, granting that although she was showing her faith in Jesus her words had in them an admixture of 'disorderly passions'. And this led her beyond the bounds of propriety:

> For when she tells herself that her brother would not have died had Christ been present, what grounds has she for her confidence? It was not conceived from any promise of Christ. It remains, therefore, that she thoughtlessly yields to her own wishes instead of subjecting herself to Christ.

She ought not to have gone beyond what Jesus had ever said. In this she is a typical example of faith tarnished by private wishes:

> ... her faith, mixed up and entangled with unregulated desires, and even not completely free from superstition, could not shine with full brightness. And so only sparks of it gleam in these words (11.21).

But even here the matter of her faults does not cease. For when Jesus says 'your brother will rise again' her reply is that she knows he will rise on the last day. In saying this, however, she is revealing an excessive timidity. She stands still 'when Christ holds out his hand'. Here too she is in the wrong:

> We must not without God's Word drink in empty and as it were windy hopes. On the other hand when the Lord speaks must he find our hearts blocked up or shut too tight? (11.24).

But Martha is not the only one with faults. When Mary comes to the tomb, in answer to the summons of her sister, she is accompanied by Jews who had gathered in her house to console her. These Jews:

> think that Mary is going to the tomb, as is customary with those who seek to excite their grief. For this is a common disease, that husbands deprived of their wives, parents bereft of their children, and on the other hand wives bereft of their husbands and children deprived of their parents or other relatives or friends, eagerly increase their grief by every possible means. It is also customary to seek various contrivances for this purpose. The affections of men are already disordered enough; but they excite them with new stimuli, so as to rush against God with greater force and violence (11.31).

But then the text says that Jesus wept and Calvin remarks that numerous readers have felt this to be inappropriate. However, since the evangelist sets down what happened it must follow that the weeping was right and in order. The explanation is that Jesus, in taking on human flesh, took on the characteristics of man, other than sin. His tears were therefore the consequence of sympathy. But sympathy is one of the passions and 'no passion of his ever went beyond its proper bounds'.

> In short, if you compare his passions with ours, they are as different as pure, clear water flowing in a gentle course from muddy and thick foam (11.35).

But if Jesus wept, Martha continued to display a fragile faith, for when Jesus told her to have the stone moved from the entrance to the burial cave of her brother she objected, saying that after four days he smelled bad:

> This is a sign of distrust for she expects less from the power of Christ than she should have done. The rest of the evil lies in her measuring God's infinite and incomprehensible power by her carnal sense.

And this is quite dependable since:

> a confused and implicit faith avails little unless it is put to use when we come to a concrete situation (11.39).

So Lazarus comes forth bound in his grave clothes, and Jesus commands that he be loosed. The simple words 'loose him' can apparently be understood in more than one way. For Calvin the purpose of the command was to ensure that the hands of bystanders might be the witnesses of what had happened. But he notes another meaning:

> The papists are extremely ridiculous when they infer auricular confession from this. They say: 'When Christ had restored Lazarus to life, he wished his disciples to loose him. Therefore it is not sufficient for us to be reconciled to God, unless the Church also pardons our sins'. But how do they guess that it was the disciples who were told to loose Lazarus? On the contrary we gather that the order was given to the Jews to take from them every trace of doubt (11.44).

And following the raising of Lazarus, the chief priests gather together to consider what to do. They are 'stupid and brutish' 'wicked men ... pitting their own efforts against the power of God' and speciously pretending a zeal for the public good, and fearful that 'their tyranny would be destroyed' (1.48). Calvin discerns in these deliberations of the Jewish priests an image for his own times:

> Those who want to be regarded as prudent and circumspect continually have this same song in their mouths about caring for public quiet and that the renovation we are attempting is not without many dangers (11.48).

But if Jesus, after the curing of Lazarus, can no longer appear freely among the Jews 'it is the priest's tyranny which prevents him from appearing openly' (11.55).

In short, the reading of the narrative concerning the raising of Lazarus proceeds on the assumption that the facts as set down by the evangelist are historically correct. What is required is interpretation and comment, and Calvin is quite ready to embark on this with an untroubled confidence born of the characteristic features of his own temperament. While acknowledging that conflicting interpretations exist with regard to specific moments in the text he is never assailed by doubts about the rightness of his own view.

The term *Logos*, for example, appearing in the very first sentence of the gospel has been given a variety of meanings, yet there is only one correct way to understand it, despite the 'quibbles' of the Arians and the nonsense of Servetus 'that most arrogant and worthless Spaniard', that 'barking dog' who engages in 'drivelling nonsense'. The fact is that one should 'disregard other interpretations which disagree with the evangelist's meaning' (1.4). And there is such meaning and it is the object of 'the grasp of my faith'. The content of that faith is what the evangelist intended to convey, but this content has been elaborated in the particular mode of explanation adopted not, of course, by papist theologians but by the writers of the early Church who chose, for instance, to employ a term such as 'hypostasis' to express the distinctiveness of the Son with respect to the Father within the unity of the Godhead. That is to say, there is a correct reading among possible readings and on themes such as that of the Logos those early writers help to bring that correct reading to light in such a way as to offer the means to rebuff those other incorrect readings which are the foundation of heresy.

Calvin, then, is not proclaiming that the last word has or indeed could be offered about the declarations of, for example, the prologue. But he is saying in effect that there is a meaning accessible to the few possessors of faith like himself. He is not claiming sole admission to this meaning but, rather, puts himself in the company of the 'chosen' who are in a position to contemplate it. Furthermore, even that small and fortunate group may not necessarily grasp all of what is adumbrated in the text. The prologue, for instance, affirms that 'all things were made by him'. But there are some philosophers who would make a similar affirmation, and Calvin clearly wishes to keep such philosophers from the same high ground as that occupied by the evangelist:

> Even some philosophers set up God as the architect of the world in such a way as to make him the intelligence behind the building of this work. They are right in this because they agree with scripture. But since they quickly slide into trivial meditations there is no reason why we should desire their witness at all eagerly. Instead we should be satisfied with this heavenly oracle, knowing that it says much more than our minds can take in (1.3).

If 'in heavenly mysteries the whole power of the human mind disappears and fails' (6.63) there is nevertheless an access code, a gift made available by God to those destined by him from the beginning to be the recipients of his generous grace. Wrapped in this confidence, with faith and assertiveness in tandem, Calvin surveys his text, ready to proclaim the meaning of what he finds, ready also to supply meaning where none is offered. When he comes to the incident of the night-time visit of Nicodemus to Jesus he is quick to characterise the visitor:

> In Nicodemus the evangelist shows us how ephemeral and weak was the faith of those who had been stirred by the miracles of Christ and who had rushed to join him. This was a man belonging to the class of Pharisees. He had a position of authority among his people, and he should certainly have been far ahead of the others ... Yet it is obvious that his reason for coming had nothing to do with the wish to learn the elements of religion. If a ruler among men is less than a boy what must we think of the general public?

This is jaundiced enough as a point of view. But there is more. 'He came to Jesus by night', a detail unelaborated by the evangelist but seized upon by Calvin, like so many before him. Why come by night? If the text proclaims no reason then it must be supplied. Calvin is quite ready to do so. It was because he lacked the courage to act otherwise in case his reputation should suffer:

> There is no doubt he was puffed up with a foolish opinion of his learning ... he had a high idea of himself and he did not wish to give it up.

But at least there was something good in him, given that he wanted to find out more about the teachings of Jesus. Yet the story of Nicodemus is valuable:

> because in it we are taught about the corrupt nature of the human race, what is the right way into the school of Christ and what we must start from if we are to make progress in heavenly doctrine (3.1).

The decision to infer the motives of Nicodemus is not an isolated one but is in fact quite typical. The Samaritan woman in chapter four is a low-grade 'prostitute ... who does not deserve that Christ should speak to her at all' (4.10). She 'jeers' him (4.9) and 'despises' him (4.11). She is stupefied by self-love, and if she has had five husbands 'we may suppose it was because her wanton and stubborn ways drove her husbands to divorce her' (4.17). And when she invokes the practices of her Samaritan ancestors Calvin is at once reminded of the many:

> proud and irreligious men who, like the Turks and the Papists looking elsewhere for a more perfect wisdom, deserve to be dragged around by endless delusions and plunged into a labyrinth of errors (4.26).

Calvin thus approaches the text on the basis of a doctrinal and moralising standpoint already in place before he reads the words, one which is actively supplementing what the evangelist has set down and which, presumably, is confirmed and enhanced by what he finds. Ironically, he is quite like Nicodemus in that he is operating from within settled habits of mind. If he is unlike him it is in the quality of his self-assurance, for in contrast to the Pharisee he is not baffled. When Nicodemus asks, 'how can a man be born when he is old?', Calvin sees him:

> tripping over a straw ... for it is a just revenge on the part of God that those who consider themselves to be the most outstanding and eminent teachers and to whom the ordinary simplicity of doctrine is cheap and low are astonished by little things.

And this thought leads irresistibly to the more general issue of 'empty subtleties' as exemplified by the theologians of the papacy:

> For they wear out their entire lives in remote speculations and, regarding all that has to do with the worship of God, the assurance of our salvation or the practice of godly behaviour, they know no more than what a shoemaker or a ploughman knows about astronomy. Besides, revelling as they do in exotic mysteries they openly despise the real teaching of scriptures as being something beneath the rank of teachers (3.4).

Anger is nourished by confidence, and the confidence enables him to deal directly with the text. He knows what previous commentators have written and he considers their assertions with sovereign ease. On one point a suggestion by Augustine is dismissed as 'foreign to Christ's meaning'. On the same point he finds Chrysostom and Cyril to be better, but though this may be so, nevertheless, 'I shall try to explain Christ's meaning more clearly and surely' (3.3).

And so it goes, eloquent, astringent and passionate, a distillation of faith and fury with not the slightest hint of gentle moments or of serene days. The sense of sin, of miasmic darkness and imminent damnation rise up to control a reading which locates meaning against the background of the chill ante-rooms of Hell. There is no pity in it, and even when the evangelist writes that 'God so loved the world that he sent his only Son', Calvin is quick to remark:

> Such is the ungodly ambition ingrained in our nature that when we think we are saved diabolical imaginings about our own merits start immediately to creep into our minds. And

> so we come to think that God is favourable to us, simply because he has deigned to look at us (3.16).

It is as if revelation and the coming of Jesus had been organised to show, beyond all possible doubt, that most have nothing ahead of them except darkness and the onset of surging terror.

RUDOLF BULTMANN

The commentary of Rudolf Bultmann[21] begins with an elaborate speculation deriving from a proposal first mooted years earlier and suggesting that behind the prologue to the fourth gospel is an earlier source – in this case, a hymn – which has been reproduced by the evangelist, albeit with interspersed comment of his own. The search for underlying sources of classic texts – the business of *Quellenforschungen* – is of course a methodological phenomenon especially familiar to students of German scholarship and it is a practice which has frequently to rest as much upon the power of assertion as on the deployment of evidence. And when the assertion is either initiated or else repeated by a formidably erudite and admired scholar such as Bultmann, the line between a suggestion and established fact grows markedly thin. So, for instance, having pronounced the prologue to be 'a piece of *cultic-liturgical* poetry oscillating between the language of revelation and confession' (p 14) and 'governed by strict rules' (p 15), namely, the rules of verse, Bultmann then acknowledges that some parts of the prologue actually do not conform to the requirements of poetry. These 'stand out as interruptions' (p 15) which disturb 'the rhythm of the hymn'. In other words, some portions of the prologue may be said to fall within the confines of a metrical pattern and, in consequence, may be classified as verse. Therefore, what does not fall within the presumed metrical pattern is, necessarily, an interpolation for which the evangelist may be said to be responsible. So says Bultmann, and, given both his reputation and the normal life span of a welcomed idea, others continue to declare that it must be so.

Yet there is nothing to hand which might provide any verification of what is being proclaimed. Hypothesis turns into fact, nor does the matter rest there because now this 'fact' is the ground for further speculation. It is not enough to declare that since verses 6 to 8 and verse 15 do not fall into a particular metrical pattern they must be taken to have been composed by the evangelist himself. They should also be regarded as polemical in character and Bultmann is even willing to sketch the presumed argument. For him, verses 6 to 8 and verse 15 were designed:

> to dispute the claim that the Baptist has the authority of Revealer (p 17). This authority must ... have been attributed by the Baptist sect to their master. They see in him the *phos* and thus also the pre-existent *Logos* become flesh (p 18).

The speculative pile-up here goes on to generate a scenario which itself prompts the suggestion that 'the source text was a hymn of the Baptist community' (p 18). And this in turn raises the idea that the evangelist might once have belonged to this community, some members of which became followers of Jesus, '... and must we not therefore assume that the Baptist tradition was taken over by the Christians?' (p 18).

Inevitably, this way of reading cannot fail to evoke a number of troubling problems, not the least urgent of which is the question of how much of himself Bultmann is putting into the text. Of course such a question has to be asked of any reader but to someone dipping unsystematically into this commentary there might appear to be an undue preponderance of moments when the treatment of the words in the fourth gospel is marked by what looks somewhat like intellectual imperialism. So, for example, when discussing the episode of Jesus and the Samaritan woman at Jacob's Well Bultmann seems to be operating on the principle that a text is to be construed in terms of its origins. It is presumed that there is a source for the episode and that the evangelist has not only recast that material but has done so in a manner which makes it possible to distinguish between his own account and the primary version of events. This being so, Bultmann feels able to talk of what the narrative 'must have included' and what 'has been lost in the Evangelist's re-writing of the story' (p 179) and he goes on to highlight in the conversation between Jesus and the Samaritan woman patterns of thought which, in his view, derive from the perspectives of Gnosticism.

Again, regarding verse 27 to 59 in the sixth chapter, those where Jesus speaks of giving his flesh to eat, words which have had enormous importance in the history of Christian thought, Bultmann feels compelled to argue with the existing text. He sees in it an erratic and unsequential layout of ideas, which he takes to be the work of an untidy ecclesiastical editor. Specifically, he insists, from his reading of the text, that verses 51b to 58 – where Jesus proclaims the giving of his body – while forming what seems to be a continuation of the discourse set down in verses 27 onwards are actually from another occasion. Two separate themes have been run together with a consequent blurring of ideas. Nor do the problems end here, for the discourse in 27 to 51 is itself marked by rough-hewn arrangements, and, whether or not one agrees with Bultmann, the point is that as a reader he feels free to insist that matters are as he claims (pp 218–222). And so it goes with many other passages of the gospel.

But it would be quite wrong to allow observations of this kind to detract from the splendour of what Bultmann has achieved in this commentary on which he worked for some twenty years. Amid the deployment of his vast and apposite erudition he never loses sight of a key motif of the fourth gospel, namely that what is asked of the onlooker and the hearer is a disposition of trust in Jesus summed up in the term *pistis*. But where other commentators, men like Thomas Aquinas and Bonaventure, drew upon institutions and upon sanctioned theologies to provide assurance for their own explanations of this idea, Bultmann is like a man on a high hill, contemplating an extensive and complicated landscape, yet able to rely upon the resources within himself to elucidate what he sees. And in dealing with the theme of *pistis* the resource to which he most evidently turns is a highly developed sense that the encounter between Jesus and individual man as set forth by the evangelist is not something to be understood in generalities or symbolism but is to be seen as a most pressing, existential engagement. That engagement is, for Bultmann, most particularly marked in the arena of self-understanding. What is at stake here is the discovery not so much of one's idiosyncrasies as of one's true status in a God-created universe, and since Bultmann takes this to be the central preoccupation of the fourth gospel he develops his comments accordingly.

When, for instance, early in the prologue the evangelist proclaims the *Logos* to be 'the light of men' (1:4) Bultmann argues that this is not the light which 'enables man to orientate himself in respect of objects' but is, rather, 'the means whereby man understands himself in his world' (p 40) and is 'the brightness in which I find myself here and now' (p 41). Brightness is the 'illumined condition of my existence, of my own existence' (p 41). Where Greek literature and the Old Testament attached the image of light to happiness, to salvation and to the realm of the divine, Bultmann focuses on personal illumination:

> For just as 'life' *necessarily included* the *definitive understanding of the self* that knows *no further question or mystery* (italics mine), so the 'light' for which man longs as this definitive state of enlightenment necessarily includes freedom from death, from the fate that makes existence sheerly unintelligible ... 'Light' therefore comes to mean revelation (p 43)

and the incarnate *Logos* is the Revealer who illuminates existence.

But this Revealer is not just another historical figure to be read about at any time. Verses 14 to 18 of the prologue proclaim not only that 'the Logos was made flesh', but that 'we saw his glory, the glory as only-begotten Son of the Father', and, near the end, they assert that 'no one has ever seen God'. Confronting these verses, Bultmann reflects on what he calls the offence in the words which posit an incarnate *Logos*. The essential point he makes is that human beings who await a revelation, which will clarify the ultimate significance of their lives, tend to look beyond the worldly, away from the quotidian to something glorious and transcendent. Gnostics offer passage out of a dark world to a direct encounter with a supra-natural deity. Philosophers prescribe the organised operations of mind as a way out of daily mire into the contemplation of supreme and timeless being. But the proclamation by the evangelist 'the Logos was made flesh' is, among other things, a warning that for man 'to attempt to make God into the direct object of his vision is to lose the true idea of God' (p 81). Man will have no true idea of God until he begins by having a true understanding of himself and of his own identity. The road of the gnostic or of the philosopher does not lead him to such an understanding. What he must do is to yield in faith to the reality and to the implications of something which happened in the arena of 'transitoriness, helplessness and vanity' (p 62), namely, the incarnation of the Logos. This incarnate Logos:

> sets each man before the decisive question whether he will accept or reject *him* ... the confrontation with the Incarnate Revealer is the decisive eschatological situation (p 66).

The character of this decisive situation is pushed into further relief by the assertion 'we saw his glory, the glory as only-begotten Son of the Father'. As he looks across the generations from the days of the evangelist to his own Bultmann sees each era tied to its predecessor and yet, in its day, having to deal with exactly the same living issue. For the 'we saw' of the evangelist is not simply the report handed in by an eyewitness – there were, after all, unbelieving eyewitnesses – nor is it the view obtained by a philosophic or a mystical contemplation evoked by particular circumstances. It is the confession of those who, unscandalised by the fact that the Logos became flesh and, furthermore, convinced that the Logos is there not as idea but as actuality, 'allow him to be for themselves what he is' (p 69). What they saw in that singular human figure was the unique 'glory' of God. They were not, as eyewitnesses, the guarantors of the truth of a particular historical event nor was it any part of their agenda to offer palatable interpretations of their response to Jesus. Rather, they were exemplars of an experience and, for Bultmann, this experience, voiced by the evangelist, this encounter with the 'glory' of God must, in fidelity to what was written, be taken out of the text and faced up to in every generation by anyone laying claim to being a believer (pp 67–70). That is, the words of the text are as much for now as for the day on which they were written and they put the one who encounters them into the position of having to take a stand.

What this might mean is shown in the description of the meeting between Jesus and Nicodemus (3:1–8). The general thrust is not in doubt. There is a call for a fundamental reorientation of a man if he is to be saved and this involves a repudiation of his human origin in favour of a new birth which will be an emergence from *pneuma*. It is an idea which baffles Nicodemus, for while he can deal with a this-worldly scene, summed up in the term *sarx*, he cannot relate at all to an other-worldly milieu. Yet Jesus insists, 'That which is born of the *sarx* is *sarx*, that which is born of the *pneuma* is *pneuma*'.

To these alternatives Bultmann brings a perspective shaped by his own characteristic stance:

> ... *sarx* refers to the nothingness of man's whole existence; to the fact that man is ultimately a stranger to his fate and to his own acts; that, as he is now, he does not enjoy authentic existence, whether he makes himself aware of the fact or whether he conceals it from himself. Correspondingly *pneuma* refers to the miracle of a mode of being in which man enjoys authentic existence, in which he understands himself and knows that he is no longer threatened by nothingness (p 141).

Man is only truly a man when he lives a life goal directed from his rebirth in the *pneuma*, and this for Bultmann is a recurring category of understanding, one which leads him therefore to interpret the words of Jesus to Nicodemus as yet another indication of the primary theme that the coming of the Revealer 'restores to man the freedom which he has lost, the freedom to take possession of his own authenticity' (p 160).

Clearly, what is touched upon here is the most fundamental and the most disturbing of issues for human beings, fundamental because a relationship with God is involved, disturbing because such a relationship cannot be built up 'from within the sphere of human works' (p 192). Just as a *milieu* unanchored in the quotidian was evoked by the words to Nicodemus concerning the *pneuma* whose coming and going is subject to no measurement or human prediction, so it is proclaimed to the Samaritan woman that God must be worshipped *en pneumati kai aletheia*, 'in spirit and in truth'. What is in view here is the idea of God as 'a miraculous being who deals wonderfully' (p 191) with believers, with those 'taken out of this worldly existence and set in the eschatological existence' (p 191). 'There can be no true relationship between man and God unless it first be grounded in God's dealings with man' (p 192). Any other kind of relationship is doomed to be false because, devised humanly, it must be locked into the only context which human beings ordinarily know. Hence the disturbance to human modes which must occur if the grounds for a true relationship are to be uncovered and, more importantly, entered into.

There is no way to avoid such disturbance, and this is strikingly evident in the comments of Bultmann on verses 27–51 of the sixth chapter when the theme of the 'bread of life' is articulated. If Nicodemus could misconstrue the meaning of rebirth, if the Samaritan woman could only think of water as something to be carried away in a pitcher, so, here, the term food can similarly be misunderstood. Of course it is the evangelist who sets down in each case the arena of potential misunderstanding, but it is Bultmann who, as it were, chooses the yardstick by which the key terms in that arena, namely rebirth, water and bread are to be interpreted. It is not merely a case of failure on the part of Nicodemus and the Samaritan woman to grasp that there is a symbolism involved, that earthly water can betoken heavenly realities. For Bultmann the point of resorting in the fourth gospel to a word such as 'bread' is to issue a reminder that to reach the things of heaven it is not enough simply to start from the worldly *milieu*. There are situations where bread can indeed be a figure of realities which are accessible to human beings. But this is not the kind of situation envisaged by the evangelist for whom one of the follies of 'man' is to imagine 'that he has criteria at his disposal to which revelation must conform to get recognition' (p 228). Knowledge of the ultimate truths cannot be sown 'within the security of human judgement' (p 231). Hence the declaration 'no one can come to me unless the Father who sent me draws him' (p 144). That is:

> ... faith becomes possible when one abandons hold on one's own security, and to abandon one's security is nothing else than to let oneself be drawn by the Father (p 231).

And the object to which one is drawn is the one who describes himself as 'the bread of life':

> The whole paradox of the revelation is contained in this reply. Whoever wants something from him must know that he has to receive Jesus himself. Whoever approaches him with a desire for the gift of life must learn that Jesus is *himself* the gift he really wants. Jesus *gives* the bread of life in that he *is* the bread of life (p 227).

But this is a reality accessible only to a faith which 'has no support outside itself ... (with a) security which can rest only in the object of faith' (p 232).

But if one must leave humanly-grounded security, then to what should one turn? In essence, one has no choice but to go to the view of reality offered by the words of Jesus, and the point is not to assess the words themselves, weighing their validity but to uncover what they offer. So, for example, there is the following:

> You know me and you know where I am from. I did not come on my own account but the One who sent me is true, the one whom you do not know. I have known him because I come from him and it is he who sent me (7:28).

The declaration that they know him and know where he comes from is 'irony' (p 297) because their knowledge of who he is serves:

> to conceal the very thing which it is important to know. Their knowledge serves only to prevent them from recognising Jesus; he cannot be the Messiah because they know where he comes from (pp 297–8).

But Jesus goes farther:

> I do not seek my own glory. There is the one who is seeking and who is passing judgement (8:50)

> If I should glorify myself that glory of mine is nothing. It is my father who glorifies me. He is the one you talk about because he is our God. And you have not known him. But I know him. If I were to say to you I do not know I would be, like you, a teller of lies. But I know him and I hold to his word (8:54–55).

And this point of view is supplemented in the course of the eighth chapter:

> If God were your father, you would love me, for I came from and am arrived from God. I did not come of myself, but he sent me. Why do you not acknowledge what I have to say? Because you are not able to hear my word. You are from your father the devil and you want to accomplish the desires of that father of yours. He has been a killer of men from the beginning and he has taken no stand in the truth because there is no truth in him. When he speaks, the lie he speaks is from what is his own, because he *is* a liar and so is his father. But because I speak the truth you put no trust in me (8:42–46).

In all of this there is a:

> colossal claim that only he, an ordinary mortal, whose origin is known to them, knows God and, moreover, that he has been sent by God (p 299).

But Jesus insists on making such assertions about himself, and thereby sets up between himself and his audiences a seemingly irreconcilable conflict.

Having emphasised this conflict Bultmann does not rest, however, but seeks to explore what is at issue, and here he resorts to a principle, voiced, for instance, by John Calvin, that while a distinction may be drawn between knowledge of God and knowledge of self these may not be had in isolation from one another (cf. Calvin, *Institutes* 1.1.1).

> It is impossible to gain a real understanding of what someone is saying unless one has some relationship to the subject matter which he is trying to express, and this applies equally to the word of the Revealer. If the revelation consists in a calling into question of the natural man, then it will be

> unintelligible to a man who is not aware of his own questionableness. Thus it is impossible for anyone who is convinced of his own security to understand the revelation; and it is equally impossible to understand it by means of a neutral assessment and objective evaluation of its claims. For all man's understanding is conditioned by his understanding of himself, and it is precisely this which is put in question by the revelation (p 317).

Nor is it just any mode of self-understanding which is invoked here. Rather, only one kind of self-understanding is deemed to be possible in the light of the fact that there is a God and that this God has sent Jesus not so much to reveal him as to *be* Him '... only in him is God visible and accessible' (p 345). There is, thus, a unique opportunity, one to be grasped without delay:

> I am only a little time with you, you will look for me and you cannot come to where I am (7:33–34).

Regarding this, Bultmann comments:

> Thus it is the historical contingency of the revelation which throws this terrible weight of responsibility on the hearer of the word. For the revelation is not generally available, but presents itself to man only at a certain limited time of its own choosing. It does not consist in universal truths, which can be grasped at all times and for all times, nor in dogma which one could invoke at any time but it confronts man in time, *it is in every case the present moment in a personal history* (italics mine). Should one neglect the opportunity, when confronted with the challenge of the Revealer, then the verdict applies too late (p 308).

And this urgent *now* operates not just for those physically present among the Jews listening to Jesus but for every human being in the ensuing ages. Prevailing truths, dogmatic systems, the tendencies to make tractable everything on the human scene, all these will be irrelevant in face of the opportunity of that now to yield to what is on offer in Revelation. The one who yields may be said to enter a true mode of being while the one who turns away is condemned to live a lie. The personal decision is crucial, because, in effect, one is what one believes:

> ... the decision of unbelief constitutes man's being ... unbelief is the very core of the unbeliever's being ... there is no neutral area of being, as it were, behind unbelief (p 317).

Equally, belief establishes 'man' in a true and living relationship with his God 'and so brings him to his authenticity' (p 321). Believing man is truly a man. Believing man is the one who has passed beyond the supportive resources of the world and who by entering into a living orientation towards the incarnate Logos finds at last his proper and self-acknowledged place in the divine scheme of things.

The reality of that place will not be a lonely one for a person who yields to the perspectives intimated by the incarnate Logos. There will be an enveloping protection there, summed up by the image of the Good Shepherd. The 'good' in that title:

> refers not only to his absoluteness and decisiveness but also to his 'being for ...'. This in itself already indicates that the title pre-supposes or demands a self-understanding of man, which takes cognisance of man's being as 'being which is dependent on ...' (p 364). Out of that recognised dependence, however, will come the sense of what is implied by Jesus in the comparison drawn between the true shepherd and the hired hand, between the one who will lay down his life for his sheep and the one who runs away when the wolf comes in to attack. '... the explanation of the hireling's behaviour ... makes it clear that true being for others must be grounded in a mutual relationship' (p 371). Such a relationship is not really possible between the paid worker and the sheep. What is required is the attitude which can only exist in the reciprocity between the flock and the good shepherd ... they mean something to him, as he does to them. But this also implies that he has a claim on them (p 371).

They will discharge that claim by following him on his terms. And this for Bultmann is a way of proclaiming that:

> the security which man finds in the Revealer is not the sort of security which can be bought and bargained for; it can be attained only by giving oneself to him as his own (p 371).

The sheep do not form:

> a society of doubters and critics. On the contrary ... the sheep recognise the shepherd with instinctive certainty, and therefore we are told: 'And the sheep hear his voice'. They have long known him, and so immediately recognise him. His 'own' recognise the Revealer with the same unfailing certainty with which the sheep recognise their shepherd (p 373).

This recognition is 'an inward realisation in which the knower's whole existence is determined by that which he knows, namely, God' (p 381). It is a secure knowledge, this disposition of faith:

> because it is a simple act of hearing and obeying; if it sought for reasons it would immediately lose its security. As the faith which hears, it is itself the proof of its security; by accepting the witness it confirms the truth of God. It is itself a proof of its security but only because it is the faith which *hears,* i.e. because it finds its security in him whom it believes, i.e. its security has in fact its ground outside itself, which is why it only finds security in hearing (p 386).

To sum up here. The words of Jesus, the Good Shepherd:

> can be believed only when they are heard as a personal address ... Man is not asked to believe in a set of dogmas on the authority of a preacher without credentials; what is demanded of man is a faith which experiences Jesus' words as they affect man himself ... man must allow himself to be questioned by Jesus' words, must allow the security of his previous understanding of himself to be shattered, and must accept the revelation of his true existence (p 391).

All this, in fact, constitutes 'the eschatalogical event'. This is an encounter with Jesus which may not be described in historical terms or within the linear unfolding of time. Rather, it is something which happens in an uninhibited 'now' where a believer lets go into the reality of the Revealer and, as a consequence, has an inner life independent of the intrusions of the world. Such a letting go is essential, for 'whoever wants to linger by the figure of the "historical Jesus" must soon become aware that he is without him' (p 493). Thus Jesus:

> has not brought doctrines or ideas, which independent of him have since become the common heritage of history and behind which he himself disappeared. He is 'glorified'. *i.e.* he has become the eschatological event, beyond which history cannot go, itself the end for the whole of history. In the acknowledgement or repudiation of him is afforded for all time the decision as to whether history is life or death (p 492).

This prospect of life or death is the particular scenario facing each particular person whether contemporary or not with Jesus, and decisive in what is to happen to the individual is the attitude each takes to all that constitutes 'the world'. That is, the putting of one's trust in the Revealer occurs within somebody who is in the world, and both the challenge and the hazard for such a one is to avoid being of the world.

Which is the point, as Bultmann sees it, of the prayers of Jesus for his followers, for 'his own':

> I do not make a request concerning the world, but concerning those whom you have given me, because they are yours and everything of mine is yours and everything of yours is mine and I shall be glorified in them. And I am no longer in the world and they are in the world and I am coming to you. Holy father, look after them ... (17:9–11).

The prayer goes on to say that he has given them 'your word, and yet the world has hated them'. The reason for the hatred is the recognition that the believers, few as they may be, are, in effect, a new community, one which has actually separated itself from the world. Indeed:

> this very hatred is the criterion for the community as to whether it does in fact no longer belong to the world, as Jesus does not belong to it (p 507).

The task of the believing community is to be the place where 'the world is annulled *within* the world' (p 508). This annulment can only occur when the believer takes the Revealer on trust and yields to what is declared to be present, namely, the glory of God himself.

Thus, Bultmann's reading chooses to bypass doctrines, dogmas and institutions. It suggests that to cast any backward look to the historical Jesus is in a sense to make a deal with him in the world's terms, and this is to run counter to what is demanded. In the aftermath of Revelation it is now the case that each possessor of an essentially incommunicable 'I' is in precisely the same situation as that of the person in Palestine who once stood looking at and listening to this itinerant preacher Jesus. The choice does not change. It is to accept him for what he affirms himself to be or else to turn back into the familiar habits and byways of the world. It is the most fundamental of existential situations.

But when one makes the choice for the Revealer it is for the truth of things 'and the truth will make you free' (8:62), which is a way of saying that one will in truth surrender one's previous self understanding (p 437), and one's existence consequently will be illuminated. However, that is not the end of the matter, as the farewell discourses of Jesus make plain. Even if allowances are made for the fact that the attitude of faith in the Revealer exists, as it were, in an expanding 'now', the basis of that faith has been the sheer palpable impact of the historically present Jesus of Palestine. That presence, for the disciples, has been the launching pad for their ability to trust. In a sense, therefore, they depend on that historical presence. But in the farewell discourse they are confronted by the reality that the historical Revealer is about to leave them, with the result that they will not be able to turn to him, to touch base with him as a way of boosting their continuance in the self-understanding brought about by faith:

> They have to learn that the Revealer has not come to be at their disposal through their faith. Jesus, in whom they believed, disappears from them, and they are left with no security ... (Which raises the question of) how can their relationship with him be retained in the face of this isolation? (p 524).

The answer is given in the incident of the washing of the feet at the Last Supper and in the words which follow. First is the act itself. It is an episode joltingly at variance with what one would normally expect in a milieu where master and follower are assembled. Indeed, lest anyone should miss the astonishing reversal of what one would properly anticipate, the evangelist describes the disconcerted reactions of Peter, at first refusing to let his feet be washed and then, if ablutions there must be, offering all of himself. The two reactions earn a rebuke, and Jesus goes on to assert that just as he has lived for them so they, as his followers, must live for each other.

That the scene has an important symbolic character has long been recognised but there has been a frequent tendency to regard the symbolism in a generalised, even bland, way, as anodyne, almost, as approval of motherhood or patriotism. Bultmann will have none of this. For him the episode has to be understood in terms of the existential imperative in every encounter between Jesus and potential disciple. The repeated demand is to be trusted, to be accepted. But at the last supper a further stage has been reached because as Jesus declares to his disciples, 'you are clean'. The washing of the feet is a practical, blunt, unromantic token of what has been available during the public life of Jesus, a service, an offering of benefit, but now those who accepted it are clean. As Jesus will say to them later 'already you are clean because of the word I have spoken to you' (15:3) a statement which evokes from Bultmann the following comment:

> Thus the *word* has cleansed them. His service is accomplished in the word which he speaks and which, by speaking it, he himself is. For his word is not a doctrine that could be separated from his person, a complex of ideas with general validity. Rather, he is himself encountered as the word, in all the separate things he says; because he is the Revealer, the presence of God – in the form of the flesh, with death as his destiny – becomes evident in him. Thus to accept his service means to believe, to accept the disintegration of all the standards which the world uses to judge what is great and divine. Whoever can do this is from the world and thus 'pure' ... Whoever accepts his act of service, i.e. whoever believes his word, needs no other means of salvation (p 471).

But it is the second element to the symbolism of this episode during this last supper which is especially important for the situation of the disciples who have broken free of the world. What they must now do is to treat one another as he has treated them. Again, this is not to be understood in a generalised and unfocused manner.

> ..... Jesus' work is not something lying open to view as an objective achievement, or as a factor to be taken into account in world history; and this is true, whether we are looking at it as part of our cultural heritage or whether we are looking at the historical figure of Jesus as such. If we look at what he did simply in order to find 'what it all adds up to' we will fail to see him ... He is only to be seen in that *which on each occasion he is for me*. Thus the imperative only holds good for the sphere in which Jesus' service has been received – only the man who is loved can himself love; and its fulfilment is not by performing a work analogous to his but by readiness for the same existing for the other (p 475).

That is 'love is not personal affection but the being of the disciple for his neighbour' (p 540). In short, the opening twenty verses of the thirteenth chapter describe 'the founding of the community and the law of its being' (p 479).

Bultmann feels the need to stress that when immediately after the washing of the feet, Jesus lays down as a 'new' command that they 'love one another as I have loved you' this is not to be taken merely as an ethical principle, one established to replace the presence of Jesus. 'In that case the future would lie in one's hands to be grasped' and the past which included the Revealer's presence (p 526) in the world 'would become a matter of indifference for the future, even if it still had educational importance' (p 526). This comment is made under the influence of the strongly existential perspective within which Bultmann works. And so he goes on:

> The significance of the *past* lies in the fact that the encounter with Jesus was experienced as his service which made the believer free; thus the significance of the *future* can only be that in it this freedom is brought to fruition. And this takes place in the fulfilment of the Command of love ... Only if they are themselves loving do they who belong to him remain in the experience of his love ... In their action, his act is present ... The association with Jesus, therefore, is not realised by possessing articles of knowledge or dogmas, nor in institutions or experiences of individual piety but in 'pupil-hood', in obedience to the command of love (pp 526–528).

And so from outside, from the point of view of the world there will be the new and strange spectacle of a community of believers whose love for one another is grounded in the divine love. From the perspective of the believing community, however, this mutual love will be the practical outcome of what happens in the expanded 'now', in the eschatological moment when each member of that community yields in faith to the Revealer.

This theme of the believing, mutually loving community is enhanced in the farewell discourses by the perspective of himself offered by Jesus when he describes himself as the 'true vine' (15: 1):

> To understand the discourse aright, we must realise that it does not draw attention to the vine with regard to its fruit, or to the wine that it bestows, but simply to the tree itself with its shoots, and that the shoots are perfused with vital power from it; from the tree they receive their power to grow and bear fruit, and they wither away if they are cut off from it: the vine is the tree of life (p 530).

Hence the injunction of Jesus to remain 'in me', for it will then be possible for the believer, who is no longer dependent upon the kind of security offered by the world, to mark his new condition by fulfilling the demand 'to bear fruit'. When, in the context of the vine and its branches, Jesus says 'remain in me (15:4) he is talking of 'holding on loyally to the decision once taken, and one can hold on to it only by continually going through it again' (p 536). In other words, Bultmann is suggesting that to avoid the possibility of faith and love being understood statically as conditions sufficient unto themselves the parable of the vine, with its emphasis on bearing fruit and on remaining 'in me' evokes continuity rather than rest in a continuing eschatological 'now'.

JOHN ASHTON

In his book *Understanding the Fourth Gospel,*[22] John Ashton begins with the following comment:

> There are many ways of approaching the Fourth Gospel. One may turn to it for enlightenment, for inspiration, for encouragement or consolation, for theological proofs (the old-fashioned rod-and-line exegesis), for evidence about early Jewish Christianity, for insight into the mind of Jesus, and much more besides. One may approach the work as an historian, a theologian, a simple Christian, or an enquiring unbeliever. What the Gospel reveals of itself will be coloured, even controlled, by the interest one brings to it. There is no disinterested reading. Nor by the same token is there any disinterested writing ... (p 3).

All this, and especially the matter of a particular interest or bias, is confirmed for Ashton by the dominant trends of Johannine scholarship from the eighteenth century up to and indeed beyond the time of Bultmann. The question of authorship, for instance, was a central preoccupation, for:

> if the author of the Gospel should turn out to be someone other than the apostle John, or the beloved disciple (the two were generally identified), then the credibility of his testimony, on which the Gospel itself insists so strongly ('He who saw it has borne witness – his testimony is true, and he knows that he tells the truth' (19:35)), must be severely reduced, if not destroyed completely (p 15).

Hence, for ideological reasons, and, in many instances to maintain the security of personal convictions, there was a deep wish in some scholars to uphold the thesis not only of apostolic authorship, but also of the derivation of this gospel from the other three. With such a thesis one could then hope to guarantee the truth and even the divine inspiration of the fourth gospel. In other words, belief and theological stance demanded of some that they consider no alternative except the view that the gospel is a haven of eternal truths set down at divine behest either by an apostle or by the beloved disciple. This in turn could only mean that the character of such a haven would itself determine what went into the act of reading the text.

Ashton, however, is not concerned, as, say, Thomas Aquinas would be, to engage in a reading where text and theology, theology and text, provide authoritative and approved answers to particular questions. Instead, he looks elsewhere for a viable route to what is in the gospel. That is, in writing his long and erudite work he takes the fourth gospel not as a foundation for personal belief but as an historical document of exceptional interest. In this he is encouraged by the outpouring of major books and articles deriving from the movement, established in the late nineteenth century in Germany and focusing on the study of religion, any religion, as primarily an historical phenomenon. One outcome of such a movement was to encourage the examination of the fourth gospel in terms of its origins, to seek an understanding of the contents of the work from a consideration of where this gospel stands in the development of early Christianity. This involved, among other activities, a hunt for sources. To what extent, for example, was the gospel text shaped by the synoptics, by Paul, by Gnosticism, by John the Baptist, by Jewish mysticism? This search for what is in the background was itself boosted by a growing conviction that while one could document a stylistic unity and thematic coherence in the text there was, nevertheless, a clear awkwardness at many points in the transition between episodes. Hence many felt able to move things around. Bultmann was not the only scholar to transpose and to relocate verses and chapter sections of the gospel in order to make his own sense of it. He had predecessors in this and he had devoted followers, and in the process the gospel was so pulled apart that for some the text as we have it could only be understood as the work of background authors, of a brilliant re-writer and of a more-or-less competent ecclesiastical editor. And all this was proposed on the basis of interpretative techniques ranging from the literary to the theological.

Although critical of some results of this approach to the fourth gospel Ashton is in fundamental sympathy with the aims of the enterprise, and so in the first part of his book he reads the text with the eyes of a scholar whose interests are mainly historical. Thus, in a chapter entitled 'Religious Dissent' he asserts the point that no accurate understanding of the gospel is possible without a lively sense of the Jewish *milieu* in which the various incidents are centred. When Jesus declares 'my Father is working still and I am working' (5:17–18), when he says 'before Abraham was, I am' (8:58–59), when Jews assert 'we stone you for blasphemy, because you, being a man, make yourself God' (10:33) such words are not uttered in a transcendent domain but in a very specific context, some details of which may be described and some speculated upon:

> Only by abstracting altogether from the circumstances of the Gospel's composition and treating it as nothing but a repository of revealed doctrine or as a timeless call to faith, as Bultmann does, can one fail to recognise in these hot-tempered exchanges the type of family row in which the participants face one another across the room of a house which all have shared and which all have called home (p 151).

But in consequence of this point of view it becomes important to seek the identity of those described by the evangelist as 'the Jews'. Is this a reference to the Jewish authorities, to the general population of Judaea and, especially, of Jerusalem, or does it point to all Jews including those of the Diaspora? The problem does not rest here but turns instead into something larger until the act of reading the gospel itself becomes a process whereby in seeking answers to fundamental questions, such as the content of the text, its author, its envisaged audience and its genre, it almost becomes necessary to spend more time on the workings of current theory and hypothesis than on the reading of the text.

At this point one is into very complicated territory indeed, given both the number of theorists as well as the absence of foreseeable hope either of verification or of corroboration of what they propose. In essence – and with due allowance for variation and nuance – what is suggested is an unfolding scenario marked initially by assembled miracle stories, by accounts of the passion, and by various sayings all having to do with Jesus. Such memorabilia become the source of controversy between those in Jewish circles who believe in them and those who do not. There follows a 'them-and-us' situation, leading eventually to expulsions from the synagogues and to the determination of the followers of Jesus to spread their word more effectively. Somewhere here comes a genius who takes previous materials – the records, such as they are, of Jesus – and who pulls them together into a work characterised by stylistic and thematic unity. This work is itself later subjected to an operation at the hands of an editor, who inserts material such as the allegory of the vine and also that of the door and the shepherd and who thereby brings to completion something present in what many scholars refer to as the Johannine Community. In short, the fourth gospel and its strata are taken to have emerged from and continue to reflect a specific and highly charged milieu which generated both the reference points of the text and the urgency of its organization.

This way of reading, this focus on origins makes it possible for Ashton to create a sense of the importunate character of the key themes of a gospel which, after all, emerged from a scenario of clashes, of bitter debate, of recrimination, of unassuageable oppositions. The evangelist, like his brethren, being a convert to the message of a man who was killed for what he proclaimed has no room in his thinking for anything bland. His writing grows out of a conviction of the peril looming over all those who refuse to acknowledge the significance of Jesus. To convey the reality of this peril he lays stress upon those insistent oppositions attending the footsteps of every contemporary: another world and this world, life and death, light and darkness, truth and falsehood, welcome and condemnation. In this view each human being is thrust into a conflict obliging him to make the choice which will yield life, light and welcome or else their grim and terrible opposites. Because of 'the fundamental bipolarity of John's vision of the world' (p 231) there is an abiding and inescapable requirement to deal with the 'option for or against Christ in the lifetime of each individual' (p 223). And in this perspective the evangelist turns to:

> the experience of the Christian community. They too will be challenged by the Jews and the world. They too will see themselves pitted against the forces of darkness.

There is, in other words, a pressing, challenging character to the Jesus evoked by the evangelist:

> He does not belong to this world at all: it is almost true to say that he enters it with the purpose of leaving it, or descends in order to ascend. He is a pre-existent divine being, whose real home is in heaven. He enters an alien world with an unprecedented confidence and assurance, knowing precisely who he is, where he comes from and where he is going. And this too is his message, that he knows both his origin and his destiny, and because of this knowledge he enjoys a special relationship with the Father that verges on total identification (p 239).

Yet, for Ashton, this sense of identity as set out in the fourth gospel can only be understood in the specific context of Judaism. That is, Ashton feels an obligation to distinguish between what he calls historical and existential intelligibility (p 243, n. 9), between particulars which are unto themselves and moments or events which for all times and in all places touch upon perennial and universal questions of human life and destiny. For him, the point of the distinction is:

> that the intelligibility of the Christian gospel depended from the first upon the framework in which it was set, that is, the framework of contemporary Judaism ... So it is important to insist that the Fourth Gospel shares this intelligibility, this rootedness in a rich cultural heritage (pp 243–244).

This being so, Ashton devotes nearly a quarter of his book to an extensive and deeply impressive historical analysis of key titles given to Jesus, namely, Messiah, Son of God and Son of Man. Because such titles are necessary ingredients out of which the portrait of Jesus in the gospel is forged it follows that the act of reading the text cannot proceed in any effective way if one does not have an informed sense of what these labels, these references to Messiah, Son of God and Son of Man could actually signify.

Thus, in regard to the term 'Messiah' as used in the fourth gospel one needs first to think of the significance of the word for Jesus. Then one has to make allowances for the successive editions and reworkings of the Johannine text, and one must especially remember the early period:

> in which the Johannine Christians, still very much associated with the local synagogue, are distinguished from their fellow Jews by their profound belief that, in Andrew's words, 'we have found the Messiah' (p 246).

Of course there are glimpses in texts other than the fourth gospel of this theme of Jesus as Messiah:

> All of these start, as Jesus himself did, from a recognizably Jewish faith: but all of them – even Matthew, the most Jewish – end with a belief that is ultimately irreconcilable with establishment Judaism, because all, though with different emphasis, preach a Christ who is very much more than a Messiah (p 251).

This is clear, by implication, in the fourth gospel when the Baptist having denied that he is the Messiah or Elijah or the Prophet goes on to affirm that there is one on whom the Spirit has come down from heaven and who is the Chosen One of God. If one adds to that the miracles such as the changing of water into wine – miracles prompting the question 'when the Messiah appears will he do more signs than this man has done?' – then the ground is set by the evangelist for the recognition that:

> Jesus fulfills in every respect the eschatological expectations of the Jews. For all the mysteriousness and otherness of his person, he is set firmly in the context of a living tradition. He is not utterly unintelligible and remote; the area of his intelligibility is limited and defined in the lapidary formula drawn from one of the most ancient of Christian confessions: 'Jesus is the Messiah' (p 279).

And yet this matter of the Judaic context requires close scrutiny if only because of the interaction between it and the evangelist. There is, for instance, a time gap between the living historical figure of Jesus the Jew and the process by which the writer of the fourth gospel comes to terms with that figure. Indeed, Ashton, like others before him, is convinced that in reading the gospel one must be conscious of the play between the historical Jesus and the Christ proclaimed by the preachers and writers of first-generation Christians. The problem for him is clearly of a kind that would occur to a historian (p 40) namely the question about the extent to which the status of the Christ affirmed in the gospel corresponds to what was actually proclaimed during the public lifetime of Jesus. This is something which is important to him, as it was to earlier scholars, and the concern obviously arises from the wish not to stray, as it were, from a strictly historical milieu. As a way of dealing with it, Ashton speaks of two levels of meaning, that which would be picked up by Jesus' hearers, the Jews, and that reserved for the readers of the gospel. There is first an obscure revelation and then there is its interpreter. A classic example is in the second chapter:

> Jesus replied to them 'Destroy this temple and in three days I will raise it up'. The Jews said 'It has taken forty-six years to build this temple, and you will raise it up in three days?' But he was speaking of the temple of his body. And so when he was raised from the dead his disciples remembered that he had said this; and they believed the scripture and the word which Jesus had spoken (2.19–22).

The puzzlement of an actual audience is succeeded later among the disciples by an understanding arising out of unspecified scriptural declarations combined with the memory of what had been said by Jesus himself. His words about raising up the temple after three days are now seen to have a reference which no listening Jew could have grasped:

> On this basis, then, we are entitled to assume, I think, that all the other riddling saying where the audience catches the straightforward meaning but miss the esoteric are likewise intended to be read on two levels (p 417).

But to what extent is the notion of the two levels of understanding to be applied, given that both are centred on the greater or lesser intelligibility of recorded events? To put the issue another way, did Lazarus rise from the dead as the evangelist declares? If a historian should feel obliged to say that he did not 'does this mean that the Gospel narrative has no truth and no validity without historical verifiability?' (p 427). Ashton quotes a remark by Ludwig Wittgenstein that Christianity:

> is not based on a historical truth; rather it offers us a (historical) narrative and says, now believe. But not, believe this narrative with the belief appropriate to a historical narrative, rather: believe through thick and thin (p 427).

Ashton would consider this 'a fair assessment of the thrust of the Fourth Gospel, and perhaps of the other three as well' (p 427).. And he goes on to add:

> Theologically speaking, one may be justified in allowing the Synoptic Gospels to shoulder the burden of historicity: in that case all that the committed Christian needs to say about the Fourth Gospel is that it is about a historical figure, Jesus of Nazareth. What it says of him is not history in any meaningful sense, but story – story plus interpretation (p 427).

Actually, Ashton is willing to go farther and to speak of 'the fourth evangelist's frequent disregard of the facts' (p 428). This is not to say that the evangelist is either untruthful or unreliable. One has, rather, to look to his purposes:

> Certainly he wants to preserve a valuable tradition and to keep its source in mind; but his main concern is to offer a new reading, one that transcends any understanding that was possible in the time of Jesus himself (p 432).
>
> The evangelists are not writing history at all (p 432).
>
> Unlike the ordinary historian, whose main aim is to write the truth about the past, the evangelists are chiefly interested in projecting a message of immediate relevance to their own present (p 433).

In short:

> … the Johannine prophet has welded tradition and belief into the shining affirmation of the finished Gospel. If the result appears new and extraordinary this is because his religious genius impelled him to disclose more and more of what he called 'the truth', that is to say the revelation of Jesus. What he saw and what he inherited are now contained in the book he wrote. Attempt to prise them apart and the consequence will be at best what Stevens calls somewhere 'an inert savoir' (p 434).

In this view, then, the reader of the Fourth gospel is dealing with a writer who is himself, as it were, a reader of a past which has been made present to him in the form of memories and records and inescapable questions. A reader of the fourth gospel is, therefore, an interpreter of an interpreter. Furthermore, when one takes into account the characteristics of what Ashton calls 'the gospel genre' one must add that the reader is the interpreter not of someone who is primarily an historian but rather of someone who, starting from actual events, has gone on to construct what in effect is a living and ever renewable work of art, one which reposes in, but is unconfined by, the specifics out of which it arose. So when Ashton comes to consider the descriptions in the gospel of the passion and resurrection he sees the evangelist 'gradually eliminating all the more painful and shameful associations of the death of Jesus' (p 496). The crucifixion, for example, is presented in terms of the 'departure' and the 'lifting up' of the Son. The vocabulary of the evangelist is concerned more with the meaning of events than with the events themselves. Indeed, Ashton remarks that:

> Jesus 'was crucified under Pontius Pilate' is arguably the only genuinely historical element in the Christian creed, the remaining articles being dogmatic additions beyond the reach of the historian's investigations (p 492).

The evangelist is in fact guiding the reader:

> to *see past* the physical reality of Jesus' death to its true significance: the re-ascent of the Son of Man to his true home in heaven (p 496).

The focus is on the glory of Jesus:

> It is as if the evangelist is gradually eliminating all the more painful and shameful associations of the death ... (p 496).
>
> ... What the world sees as a defeat is really a triumph, and what the world sees as the end of Jesus' hopes and aspirations is really the beginning of his ascent into glory (*ibid*).

Similar considerations are brought to bear even more pressingly on the matter of the resurrection, for while the historical reality of the crucifixion may be affirmed it is, for Ashton, much less easy to do so in regard to the claim that Jesus rose literally from the dead. Of course there is a resurrection narrative or, as Ashton and others would have it, there are four stories brought together in the text centering on the risen Lord. But 'nowhere, it has to be said, does the evangelist move farther from history than in these four episodes' (p 502).

> Only a reader whose own imaginative responses have been blunted by familiarity or credulity will be left undisturbed by the shift from the elegance and finesse of, say, the farewell discourses to the fairy-tale atmosphere of the resurrection stories. It is like finding Hans Christian Andersen hand in hand with Soren Kierkegaard (p 511).

There are too many oddities in the account, such as a:

> corpse that apparantly unaided, slips out of its burial wrappings, angels who ask a single question and disappear without waiting for an answer, a man whom Mary now knows to be Jesus rejecting physical contact because he is about to ascend into heaven. And so on (p 512).

Such stories, in Ashton's view, can hardly be credible at the historical level and it is not even clear that the evangelist himself could have believed them. Yet that does not make a nonsense of what he writes. If John invented the story of doubting Thomas:

> it was not, surely, to stimulate his readers to reflect upon the tangibilitv of risen bodies, but to impress upon them the need for faith (p 514).

In other words, remembering the point made by Origen concerning the spiritual meaning of this gospel, one should look in the resurrection narrative for light on the great themes of faith, of the glory of God and of the modes of responsiveness to all that the historical Jesus signifies.

Being neither theological tract nor historical text but something of both and something uniquely itself, the fourth gospel embodies the reflections of the evangelist upon the meaning of the life and death of Jesus. That meaning can be summed up as revelation. But revelation of what? Put that way, one is in for a disappointment, according to Ashton. Indeed Bultmann claimed that the evangelist presents only the fact of the revelation without describing its content. This, to Ashton, is a misreading. The fourth gospel is actually a writing of genius, sparked by the words and the works of Jesus which are not unto themselves but are the carriers of God-centred truths. The genius of the text lies above all in the fact that in an important sense it is not 'about' anything. It is in its own fashion what was on offer in the days of Jesus. As Ashton puts it,

> … no understanding of the book is possible if one loses sight of the simple fact that it is not a theological tract but a Gospel. What the divine agent 'heard' from God is disclosed not in his words but in his life; the 'what' is displayed in the 'how'. The matter of the Gospel, its true content, is indistinguishable from its form: the medium is the message (p 553).

DIARMAID MCGANN

Journeying within transcendence offers a good example of the process which one might characterize as the gospel for significant personal use.[23] That is to say, the text is scrutinized by a reader whose understandings and insights are then applied to something that is going on within himself. This particular reader believes in God, in Jesus and in the truth of whatever the evangelist has proclaimed. He is determined to live more profoundly and, as he sees it, the gospel provides him with a necessary framework for doing so. The reading of the text thus becomes not an excursion into historical events as such but, rather, the establishment of a focus for reflection and self-understanding. Two stages are, therefore, to be recognized; first, the construing of the text and, secondly, the application to a private landscape of whatever has been so construed. This second stage is entered not by way of thesis or argument but as an exercise in personal prayer. The reader, in short, is not a dispassionate witness to what he has found in the gospel but is openly using the texts for purposes which, ultimately, are strictly his own. And the reader of his reading is someone invited to overhear.

It is important to stress this commitment to the text. The words of the evangelist are looked to not as a possible way out of something, an escape from ignorance, say, or from a personal crisis. They are approached in utter belief and, therefore, in the confidence that, if taken prayerfully, they will open up the most uncommon of vistas. So, for example, when considering the details of the first chapter, with its prologue and its attention to John the Baptist, McGann picks out the affirmation that nothing was made without the Logos and he takes it that in consequence one has oneself emerged from God. 'But this means that I too am alive with the presence of God' (p 12), and the task then is to transmute such an idea into a felt and encompassing realization. One has to stake out a new perspective, yet it will be one for which there is the warrant of the gospel:

> I accept what John points me towards in the prologue
> and that it is true of my life that I am on a journey
> under providence, *towards meaning, intelligence*
> *and love* (italics mine) and that the process of my
> life is awakening to that journey. I accept that my
> journey in life is a journey towards transcendence (p 13)

These are not the words of a heart for whom life is a brief and pointless excursion confined within the prosaic immediacy of stones, an old boot and a blasted tree. There is, rather, a sensibility buoyed up by the conviction of the existence not only of God but also of an inner milieu which is present in the world not as an artifact divorced from its maker and consequently alone but as, in some important way, a living manifestation of the creator. To travel within that milieu is therefore to be already on a direct route to an existing God. In this situation every word of the first chapter in the gospel becomes both fact and guide. If, then, John the Baptist is the witness testifying to and making way for the unique and vitally more significant presence of Jesus he is thereby the exemplar of what should and could occur within the privacy of the person. For, as McGann sees it, there is within that privacy an ongoing drama of which the protagonists are a mastering ego and an infrequently encountered but undeniable 'deeper self'. The ego is the executive, more or less worldly-wise, directing a life in accordance with the habits and perceptions of the quotidian. The more domineering the ego the more miniscule the space for that profound self. Yet the reality of that self is not in doubt. It is sensed in those moments when having touched one's limits one is:

> nevertheless drawn beyond them ... In those moments I discover a deeper self within me that I want to testify to and that I want to surrender my whole being to forever.

The glimpse of that self is rare, a gift and a blessing (p 22). But once sighted it confers a proper sense of proportion within the person, and the ego, regardless of efficiency or splendour, will recognize that it must step aside, make way for what is infinitely more valuable. 'The John the Baptist within me senses the Christ in those moments' (p 21) when the deeper self is noticed in the offing or even admitted for a moment to center stage.

But ego and the momentum of habit will surely prevail unless there is a crucial change within the person, and so the events related in the gospel become the tokens of how that change could proceed. 'The question for us is to discover what all this looks like in our life. How do we understand it as a story of the self' (p 37). In other words, the narrated events are given a symbolic character by this reader who, taking for granted the historical truth of what the evangelist has written, chooses rather to consider what these events portend for the life within himself. Of course McGann is not the first to operate in this way, since after all there are temperaments which respond expansively to the presence of symbols. One needs only to think here of Origen or Augustine. What is perhaps new is that this reading of the gospel proceeds under the aegis of psychological ideas and insights associated especially with the work of Carl Gustav Jung. The reference to the conscious and unconscious life of the person, to the interaction of ego and deeper self, to the problems of psychosis and neurosis are adumbrated from within Jungian perspectives albeit in a framework of prayerful meditation rather than of clinical discourse. And so the gospel provides, as it were, the vivid tokens of a drama, real or potential, within the self.

Consider, for instance, the reading of chapter five by McGann. This has to do with the cure on the Sabbath of the man who for thirty eight years has been lying by the pool at Bethesda waiting in hope to be first into the waters after the angel has stirred them. Jesus heals him and is assailed by the Jews not only for breaking the Sabbath but, worse, for making himself 'equal to God'. This latter charge evokes from Jesus words astonishing in all that they claim for himself. But it is not the historical or theological import of this which draws the attention of McGann. He sees the chapter as portraying the interaction of three types of character within the context of the Sabbath, itself a sign of the covenant between God and his chosen people. There is, first, the paralysed man, lonely, bitter, with all hope gone of ever getting on time to the pool:

> This man seems dulled in his sensitivities. He has become accustomed to disconnectedness, not only from his family and friends, but it appears, even from himself. He is not able to express his own needs, and he is no longer in touch with his own emotions, feelings and desires ... The overall tone is that of an isolated, disconnected person, frustrated over his inability to reach the water (which of itself is an interesting symbol of life, unconscious, etc) and who in consequence is feeling the burden and terror of despair and depression (pp 65–66).

Then there are 'the Jews', increasingly symbolic of everything negative. And there is Jesus, the harbinger of wider horizons and perspectives.

These three characters are themselves the exemplar of three forms of the outsider or, as McGann puts it, of imagination. The paralytic 'sees the world as dangerous and destructive and in consequence everything has to be distrusted' (p 66). The Jews, looking only to a past which they have institutionalized identify 'all of a reality with a little piece of reality' (p 68), their own, and, as a result, can take only 'an inquisitorial stance' (p 68) towards any point of view other than what they themselves have settled into. And, finally, there is Jesus, the sublime maverick, capable of integrating all realities and perspectives within his own unparochial horizons and offering, thereby, a liberating way out to all who might otherwise be blinkered and bigoted.

The three, then, represent potential alternative conditions of the psyche, as McGann comes to see after 'praying this story for the past four or five weeks' (p 73). The contextual Sabbath is 'a quiet space within me' (p 73) where the lonely fearfulness of the paralytic and the backward-looking mentality of the Jews may give way to the loving integrative openness exemplified by Jesus. From a consideration of the three points of view delineated in the text it becomes possible, indeed necessary, to focus upon one of them, that which respects and responds to the diversity of being and which, furthermore, does not seek to impose upon reality either the logic or the expectations of approval. But for McGann the reading of chapter five is part of the ongoing career of introspection undertaken by the meditative believing reader who:

> brings to the story his own life with all of its strengths and weaknesses because he wants to receive the vision of the story by handing himself over to it. The eyes of the reader are the eyes that want to be, expect to be, hope to be changed by this contact. These eyes are the eyes that want to see the new vision projected by the images. They are the eyes that are willing to risk the transformation of life. In the process of the transformation we come to see that all the eyes of the story are our own eyes … (pp 115–116)

That is, the psyche in all its complexity is brought to recognise its own capacity for multiple ways of seeing. Its point of view can be that of the paralytic, of the Jew or of Jesus, and the problem then is to decide which of these is appropriate to the life not of the ego but of the deeper self. The Jesus of chapter five becomes manifestly the best option, and he does so because he lives a perspective to which the deeper self aspires as it seeks to break loose from all that constricts it. And for the believer the breaking free in this way receives its encouragement and its justification in these pages of the fourth gospel.

And so it goes throughout this reading of what the evangelist has put together. Thus, the meeting between Nicodemus and Jesus becomes the encounter within the psyche between the diligently acquired knowledge of a succession of yesterdays and an uncatalogued but beckoning and potentially rich present. 'It would mean coming home to the depths within me, coming home to water and to Spirit' (p 50). The episode of the Samaritan woman 'becomes my own story in prayer. She, like Jesus, corresponds to something within me' (p 58). The feast of Tabernacles turns into:

> a story of self. It means coming to that place in me where I appreciate life ... In this place I am confronted with a decision about the deeper self. Is this deeper self, this Christ within, in reality the light I can trust and the water that will slake my thirst? (pp 91–92)

Even the details of the passion constitute at one level:

> my story. I see in it not only the culmination of the gospel but through it the gathering of all the facets of my own personality (p 178).

Judas, the hostile crowd, the denying Peter, all portray the varied faces of the self. So too does the cross:

> The vertical bar reaches up to the sky, to the light
> To consciousness. It is the masculine pole of my
> existence. The vertical bar also reaches down into
> the depths, the dark, the earth, the unconscious.
> It grounds my being. It is the feminine pole of my
> life, the reservoir of life itself (p 180).

Like M. Scott Peck in *The Road Less Travelled* McGann is concerned, then, with the release of what is best in the self. Such a release can only occur when one has learned to recognize and to confront those varied and often hampering ways of seeing which are alive within us. However, while Peck works towards this end from the basis of mutually illuminating ideas in psychiatry and Christian belief, McGann focuses, rather, on prayerful attention to the numerous scenes in the gospel of John. These, on inspection, are taken to be the mirror not so much of particular events as of the operating dynamics of that field of force which is the individual psyche. Of course historical reality is neither denied nor overlooked. But these episodes help to ensure the correctness of the analysis of the inward life of the person. For McGann, this strength lies precisely in their capacity to serve as vibrant and confirming images of what is happening to someone 'journeying within transcendence'.

CHAPTER THREE

If it is the case that character, calibre, personal interests, complicated purposes and much else besides may be said to mark the event where a reader of the gospel of John makes sense of the words on a page does it then follow that in the matter of interpretation anything goes?[24] Is every reading so very private an episode that it simply adds to the sum total of such events without contributing in any way to some common pool with which other readers may identify? Is the discovery that other readers may have arrived at the same sets of understanding as oneself nothing more than an encouragement to continue on one's own solitary way?

In dealing with this issue it is important to avoid open-ended generalisation. A distinction has to be made, for instance, between the contextual information gleaned from the words of the evangelist and the meaning to be assigned to what is said and done in the text. There may not always be a clear line between the two but the distinction has to be acknowledged nevertheless since it helps to ensure that the potentially difficult matter of interpretation is not confused with the uncovering of useful information in the gospel.

Clearly, there are certain facets of the text where the reading is relatively unproblematical and where the achievement of shared understandings among the readers may be said to offer no great difficulties. It is unlikely, for instance, that the essentially private event of reading will lead to public disagreement about the fact that the narrative unfolds in a Jewish ambience which has been shaped by a particular history and by a contemporary set of problems. It is hard to imagine any dissent from the perception, common among students of the text, that the Temple in Jerusalem is a significant setting for several of the incidents described by the evangelist. If something is to be grasped of the significance of this setting for the many encounters between Jesus and the crowds, the less informed reader will turn profitably to the commentaries and to the works of scholarship which are concerned to illuminate such matters. Again, the episode of the crucifixion as related in the gospel is unlikely to support any argument that the Parthians rather than the Romans were the perpetrators. In short, there are many moments in the text which can only evoke from the most diverse readers a shared appreciation of what is going on.

Not so with other parts of the text, as must be obvious when an Origen, a Thomas Aquinas or a Calvin descends upon the scene.[25] Since a detailed history of competing interpretations would fill too many volumes the question to be asked now is whether some kind of minimal assent could be imagined or else some arena where diverse readings might meet without any requirement to compromise or to make unwanted concessions. The impetus to envisage this might be brought into sharper focus if for instance one were to think of a language where something shared is in being but where speakers may also make idiosyncratic use of the semantic ingredients of what they have in common. Or more to the point, perhaps, might be the way in which a number of people, each with a distinctive angle of vision, can nevertheless sign up to a more or less agreed appraisal of someone without exhausting the mystery and the uniqueness of that person and without necessarily empathising with what they see. Could something like this be possible in the case of the readings of the fourth gospel?

To make some progress on this issue one might focus on the Jesus evoked in the text. An advantage of doing so would be to highlight the fact of a relationship not between reader and writer but between both and the man from Nazareth who occupies the centre of the narrative. The evangelist in his selection of relevant material and in the description of a series of episodes is offering a view of Jesus. The reader, travelling along a path laid down by the writer is also trying to reach a perspective on this very distinctive man. The writer has the advantage of proximity to the events. The reader, however, has the freedom to arrive at a perception of Jesus which may differ fundamentally from that stated or implied in the text. The writer may operate on the basis of a conviction that there is a God and that Jesus, through his words and actions, has demonstrated that he is a divine presence offering rescue to everyone. The reader may decide, on the evidence of this same gospel, that Jesus, while undoubtedly fascinating, was someone hopelessly deluded by what he imagined himself to be. On the other hand, if it should happen that the reader chooses, for whatever reason, to accept what appears to be the attitude of the evangelist regarding Jesus this decision does not alter the reality that two views, not one, have in this instance circled around the historical figure and that in this case the convictions of the evangelist merely precede those arrived at by a sympathetic reader. Indeed sympathy and the lack of it need not inhibit at all the construction of a shared description of the Jesus presented in the narrative.

So, then, what kind of man is this Jesus?[26] The usual guiding adjectives and the convenient labels are missing. Nothing is said about the quality of his voice, the way he stood, the gestures which were as much a part of him as the colour of his eyes. He moves around with his followers. He is rarely alone. He slips in and out of crowds, and it is reported that there were listeners and bystanders who put their trust in him simply because it was enough to have been there and to have heard him. Yet the charisma and the chemistry of interaction between himself and his audiences are absent from the page.

The man remains constantly elusive, so far as the reader is concerned. Images of him constructed in abundance throughout the centuries since his crucifixion have to keep company with the blankness of a text where his physical presence remains uncharacterised and undescribed and where the only sighting of him is either in the episodes in which he is the protagonist or else in the words which he is said to have uttered. The scene where he clears the hucksters from the Temple is typical:[27]

> The Jewish Passover was near, and Jesus went up to Jerusalem. In the Temple he came upon the merchants of cattle, sheep and pigeons as well as the moneychangers who were sitting around. Making a whip out of reeds he drove them all from the Temple – the sheep and the cattle – and he

> scattered the coins of the money-changers, overturned their tables, and to the sellers of pigeons he said 'Get these out of here and do not make the house of my father into a business store' (2: 13–16)

To these brief and bald sentences the evangelist adds, by way of comment, that followers of Jesus, seeing what was happening, remembered a saying in the Old Testament 'zeal for your house consumes me'.

This is not the end of the incident. Nevertheless there is enough so far to highlight the situation of the reader who confronts the fact that with fewer than one hundred words of Greek the evangelist has summoned a memorable image of a man on the rampage. The raw details are laid down, the dealers, the whip, the scattered coins, the overturned tables, the demand that the Temple be liberated from worldly business concerns. But much is also left out, especially the crackle and the feel of the actual moments. Indeed the only hint of the atmosphere is suggested with the scriptural quotation focusing on zeal.

Few readers will settle for this. Implication and imagination inevitably go to work,[28] supplying the drama of the incident, pausing over the apparent inertia of the dealers in the face of this assault on their vested interests, wondering why Jesus was not set upon and himself kicked out since, after all, he was but one man in a crowd. Could nobody restrain him? Why not? Was the 'zeal' the decisive factor here? The questions multiply. But of course they are those of a reader who is drawn into the gaps in the account and who feels the urge to import more substance into the sparse narrative. And this is the situation of the many readers who engage with what is recounted by the evangelist. But even when emphasis and nuance may vary in what is read into the text there can still be a coming together and a broad agreement among those who are trying to form a sense of what Jesus was like.

This too is the case with the simple episode at Bethany when Mary anoints the feet of Jesus:

> They made a meal for him. Martha served and Lazarus was among those at table with him. Taking a pound of very expensive ointment – pure nard – Mary anointed the feet of Jesus and wiped them with her hair. The house was filled with the smell of the ointment (12. 2–3).

As in the Temple episode the bare details are themselves uncomplicated and present no obvious problem for any reader. But, again, the imagination begins to work, lingering on the perfumed air of the house, on the hair which must have been long if the feet of Jesus were to be wiped, on the ointment which did not come cheap. But most of all there is the gesture. Why did she do it?[29] The answer for some readers appears to lie in the few following sentences:

> Then Judas Iscariot, one of his followers, the man who would betray him, said 'Why was this ointment not sold for 300 denarii and the money given to those in need?' He said this not because he was worried about the poor but because he was a thief. He was in charge of the common purse and used to help himself to the contributions. So Jesus said 'Leave her alone. She has been keeping this for the day of my burial' (12: 4–8).

These words of Jesus have led many readers to suppose that the narrative moves in anticipation of the time when the body of Jesus will lie in the tomb awaiting the administration of the spices and ointments which are required for the fulfillment of Jewish burial custom (cf. Luke 23: 55–24.2). So on this reading Mary is simply a precursor of the women who will be involved with the rites of burial.

But is that all there is to it? The evangelist is looking back on the scene and has taken the words of Jesus to imply that Mary is anticipating what is to happen soon. A presumed meaning is given to the incident.[30] But does this really exhaust the moment? Being male, could the evangelist have missed out on something important, on the possibility, for instance, that the gesture was that of a woman responding in love and admiration to a truly remarkable man? To claim she was anticipating the burial of Jesus is to presume she had some awareness of his fate or else that she was acting under some kind of inspiration. The fact was that he was passing through

Bethany and there was reason in her household to be truly grateful to him. Why, then, could she not have been responding out of a full heart and in the only way she could think of in the presence of this man?

The narrative in which these episodes appear may evoke elaborate and diverse interpretations. Nevertheless it points any readers towards a growing sense that Jesus was a truly emphatic presence among those who encountered him. This, at a minimum, is what the writing achieves. In so doing it enables the ultimate privacy of each reading to proceed in the company of other readers travelling towards the same outline image of the man Jesus.

But, of course, narrative is not solely a register of detail. The deployment of words is also a process where tone and nuance matter significantly. This is why conversation is direct in more than the obvious sense, for the experience of understanding what is said during a living exchange can move forward with greater assurance on the basis of expression, emphasis, hint and much else that is part of any ongoing face to face discussion. Such elements can be of crucial importance in preventing misunderstanding. But these are not available to the reader who is dealing with what is fixed on a page. And for two millennia the same words of the fourth gospel have remained in view, waiting for whatever it is that can be read of them and into them. They are the silent partner in that exciting event which constitutes the act of reading. But their tone and nuance – however much these may have vibrated in the mind of the man who wrote them – can only be, at best, a matter of guesswork on the part of the reader. Consequently, the accounts of the incidents in the Temple and at Bethany impose restricted access to the man Jesus, which is not to say, of course, that individual readers do not go on to construct views of Jesus which may well be accurate but which, strictly speaking, are not condoned by the actual text.

The issue of tone is only one among many ingredients in the ongoing situation of the reader who wishes to take aboard as much as possible of what the text is seeking to convey about Jesus. Nevertheless this issue has its own importance in the scenario put together by the evangelist, and especially so when the effort of the reader is to get as close as possible to the main figure in the narrative. An example of this occurs in the exchange between Jesus and the Samaritan woman. The principal elements of the conversation are set down like the notes of a musical score or the words of a play but, shorn of its trimmings, the dialogue between Jesus and the woman lays on every reader the demand to be the new director of an old drama:

> Give me a drink.
>
> How come that you, a Jewish man, are asking me, a Samaritan woman, for a drink?
>
> If you knew God's gift to you and who it is that's saying 'give me a drink' you would ask him for living water. And he would give it to you.
>
> Sir, you haven't a bucket and the well is deep. So where are you getting living water? Are you greater than our father Jacob who gave us this well and who drank from it himself, along with his sons and his herds?
>
> Everyone drinking this water will be thirsty again. But anyone drinking the water I give him will be without thirst for all time and the water I shall give him will be a fountain leaping out of him for everlasting life.
>
> Give me this water, sir, so I won't be thirsty and won't have to come here to draw buckets.
>
> Call your husband and come here.
>
> I haven't got a husband.
>
> 'I haven't got a husband'. Well said. You've had five and the one you have now is not your husband.
>
> I see you're a prophet, sir.

How did they play it, these two, this Jewish prophet and this Samaritan woman? Did Jesus talk down to this woman in the way a certain kind of self-righteous white person talks to somebody black? Or that an ageing ecclesiastic of a nearly bygone era addresses a woman, any woman? Or is the exchange conducted at a completely different level? Is a responsive man giving of himself to a stranger whose life is there to be enhanced?

And what of the woman? Three times she addresses Jesus as *kurios*, a term regularly translated as 'lord', with its attendant implication of relationships conducted in hierarchy. Does she therefore speak with downcast eyes, as many would have her do, given whom she is talking to and given also the number of acknowledged men in her life? But might it be that she really means only to call him 'sir', or 'mister', and this because the evangelist is actually presenting an unbrowbeaten woman? In short, where is an interpreter to place the emphasis in a scene at the centre of which, is on one view, an extraordinary being and a submissive woman or, on another view, either two unsentimental strangers in a place of refreshment or, else, in Rilke's phrase, two solitudes saluting one another?

But more complex issues now emerge in the company of such questions. For when the Samaritan woman calls Jesus a prophet she opens up in explicit fashion the domain of religious belief. And this is undoubtedly a context where a prospective alliance of readers may in fact begin to move out of reach. Not that there need be much doubt regarding what the narrative says. Rather, the phenomenon here is that readers will inevitably bring to the gospel their own perspectives on the validity or otherwise of religious convictions. Even if they themselves are believers they may still differ significantly on what they find in the text. All this in turn must result in a plurality of approaches to the one set of words fixed on the page by the evangelist.

It is the woman who extends the reach of the conversation, for having called Jesus a prophet she goes on to say:

> Our fathers worshipped on this mountain, though your people say that Jerusalem is the place where one should worship

> Believe me, woman, the time is coming when you will worship the Father neither in this mountain nor in Jerusalem. You worship what you don't know. We worship what we do know, because salvation is from the Jews. But a time is coming, is now here, when true worshippers will worship the Father in spirit and in truth. These are the kind of worshippers whom the Father seeks, for God is a spirit and those who worship him should do so in spirit and in truth
>
> I know that a messiah is coming, the one called 'Anointed'. When he comes he will make everything clear to us
>
> I am that one, and I am talking to you (4: 7–26)

Some of these words would be meaningless in the twenty first century if they stood alone and unaccompanied by available scholarship. The reference to the 'anointed one' is an obvious example, for who could guess what it signifies if historians had not already illuminated a Jewish context in which the notion of an extraordinary rescuer had taken root?

On the other hand the idea of worship will strike a more familiar note among readers since it has long been the case that human beings find themselves confronted by the fundamental question of whether a God, of whatever name, exists, a being to be worshipped, to be sought amid the contingencies of being, a presence to be acknowledged somehow during the transience of a lifetime. To some – for many reasons – the answer to this exigent question is a ringing negative, reflecting a decision that the limits of the universe have been perceived, however dimly or indeed theoretically, and that these impose no demand for belief in any divine being. The conglomeration of worlds is there and, ultimately, nothing more remains to be said, apart, perhaps, from multiplying the descriptions of what is available. And so one philosopher can say 'I don't want there to be a God',[31] while a poet writes:

> And I know that the sacrificial smoke drifting into a cold sky
> braids a pigtail for a deity without a head.[32]

Not so for the evangelist, however, nor for the many figures in the narrative. And especially not so for the Jesus who speaks of God as a spirit, a being both elusive and firmly there like a passing wind which is confined neither to a mountain nor to a venerable holy city. In other words there is an important issue of personal orientation here, and it is one which runs throughout the gospel, emerging for instance during the night-time encounter between Jesus and the prominent Jew Nicodemus, a Pharisee who has taken to heart a sense that this Galilean is someone out of the ordinary and who is troubled by the implications of what he has seen and heard. A believer in the fact of God, Nicodemus detects a connection between the public activities of Jesus and the God he worships:

> It is clear to us that you have come as a teacher from God, for no one, unless God were with him could do portentous things such as you do (3.2).

While the text offers only a distillation of the conversation between the two men, it is safe to presume that the existence of God was not an issue. Nicodemus, after all, is a religious teacher in the Jewish community. But what is central are the spiritual and intellectual horizons within which these two men function. So when Jesus speaks of 'the kingdom of God' (3.3) and goes on to declare that this is a realm which can be entered by any person who fulfils the essential condition of 'coming to birth from above' (3.3) the idea proves baffling to Nicodemus. How can an old man be born again? Can he enter a second time into the womb of his mother and be brought to birth? Missing the phrase 'from above' Nicodemus directs his attention to the notion of a second birth and is understandably puzzled. But – and this is the decisive point – the puzzlement will remain even after he has listened to the words offered by Jesus in explanation. 'How can such things be?' (3.9) he will ask, drawing from Jesus the surprised question 'How is it that you, a teacher of Israel, do not know these things?' (3.10)

It is a poignant moment this, the first of several in the fourth gospel, when Jesus finds that the central notions which underlie and shape his own most urgent words are met by painful incomprehension, even in a man, a teacher of Israel, who could be expected to know better. Yet at the same time, such incomprehension cannot be wholly surprising because what Jesus has said to Nicodemus, in the summary version of the evangelist,[33] constitutes both a challenge and a threat, a challenge to look beyond the known boundaries of existence and a threat to that most commonplace of human phenomena, namely, settled convictions regarding the makeup of reality. 'How can such things be?' Nicodemus, a religious man, has accumulated a baggage of more or less explicit certainties about the way things are and, even though his frame of reference includes a belief in God, he still cannot cope with a discourse which, nevertheless, centres on the relationship between the human and the divine. What is striking about Nicodemus is not his inability at the beginning to understand the language of Jesus but rather his continuing blankness in the presence of the substantial attempt to get him to attune his thinking to the extra-mundane. With a notably potent image Jesus adverts to this domain of spirit:

> The wind blows where it pleases, and you hear its voice. You do not know where it comes from and where it is going. And everyone born of the spirit is like this (3.8).

Words of this kind, evading the usual categories of the manageable and the comfortable, are a source of disquiet to every Nicodemus. For words such as these are spoken by some, poets especially, who have a sense that the real, the truly there, is not always co-terminous with human powers to observe, to classify, to encapsulate in tried language and in the complacencies of yesterday's discourse. Faced by mystery, which is not to be confused with the merely unexplained or with the first advance pulse of what will eventually be the obvious, there is a choice to be made. One can acknowledge the possible existence of that which refuses to be confined, pinned down, grasped; or else one can decide to retire into the relative comfort of one's routine habits of thought. Of these choices it is the first which is the most unsettling since it implies a willingness to accept that one cannot count on being the measure of all things, that one has to be humbly open to much that may refuse to submit to the capacity of one's self and of one's neighbours to understand. It is a disturbing choice, too grievously so for Nicodemus. He finds himself unable to allow for the unknown. The buoyant ambiguity of 'mind' and 'spirit' is too much for him and Jesus is left to make the wistful comment that:

> if you cannot trust what I say to you about the things of earth how will you come to trust me if I talk of the things of heaven? (3.12)

The 'things of heaven' are indeed at the core of the encounter between Jesus and Nicodemus.[31] But this is also a problem for the reader who, living 'in the narrow bed of our flesh' (3), is so shaped and moulded and prompted by 'the things of earth' that an opening out towards any other domain requires a surrender of the self, a re-deployment of familiar resources in the way which, in the kind of circumstances facing a Nicodemus, can prove simply too daunting or too unacceptable to contemplate.

But no concessions are offered by the text. Not only does Jesus speak up to insist that the domain of spirit actually exists but he also moves on to give voice to words which combine the dense, the explicit and the dramatic:

> I tell you that we proclaim what we know and give witness to what we have seen, and you do not accept our testimony ... you do not trust ... No one has gone up to heaven except the one who has come from heaven, the Son of Man. And just as Moses lifted up the snake in the desert so must the Son of Man be lifted up in order that everyone who trusts him may have life for all time (3:13–5).

The claim to be a direct witness, the implication that when referring to the 'Son of Man' Jesus means himself, the allusion to the one 'who has come down from heaven', the co-relation between the lifting up of the Son of Man and unending life for those who trust him – all this is startling, bewildering talk. It cannot be softened or played down. It refuses to be tractable. It corners the reader, who has to decide whether to close this book now, merely note its contents or, finally, carry on in growing scepticism or else in the hope of some enlightenment.

The evangelist seems to recognise the problem for he abruptly begins to sketch a perspective within which everything said thus far should be placed:

> ... God had such love for the world that he gave it his only begotten son, so that everyone trusting him might not be lost but would have life without an end (3.16).

Such a statement, however, does not ease matters too greatly since many a reader throughout the centuries would find the notions of a loving God and unending human life difficult to absorb or accept. More intimidating still would be the emphasis on trust, and, as if to acknowledge this, the notion is adverted to repeatedly:

> For God did not send his son into the world to pass judgement on the world but in order that the world might be saved through him. The one who trusts in him is not judged. The one who does not trust in him is already judged for not putting his trust in the name of the Son of God (3:17–18).

Trust. This theme is not a transitory one in the text. It will be emphasised more and more with every turn of page. Here it is directed towards a name. And that this 'name' does not refer to someone out of sight and out of reach is emphasised by the remark that light has come into the world, a light which has nevertheless been rejected by those who have failed to see the intimate connection between God, light and the human need to be in the truth.

And as if to buttress all this presentation of what to a Nicodemus would be the difficult and the obscure – especially since unusual status is now being implied for Jesus – the evangelist reverts to the more familiar, more reassuring figure of John the Baptist. For just as the reader might be tempted to ask regarding Jesus, 'who does he think he is?', so the followers of John are moved to seek reasons for the increasing numbers flocking to the Galilean for baptism. John, whose style of living has matched his deepest religious convictions and who will soon have to die because of speaking publicly what lies in the privacy of his beliefs, this figure, described elsewhere as wearing only animal skins and eating locusts and wild honey, will now summon the authority of his formidable character to perform one last deed of service for Jesus:

> You are my witnesses that I said to you 'I am not the anointed one but was sent on ahead of him'. It is the bridegroom who has the bride. The friend of the bridegroom stands nearby, listens to him and takes delight in the voice of the groom. That is my joy, and it is abundant (3:28–29).

An impressive man, John, nevertheless, is now asserting that he must step aside to make way for someone whose singularity leaves him no other option. 'His measure has to grow, mine to diminish' (3.30) and these words are more than a valedictory, for the Baptist had earlier indicated to his followers that a human cannot grab, seize, lay hold of the real so as to package it and manage it in ways that are a comfort. One has instead to be open to it, for 'a man can lay hold of nothing unless it be given to him from heaven' (3.27). It is in keeping with this that John here chooses to yield centre-place to someone whose coming is for him the manifestation of a reality far greater than himself.

In a drama involving heaven and earth something, indeed, has been given. Or so the evangelist now argues in comments which, to some, might appear to be strangely laboured and incoherent. It is as if the evangelist were trying to catch words tossed at him from the opposite bank of a tumbling stream:

> The one coming from above is over all. The one coming from the earth is of earth and his talk is of earth. The one coming from heaven is over all and he bears witness to what he has seen and heard, and no one accepts his testimony. Whoever accepts his testimony proclaims the authenticity of God's truth. For the spirit does not dole out measures. The father loves the son and has given everything into his possession. Whoever trusts the son has life without end. Whoever has no trust in the son will not see life, and the anger of God lingers over him (3:31–36).

These words lay down a view of an emerging landscape, some of whose colours will be brought out more and more sharply in the pages ahead. But for the moment they make it possible to appreciate the reasons for the troubled, uneasy reactions of Nicodemus, for they invite acceptance of the notion that the horizons of reality stretch far beyond the paths along which human beings ordinarily stride with unimpaired confidence.

They propose that it is not enough to rest in known waters, that an assured life depends on striving to reach a world outside any apparently safe and constructed haven including the 'safe' haven of 'authorised' interpretation.

So when Jesus is quoted as proclaiming the presence of an unconstrained God this is not necessarily matched by human willingness to be responsive. This fact underlies the intimations of mission and of urgency in all that Jesus has now to declare. 'My food is to do the will of the one who sent me and to bring his work to completion' (4.34). But which work? He does not explicitly say, at least not in the text, but, as already noted, he had described himself as the one who would bring clarification, making things understandable presumably in the arena where a human being may, if he chooses, go forward to meet God. And despite the visible apparatus, not to mention the venerable traditions, of an old religion in this land where talk, where commitment, where passion were rife, it is evident that, for Jesus, a formidable need is nevertheless there to be met. For instance, before going to spend two days among the Samaritans he would speak to his followers of an immense ready harvest. 'Lift up your eyes and look at the lands that are white for the reaping' (4.35). Nor is reaping a task for him alone. It is there also to engage his followers and the stakes are high, for what is in store is 'life without end' (4.36).

In fact Jesus is a man under pressure. During the encounter with Nicodemus he had spoken of proclaiming 'what we know' and of giving 'witness to what we have seen' and yet of not being trusted. He had talked insistently of 'the things of heaven'. He would tell the Samaritan woman that he had something extraordinary to give. He would seek to impress on his followers the magnitude of the job now to be done. And so it would continue. In episode after episode the evangelist portrays him urging, asserting, making claims.

Still, many have passed through the world like Jesus with a sense of mission, but the evangelist, coming as he does, from a region of prophets and proclaimers, moves rapidly to emphasise the special and unmistakeable impact of the Galilean. The Samaritan woman is described as encouraging the men of her town to go see this visitor who must surely be 'the anointed one'. Some are convinced. Others will react similarly by the end of the two days spent by Jesus among them and – a neat touch this – they will make a point of asserting that they were putting their trust in him not because of her *lalia* (blather) but in the aftermath of hearing his *logos* 'We ourselves have listened to him and we know that this man is certainly the rescuer of the world' (4.42).

A gullible public? The evangelist seems to anticipate the possible jibe, for he moves on immediately to relate the episode of the aristocrat who travels from Cafarnaoum to Cana to plead with Jesus to come and heal his son. Jesus gets close to taunting him and all the others. 'Unless you see signs and wonders you will not trust'.(4.48) But the aristocrat persists 'Come before my child dies' (4.49). So Jesus offers him a direct challenge. 'Go home. Your son lives' (4.49). The man goes, finds his son alive and safe, and, back home and away from Cana, 'he put his trust in him as did his entire household' (4.53).

Something indeed is getting through to all these people and the text implies that not only are they responding to a discourse, a *logos,* which is directed to the relationship obtaining between human being and God but that Jesus himself, by word and action, is giving them to understand that he is in an unusual and special position to illuminate that relationship. Yet, surprisingly, there is no detailed report of what Jesus has been saying in regard to so weighty a theme and the reader is turned instead towards the reactions of those who heard and saw him. The spotlight is on the man in such a way as to suggest that, whereas other discourses can be evaluated by themselves without continual reference to the speakers who deliver them, the position in this case is that Jesus and his *logos* have to be seen together for what they are, a unique un-repeated presence to which contemporaries could not be indifferent. And the narrative makes the point that every reaction to this presence was not inevitably one of trust. This is indicated suddenly and shockingly when the writer begins to describe events in Jerusalem during which the words of Jesus, his *logos,* evoked in some of those who listened not a mood of benignity or boredom but, rather, the blunt desire to murder him. Even as the notion of trust comes more and more into view, the evangelist, nevertheless, switches sharply to this surfacing desire to kill Jesus. That the Galilean was a vibrant disturbing man has been made increasingly clear in the text, but now, more starkly, the reader is drawn to where the onlookers at the Temple were impelled to turn, to an arena whose decisions lie there to be taken up, where reactions are there to be shaped. And all because of a *logos* which grows ever more explicit, for this *logos* of Jesus, the words to which he gives utterance, lay claim – and are perceived to lay claim – to a unique situation in everything that has to do with the interaction of God and of human kind. When Jews complain in the Temple, the holiest of all places, that Jesus has broken the sabbath rules by healing a cripple at Bethsaida they elicit the reply 'My father continues to work and so do I', (5. 1–7) a powerfully direct statement allowing for no ambiguity. 'It was therefore because of this that the Jews sought all the more to kill him, for not only did he break the sabbath but he called God his father, putting himself on a level with God' (5.18).

Nowadays, when a man rises in a gathering of believers to proclaim that he is the son of God the ushers and security are quick to take him away, leaving behind him reactions of pity, amusement or exasperation. But a man who speaks up in the Temple to suggest that he is 'on a level with God' is something more than a harmless nuisance, for he is talking to a people disposed to take offence at anything that would seem to undermine the majesty of their God. It was, after all, among their own ancestors that a hunch was translated into a prohibition, that a sense of God grew so profoundly that the idea of enclosing him within the confines of a name or of an image was seen to be arrogant blasphemy. The old condemnation of strange gods was but one of many devices to keep open the sense of a deity untouched by any human capacity to humiliate. A God made tractable is no God at all. And yet here is Jesus affirming the intimacy of his own relationship with the God of Abraham of Isaac and of Jacob, this ultimate higher power whom he calls his father. The words, as deployed, owe much to the intentions of the evangelist but their stubborn substance lies in what was openly declared in the Temple:

> The father loves the son and shows him everything he does, and he will show deeds greater than these so that you may be amazed ... The father judges no one but has handed over all judgement to the son in order that all may honour the son as they honour the father. Whoever does not honour the son gives no honour to the father who sent him... I tell you that anyone hearing my *logos* and putting his trust in the one who sent me has life for ever ... The deeds that I do are my witness that the father has sent me (5.20ff).

It is not as messenger that Jesus comes but as son and, moreover, a son to be honoured on a level with the father.[47]

There is no place here for ambiguity, for the softened interpretation. And the narrative, allowing no respite, continues to pile challenge upon challenge. The words at the Temple have scarcely been set down when the action is moved to the sea of Galilee to the story of the feeding of five hundred men, to the strange passage at night across the lake and the image of Jesus walking on the waters, and, above all, to the words spoken at Capernaum in a mixture that is strange, assertive and sad:

> Whoever eats my flesh and drinks my blood has life forever and I will raise him up on the last day (6.54)

> I ... am sent by the living father (6.57)

> I am the bread of life. Whoever comes to me will never be hungry, whoever puts his trust in me will never be thirsty. But I have said to you that you have looked upon me and that you have no trust in me (6.35–36).

No wonder there was controversy. No wonder there were those who walked away from his 'unyielding *logos*', as a reader might walk away from the text. The claims are too astounding. A being on a level with God, the bread of life, the provider of his own flesh to eat – such a *logos* is unheard of, demented, scandalous. And yet he does not talk completely like a fool, and there are the signs which accompany him as he travels throughout the countryside. And there are the repeated moments when those who see and hear him cannot, will not withold their acknowledgement of his resonant, unique presence. 'What are we to do?' (6.28) The question bursts from the audience, from an audience, moreover, convinced that there is a God to be reckoned with. 'What are we to do to perform the tasks of God?' (6.28) Tasks are visible and, in the common view are measurable, and it is characteristic of the Jesus so far presented in the pages of the evangelist that the reply to the insistent question about what to do includes a reminder that convenient, humanly comforting terms of reference do not apply here. For just as he had said that there exists a domain above the world, just as he had asserted that God is a spirit to be worshipped in spirit and in truth so now on this matter of deeds he diverts from what can be seen and computed and sends his audience towards the inner world of the individual, to the realm of mind and disposition. 'The work of God to be done is this, that you put your trust in the one whom he has sent' (6.29). Not exploits, not the performance of listed actions, not the visibility of gesture, but the decisive re-orientation of the heart's impulse.

So the theme of trust grows evermore persistent and inescapable. 'The disciples put their trust in him' (2.11). 'Many put their trust in his name as they watched the signs that he gave' (2.23).

> If I have spoken to you concerning the things of earth and you do not trust me how will you trust if I speak to you about the things of heaven? (3.12).

But more is involved than some indeterminate bestowal of credibility, for the act of trust will also have dramatic significance:

> I tell you that the one who hears my *logos* and puts his trust in the one who sent me has life forever (5.24).

> Whoever trusts the son has everlasting life; whoever does not trust the son will not see life but has the anger of God remaining against him (3.36).

And this reiteration of the idea of trust is inseparable from his *logos,* from what it is that Jesus has to say, so that, even if one leaves aside for the moment the problem of how to understand the dynamics of trust, the principle determinants of the text here seem unmistakeable. There is a *logos*, encapsulated in the words reported by the evangelist, and, as it were, made visible in the man, and since the indifferent nowhere appear, there is the polarisation between those prepared either to grant or to deny their trust to what this Galilean has been affirming. A yes or a no, with, it is claimed, the profoundest consequences for each.

The issues are all in the open now and the narrative structure from here on reflects the cadences of the encounter between proffered word and listening world. And so in the pages stretching from the seventh to the end of the eleventh chapters the unique character of Jesus and the responses to him are played off, one against the other, in an ever more assertive choreography. As the issues become increasingly compelling, the *logos* of Jesus appears either as direct claim by him or else as a reply to the hostile onlookers among the crowds who have gathered around him. To this larger public he insists, as he had with Nicodemus, that to channel the search for reality within the banks of the visible is already to miss the truth of things and, worse, to turn on to a highway to death. Nor is this some vague generalisation, for he pointedly claims that those in his audience who withold their trust, those who refuse to open towards him are showing themselves to have opted for loss:

> You are from the things below, I am from the things above; you are of this world, I am not of this world. I have told you that you would die amid your wrong-doing. If you do not put your trust in me as I am you will die amid your wrongdoing (8:23–24).

And the pity of it is that much in fact is waiting there to reward the act of trust:

> If you stay with what I have told you then you will really be learning from me and you will know the truth and the truth will set you free (8.31–32).

Truth, death, trust, freedom. These are heady issues indeed, and it is clear that, as so frequently in his utterances, Jesus is talking to a people many of whom do not really understand him at all. So when he speaks of freedom it is to an audience conscious of a past where servitude bulked large and tragic in its many effects and they angrily deny that they are now to be thought of as slaves. They refer his words to parameters within which they normally operate and, therefore, they reject him. But the freedom of which Jesus speaks is plainly something else, something to be looked for, however uneasily, however uncomfortably, within the context of spirit, of personal disposition, of those interacting domains of 'the things of heaven' … (and) 'the things of earth' (3.12). In short, this is a further version of the dialogue with Nicodemus, though this time in the open, not in the furtive silence of the night but amid the stirrings, unpredictable and vaguely menacing, which are called up whenever a man confronts a crowd. And, as with Nicodemus, there is no confluence of word or thought.

But he presses on, this Jesus, insisting that a freedom and a life without end are there for the taking, insisting also that this journey to freedom lies through him:

> I am the light of the World. The one who follows me will not wander about in darkness but will possess the light of life (8.12)
>
> If anyone gives heed to what I have to say he will never see death, will never taste death (8.52–53).

And from the audience, from the listeners to this astonishing and baffling claim, comes the wholly predictable riposte 'prove it'. But his comeback is that there will be no proof of the expected kind, since those challenging him are doing so from within the guidelines of the quotidian, attacking him because they think 'in accordance with what can be seen', 'in the terms of the corporeal'. 'Do not judge by what you see. Instead make a just judgement' (7.24). And the making of such a judgement will only be possible to someone willing to trust, willing to open the gateway of mind and heart to a truth unconstrained by human expectation as to how the truth must be and also originating in God himself:

> My teaching is not my own but is that of the one who sent me. Anyone ... will recognise if this teaching is from God or if I am speaking for myself (7.16–17).

But the will to recognise is not there, at least not among his present listeners, and a sign of the fact that so many of his audience remain in their old habits of thought comes with the desire they have to kill him. For 'what I have to say to you has no place among you' (8.38).

The impasse remains. Breaking free of the momentum of settled modes of seeing the world, the trusting become more numerous in his presence, but the doubters and the hostile continue to harry Jesus with their demands to be convinced. And the controversy will roll on with the tale of the healing of the man born blind and with the unfolding story of the raising of Lazarus. The narrative moves back and forth to present and re-present the essentially same conflict.

> I am the resurrection and the life. The one who trusts me will have life even if he should come to die. Everyone who lives and who continues to trust in me will not die, ever (11:25–26).

> He is possessed by a devil and is demented, a madman (10:20).

Yet even now Jesus might have got away with the image of himself which he was projecting to the crowds who saw him. Doubtless, controversy would have continued but the end need not have been violent and the arguments, for all their fury, could have run their course into the common sand. That is, had it not been for the event known thereafter as the entry into Jerusalem. The demonstrations, the shouts hailing him as King of Israel, the roadway strewn with palm branches, like the purple path trodden by Agamemnon home from Troy and about to be killed – all this has implications, political, social, as well as religious for both the Roman authorities and for the Jewish ruling elite. Neither the administrators of the occupying power nor the uncertain leaders of the Jews could now stand aside from the prospects of a disturbance of the peace centred on this one man. Too many interests would now feel the breath of the crowd. And so the ride on the donkey was, indeed had to be, the start of a last mortal journey.

The evangelist tersely conveys that a point of no return has been reached, and the narrative is so worded as to embed the entry into Jerusalem in a context wider than the particular moment. Not only is Jesus hailed as *basileus*, but the very notion of *basileus* is itself seen to be intelligible only in terms of those Old Testament allusions where kingship and God are interelated. Hence the inevitably political character of what is now happening. 'All praise to the one coming in the name of the Lord, the King of Israel' (12:13) is the cry of those gathering around Jesus – a cry which could not fail to be reported to the authorities, Roman and Jewish – and for the evangelist, this is more than the exuberance of a moment. It is part of a larger scheme, a moment also foreseen by scripture itself. 'Do not be afraid, daughter of Sion. See, your king is coming seated on the foal of a donkey' (12:15). All of which inevitably means that in the time remaining to him the *logos* of Jesus, what he has to say, is bound to be shadowed by ever more burdensome themes.

In fact, the words assigned to him following his entry into Jerusalem are ringed by an awful melancholy, carrying within them the sense of a death to be endured, of trepidation at what has to be, and of realism about the numbers of those who, having heard his call for trust, will nonetheless go their own unheeding way:

> I tell you, if the ear of corn which falls into the earth does not die then it remains alone. But if it dies it bears much fruit (12:24).
>
> My spirit now is made uneasy and what am I to say?... (12:27)
>
> ... The light is among you for only a little while longer. Go about so that you may have the light, so that darkness may not bring you down. Whoever walks around in darkness does not know where he is going. Trust in the light so that you may have the light, so that you may become sons of life (12:35–36).

This theme of trust with its outcome of life and light continues to dominate. Quoting Isaiah to validate that it must be so, the evangelist adds that many of the community leaders were actually willing to put their trust in him but would not openly acknowledge this out of fear of being expelled from their synagogues. And Jesus himself refers to the same theme in words of almost desperate intensity:

> The one who puts his trust in me trusts not me but the one who sent me, and the one who looks to me looks upon the one who sent me. I have come as a light to the world so that everyone who trusts in me will not remain in darkness (12: 44–46).
>
> I have not been talking from within myself but it is the father himself, the one who sent me, who has given me a command as to what I say and what I utter. I also know that what he commands is life without end (12: 49–56).

In these words there is much more than missionary zeal. There is also the open urgency of love. The evangelist knows it. 'He loved those in the world who were drawn to him, and he loved them to the end' (13:1). Including Judas. For who would insist on the exclusion of Judas from these words 'love each other as I loved you' (13:34) or from the example set during the washing of the feet when Jesus said:

> If I, your leader and teacher, have washed your feet then you owe it to each other to wash one another's feet (13:27).

It is love as fact. It is love as precept. But it is also love encumbered by the circling doom. The text becomes unusually detailed as it seeks to anchor the scene precisely. There are the lounging figures. There is the nudging by Peter as he tries to grasp the point of what Jesus appears to be saying. There is the ambiguous gesture as the piece of dipped bread is handed over. There is the powerful tense simplicity of the circumstance of Judas' departure. 'He took the morsel of bread and left immediately. It was night' (14:30)

And it is in this moment of darkness that Jesus must summon the words which will give to these men of varied talent, intelligence and character something by which they may live in the coming times when he will no longer be among them as a palpable encouraging presence. It is his last opportunity to reach them, to draw together for them the main themes of the previous months, to leave them with a final sustaining *logos*. It is also the hour when words must be pushed to the limit if anything at all is to be conveyed of his urgent sense of how things are.

Poets, those supreme makers of *logoi*, know that burden well, Osip Mandelstam, for instance, trying in anger and near desperation to fit the right words to the powerful but elusive song rising within him, Zbigniew Herbert searching to break free of the roundabout devices by which language tries to speak the real.

> I would give all metaphors in return for one word drawn out of my breast like a rib, for one word contained within the boundaries of my skin.[34]

And the words which Jesus must find will not only have to match the vibrance of his own living sense of the real but they must travel with the added burden of having to express what transcends the horizons within which man usually operates. He has to speak of dimensions of being of which the familiar constitutes only a portion as tiny as a falling pebble whose ripples are a miniscule passing configuration on flowing waters. But it is all he has, these humanly devised words, and he has to offer them to men of ordinary mettle for whom the meanings of discourse lie within the habitual and the experienced.

So, under the shadow of his imminent departure, when he declares that he is 'setting out to prepare a place for you ... and you know the way where I am going', there is dissent at once. 'We don't know where you are going. How, then, could we know the way?' A simple commonsense reaction, yet one which evokes a reply resonant with a mystery lying behind the usual human powers to grasp or to make one's own:

> I am the way and the truth and the life. No one comes to the father except through me. If you were to have knowledge of .me you would also know my father.

To describe himself as the way and the truth and life can be coped with and may be fitted into the incidents, described earlier in the text, when Jesus was claiming a status and a knowledge unique to himself. The repetition now of this claim, despite the opaqueness of some of its ingredients, has certainly the touch of the known. But what is one to make of the assertion that no one can come to the father except through Jesus himself, that to know him is to know the father? Is this megalomania? Is he declaring himself to be the only channel to the knowledge of God? If so, what of all those human beings of earlier days – the Old Testament prophets, for example, – who sounded their own allegiance to an omnipotent God? Were they all deluded? Or is it the case that Jesus refers here not so much to a knowledge that God exists as to the fact that he has certain characteristics such as fatherhood and a disposition to be loving, characteristics hitherto unremarked and unproclaimed?

They come in a rush, these questions, and another of the followers, Philip, tries, like Thomas, to force a halt in the practical. 'Show us the father, and that will be enough for us', a request that seems entirely reasonable. But again there is a reply which refuses to be limited by the manageable and the tractable:

> Have I been all this time with you, Philip, and you do not recognise me? The one who has seen me has seen the father. So how can you say 'Let us see the Father' (14:9)

Philip deals in what he knows. But what he is given leaves him, as it leaves others, in the coils of dilemma, where mind and heart must ponder a basic option, to turn away in sadness, in exasperation, in boredom, even, from a discourse, a *logos*, which has the look of being empty, or else, gambling on the truth of what is being said, to move out from the sanctuary of the evident to the open seas of being.

What, then, is he given? 'I am in the father and the father is in me' (14:10). It is the assertion that had sent many in Jerusalem to look for the nearest stone to cast at him since, as they saw it, he was putting himself on a level with God. Yet here it is again. 'The one who has seen me has seen the Father' (14:9):

> The words which I speak to you I do not utter from within myself. It is the Father as he abides in me, who does these things (14:10).

Or again:

> I will make a request to the Father and he will give you another help to be with you for ever, the spirit of truth which the world cannot take because it cannot look at it nor recognise it. You, however, will recognise it because it will remain beside you and will be among you (14:15–17).

> This help, the spirit of holiness, which the other will send in my name, will teach you everything and will remind you of everything I told you (14:26).

This is all in the context of relationships. 'Believe me that I am in the Father and the Father is in me' (14:11). 'I will not have you abandoned' (14:18):

> ... you will come to know that I am in my Father and that you are in me and that I am in you (14:20).

But, to quote Nicodemus, 'how can such things be?' How can such relationships exist at a level deeper than mere talk? The answer comes in a repetition of a term constantly invoked throughout the text and central, it would seem, to the creation of a flow between the individual and Jesus and God. The dynamic proposed now as before, is *pistis*, trust. It is the dynamic which must be at work if Philip and his like are not to suffer the fate of those prisoners in the cave of Plato's story, looking forever in the one direction, shackled within a point of view which they never question and never doubt, satisfied that the real is what they see. Just as at another time Jesus had warned against making judgements on the basis merely of what is visible, so now he repeats his call for *pistis*. 'Trust me for the fact that I am in the Father and the Father is in me' (14:11). 'Be trustful because of what has been done' (14:11):

> I tell you that the one who trusts me will himself do the deeds that I do and he will do even greater things (14:12).

But since trust is especially a stance of the heart and is the last milestone before the free spaces of love it comes as no surprise that the call for *pistis* shades quickly into something more profound. Jesus does not simply ask for trust. And indeed to look for more in the passing crowds would scarcely be realistic. But among those who wished to be with him and who would seek to learn from him he clearly hoped for love. In fact a decision to guard and to adhere to his *logos* would be taken to be a token of love, and the consequences would be beyond all telling:

> Anyone who loves me will hold onto my *logos*, and my Father will love him and we will come to him and will make in him a place for us to live (14.23).

So he exhorts them to be brave. 'Do not allow your hearts to be shaken. Put your trust in God and put your trust me' (14.27). And bound into this trust and this love will be peace:

> I leave you my peace. I give you my peace. But I give it to you not as the world does (14:7).

It is the phrase 'not as the world does' which helps a little to give focus to the perspectives dominating this *logos* of Jesus. 'World', unfortunately, is a bland, slack term, devoid of the more precise and assertive presence implied in *cosmos*, the word used by the evangelist. *Cosmos* means the way things are, the way things are arranged, including the arrangements by which people live amid the cherished perception of their surroundings. And since people can react ferociously to any aspersions, real or imagined, upon their convictions Jesus can therefore speak quite properly of the active hatred of which the *cosmos* is entirely capable. Indeed he warns his followers to anticipate such hatred:

> If you belonged to the *cosmos*, the *cosmos* would love you as one of its own. But because you are not of the *cosmos*, since I have picked you *out* of the *cosmos*, for this reason the *cosmos* detests you (15: 18–19).

But in what sense has he picked them out of the *cosmos*? Is he leading them to a withdrawal from society in the way, for instance, of the community at Qumran? In which case why should society even bother about them, let alone hate them? Or is he warning them that adherence to the *logos* may cost them their place in the synagogues, with all the opprobrium which this may entail? Indeed the evangelist has earlier referred to those in Jerusalem who have masked their sympathetic response to Jesus precisely because of such fears. Is this, then what the followers of Jesus are now invited to confront; some form of social death?

Although not excluding such considerations, the words here, the *logos*, clearly point in the direction of more fundamental realities. Indeed, what is evoked is the polarisation adverted to during the talk with Nicodemus when Jesus drew the contrast between those who are 'from the things below' and those who, like himself, are 'from what is above'. He is inviting his followers who, at one undeniable level at least, are and, until they die, must continue to be in and of the world to operate now within horizons wide enough and sufficiently different to evoke the scandalised opposition of those others who settle for the current perceived parameters of the *cosmos*. To enter within such broader horizons one must exercise that fundamental act of trust for which Jesus has appealed consistently in his public discourses and for which in these last hours he especially looks among his immediate followers. This act of trust is held out as the gateway to a domain which is never static, which may be entered by anyone with the disposition to learn from him and which is marked above all by a strangely potent unity of relationship centred on Jesus and on the Father:

> I am the vine. You are the branches. Someone dwells in me. I also dwell in him and he bears much fruit, because without me you can do nothing. Someone who does not dwell in me is thrown out, like a branch, and dries up (15:5–6).
>
> I am the true vine and my father is the vine dresser. He takes away every branch in me that is without fruit. He cleans up every fruitful branch so that it may bear even more fruit (15:1–2).

What is affirmed here is a life of growth to which the followers of Jesus are invited and it is a realm entered by the channels of trust and of love:

> If you dwell in me, if my words remain in you, then whatever you ask for will come into being for you (15:7).

Growth is founded on trust, trust is granted to that *logos* which is itself a manifestation of the being of Jesus. This, it would seem, is what is in prospect between master and follower. And this relationship with him must go hand in hand with another, namely that between followers. 'This is my instruction to you, that you love each other as I have loved you' (15:12). What is adumbrated is not a series of one-to-one modes of being but, rather, a network of relationships functioning at a level beyond the normal workings of the *cosmos* and depending for existence on the giving of self by each free heart.

Because he is, for the moment, among his own, there are none to denounce him now, to scoff, to turn off. No stones are hurled. But the challenge remains present, unequivocally the same as during the times amid the crowds in Jerusalem. It is the challenge to trust that things are as he says they are and especially to trust that the words shaping his *logos* have not merely taken on a life unto themselves, giving heart and hope, as some words are inclined to do, but that they are actually, truly the harbingers of a reality, ample, profound and transcending all daily experience. He is asking his followers to believe that he is talking about what is, and, furthermore, that he is doing so on the basis of direct knowledge. He is also promising them help:

> I am going now to the one that sent me ... It is a good thing for you that I am going. For if I do not go the helper will not come to you. If I set out I will send him to you and when he comes he will show the cosmos how wrong it was... When he comes, this spirit of truth, he will lead you to all truth (16:8–16).

Mysterious and troubling, this *logos* proceeds, speaking of sadness and of joy to come, circling around the Father and 'the spirit of truth', assuring the followers that anything they request of God will be granted 'in my name', talking of a day when they will not have to be asking questions:

> In what I have been saying to you I have been using figures of speech. But a time is coming when I will no longer speak figuratively to you, but will tell you openly about my Father... The Father loves you because you have loved me and because you have put your trust in the fact that I have come from God (16:25–27).

They grab this reference to figures of speech, these followers who have been trying to make sense of what he is saying. They understand about figures of speech:

> 'Now you are talking plainly', they say. 'You are not saying anything figuratively. Now we see that you know everything and there is no need for someone to question you. And so we put our trust in the fact that you have come from God' (16:29–31).

'So at last you believe?' (16:31). He asks from within that melancholy realism which had surfaced before:

> Ah, the time is coming and has already come when you will be scattered, when each will go his own way leaving me abandoned. Yet, I am not alone, because the Father is with me. And I am telling you this so that you may have peace in me. There will be trouble for you in the cosmos. But have courage. I have won a victory over the cosmos (16:32–33).

Trouble in the *cosmos*, trouble within the perceived schemes of things, trouble because of the acceptance of a *logos* which refuses to operate within the perspectives of mortality, such is to be the lot of those who would learn from Jesus. To Pilate who asks him to explain the reasons for the hostility he has provoked he says:

> if my domain of power were of this *cosmos* then those subject to me would fight to prevent my being handed over to the Jews ... My domain of power is not of this *cosmos*' (18:36). 'For this I am and for this I came to the *cosmos* that I might be a witness to what is true (18:37).

That witness is by way of a *logos* which he has continually uttered both publicly and among his followers. It is a *logos* which has articulated a particular, idiosyncratic view of the nature of the real. Ultimately, it has asked only one thing of every individual in every audience, a response of trust, trust that things are as Jesus says, trust in Jesus himself.

And the narrative claims that the response did come. Many put their trust in him. But of course very many did not, and the last discourse would be followed by what the *cosmos* has always known too well, a squalid cruelly efficient dealing out of death, accompanied by the howling self-righteousness of the perpetrators. So he would die a criminal, this Jesus, his body broken, his last brief *logos* proclaiming, ambiguously, that 'it is all finished' (19:30).

The narrative of the aftermath of the crucifixion seems at one level to have nothing new. The clear focus up to now has been on someone unique, on a man speaking passionately to gathered crowds, on a leader sharing his life with sometimes mystified companions. The presence of the man has been marked especially by far-reaching *logoi* and by the repeated call that he be the object of *pistis*. And so it continues. He is once again talking, to Mary Magdalene, to his friends the fishermen, to Peter. It is as it has been. Except that he was dead and has reappeared among them. The killing and the return to life are incidents. If there is drama, it is when the tomb is found to be empty, when the figure thought to be the gardener proves to be the master. But no trumpets sound. The prose is unexcited, as unconfused in its description of the charcoal fire and the breakfast by the shore as it is in listing the clothes in the empty tomb. Of course the refusal of Jesus to be hugged by Mary Magdalene suggests that things may not be quite exactly as they were. And the absent Thomas baulks when told the news. But under the impact of what he sees and touches he changes his mind. Nothing, after all, may have changed. For there is a continuity. The pre-crucifixion Jesus is no different from the post-resurrection master. Before he was killed he spoke *logoi* which 'many' came to trust, and since these *logoi* implied that he had a particular status and a startling set of characteristics then those who really took him at his word could not be ultimately surprised that he was the sort of being who could re-emerge from the dead.

Or so the narrative implies. And it is important here to be faithful to the text and to resist, at least for the present, the temptation to interpose one's own reaction to it. As elsewhere, there is here an 'intention of the text', one which supplies the unity which marks the fourth gospel from beginning to end:

> What is here has been written so that you may trust that Jesus is the anointed one, the son of God, and also that through your trust you may have life in his name (20:31).

Always the same theme of trust, and for the reader who has persevered through these pages, always the same problem of reaching some view of what this might mean. 'Trust in God and in me' 'The work of God to be done is this, that you give your trust to the one whom he has sent'. When words such as these recur it is in the context of assertions by Jesus concerning the realities enmeshing man and God, so that the trust he seeks has to do with what he is proclaiming about such realities and also with what he himself is. He seeks acknowledgement as the particularly authoritative exponent of the encounter between the things 'from below' and the things 'from above'. He claims to be 'the way, the truth and the life', and to trust is somehow to take a chance on the fact of this being actually the case. But merely to say this is not enough. Even among those who were first to read or to hear the fourth gospel there had to be some who never laid eyes on Jesus, never saw how he walked and spoke, never felt, as had the Samaritan woman, the impact of his presence and personality, and the evangelist would have known this as he composed his text. Yet no allowances are made, no literary devices are summoned to entice the reader into agreeable malleability. The issues are presented starkly in this gospel, as they were put to the listening crowds in Jerusalem, and the blunt challenging call to *pistis*, to trust, remains there to be faced.

There are, of course, the self-evident ingredients of the situation. Trust is, ultimately, a personal stance, reinforced perhaps by the supporting attitudes of others, but alive, if at all, in the privacy of the self. Each person has do deal alone with the subjectivity, with the moods and the perceptions which ensure that trust will sometimes be like a figure borne upward on a hang-glider by abundant breezes, will sometimes be a hollow-eyed victim of the desert, will in other circumstances, be no more than a stone immobile in its surrounding lair. Trust is in essence a special impetus and its opposite is a quite particular absence of movement within the innermost regions of the self. Deeper than a certain kind of rationality to which philosophers have tended to look, it is, present or in abeyance, at any given moment within the domain of the individual life space.

For assuredly, there is in each person a field of energy which is part inchoate, part sculpted. It is the dwelling place of the 'I' and of the human potential for growth or sterility. It is the area where past and present, joy or indifference, fear or expectation come together with much else besides to forge the characteristics of individuality. For its tentative, provisional sense of itself it needs the exclusions visited upon it by the complex assertiveness of whatever crosses its path. To survive it needs to learn both how to measure the extent to which the outside will be allowed to impinge upon it and also how to give of itself to what lies beyond its own unshared boundaries. Active and passive, clinging here, independent there, predictable sometimes and sometimes not, it is never still, and for its sum, as for its parts, a central dynamic during its hour in the sunlight is either to grow or to wither, to open out as being or simply to exist.

And it is to somewhere within this personal space that the Jesus of the fourth gospel looks, not for adherence to a party line, however well formulated, but for something more fundamental and certainly more difficult, namely, the act of trust directed to him and to his *logos*. Adherence to a party line may frequently require no more than accommodation to some kind of pressure outside oneself. Alternatively, one may insist upon oneself being the measure of all things. But only a clouded vision would belittle or underestimate the interplaying factors which go into the making of that solitary stance which in this case is the sought-after giving of trust to Jesus and to his *logos*.

In more general experience a stance of trust does not operate in and by itself. It looks to specific situations, to the numerous revelations of being. Furthermore, there are times in the lives of individuals when the conferring of trust will be seen to have been justified, when the rightness of a particular activity of trust will be obvious and confirmed. Or, sadly, the opposite will occur, leaving the individual to pull back behind a barrier of bruised feelings and even of despair.

In this general scheme of things, justification or disappointment would seem to be the necessary co-relatives of trust. That to which one has extended one's trust either grants or witholds validation, and one reacts accordingly. But what of the apparently special act of trust which Jesus seeks among his listeners? For he asks acceptance of the view of reality which he has been proclaiming, one of such character, moreover, as to defy the routine procedures of assessment which operate within the horizons of the *cosmos*. How is one to know if he is talking sense? Does the meta-cosmic realm proclaimed by his words give any responsive assurance to the act of trust extended towards it? To the spectator there would seem to be no criteria of judgement which would offer some reason to hope that one is not being summoned to illusion.

But there are experiences to suggest that a spectator may not always know the whole story, that in the life space of the observed individual there is a subtlety, a nuanced complexity which refuses to be packaged and managed by processes of analysis brought to bear upon it from outside. In certain modes of being there is an inwardness which eludes even the disciplined and rigorous observer, so that, for instance, the most exhaustive account of the phenomenon of love will helplessly roam outside the enchanted privacy of that specific garden created by two people who actually love one another. Indeed, the words of love are themselves remarkable for their poverty especially when they are compared with the articulate cascades of hate. Again, an encounter with a landscape, with a poem, with a terror can rob all available descriptive words of their presumed capacity to reveal what happened. In short, there are currents of feeling and of reaction rising up within the person which will unfailingly stand with essence forever untouched by the numerous classifying resources of language, especially the language of the outsider and of the onlooker. And it is in such circumstances that the nimbus of expertise on the self-confident reductionist and on the suave merchant of reality begins to look rather comically misplaced.

Inwardness is quite clearly too common an experience to be shunted aside and there are too many people who are well aware of the fact for instance that irrespective of the judgements of convention or of the pronouncements of party chieftains, the inwardness of a loving relationship is profoundly and astonishingly real. And so it is, for instance, that someone for whom living had turned into a grey wait in the ante-room of death but who is now conscious of the unexpected gift of being loved will know, regardless of what the world may say, that there is an extra brightness in the air and a new sheen on the grass. This is so because there is in being the heart-clutching awareness of an offered love that is received and reciprocated.

A specific knowing relationship directed towards a specific mode of being can flourish in the privacy of the self. Occasionally its presence may be detected by the outsider on the basis of analogical experience, but, ultimately, the flow and the contour of that presence lie only within the frontiers of the directly experiencing person. And this way of experiencing is not, as it were, an instance of someone combining a giving of self with a standing on the sidelines to measure and evaluate what comes in return. The involved actor and the detached critic do not join to make the play. Rather, the pair implicated in the particularity of a truly loving responsiveness are caught up into what has come into being and, no longer observers, yield and let go into what is wonderfully there and theirs.

This being-caught-up-in is not exclusive to the drama of love. It happens also in the relationships to other manifestations of being when the calculating appropriating, managing 'I' is so taken over by exigencies or presences that if one is to swim at all it has to be with the tide. The real has its own way of laying claim to the responsiveness of the person and only the self can finally sense the extent of the take-over. Sometimes it is a dark grim invasion, as anyone in the legions of the tormented will know. Sometimes it is an overwhelming radiance. Sometimes it is no more than a stirring as unassertive as that of a forest leaf. But in every case it is a particularity of being which comes in to dominate, however briefly, the resourcefulness of a personal space.

And it is this resourcefulness which is addressed by the *logos* of Jesus, and especially by his call to trust. Just as poets know that a poetry of being is waiting every day to be articulated, so the evangelist in the way he presents the figure of Jesus is asserting that a truth more spacious than the habitual boundaries of the *cosmos* is waiting there to be lived in. Of course, every Nicodemus, cushioned by those familiar arrangements of word and object which constitute the *cosmos*, will ask how such things can be and will want his portion of truth to be measurable and quantifiable. But there are others who have sensed the anaesthetising power of the familiar and have cried a warning against it. Marina Tsvetayeva speaks of the 'terror of words already mangled by use, already ambiguous', and Boris Pasternak talks of the name given to things of the spirit as being no more than an approximate generalisation. Which is a way of hinting that those whose inwardness is actually caught up in some manifestation of being will know that to rest in the banalities of description is already to opt for a kind of death or, indeed, of untruth.

Some words of St. Exupery may help here:

> If orange-trees are hardy and rich in fruit in this bit of soil and not that, then this bit of soil is what is truth for orange-trees. If a particular religion, or culture, or scale of values, if one form of activity rather than another brings self-fulfilment to a man, releases the prince asleep within him unknown to himself, that culture, that form of activity constitutes his truth.[35]

Since that release of the prince can happen only in the privacy of the self what the call to trust seems to imply is that if one lets go into and surrenders to what is asserted in the *logos* there will follow a being-caught-up in light and life and truth in a manner impossible for anyone who relies solely on the schematising *cosmos*.

To let go. But how? That will be the cry of Nicodemus from the sidelines. Yet it has been done by countless men and women since those days when Jesus spoke his *logos*. Yet how? From within many individual life-spaces will come many answers. Or in other cases none. For only the solitary 'I' can let go, if at all. This letting go can sometimes be described as a leap into apparent darkness, and some who are not obviously foolish do indeed make the leap. The story told of Nijinsky is apposite:

> ... the dancer Nijinsky was once asked how he managed to leap so high. He is reported to have answered that he saw no

> great problem in this. Most people when they leapt in the air came down at once. 'why should you come down immediately? Stay in the air a little before you return, why not?'[36]

This appears to be what the narrative is proposing, that there is a letting go, when the private space in each person is allowed by some intuiting orientation to be taken over. And this happens with an accompanying sense, sometimes faint, that it is not all gamble.

Clearly, the evangelist had himself let go into a quite specific view of Jesus. Certainly, he had done so before he began to write his gospel, as he makes evident in the celebrated preface. There he sums up what he accepts, namely, that a nomad *logos* had passed by in the person of Jesus, a being who could only be described as divine, one who gave meaning, sense and principle to things. People such as the evangelist himself had been fortunate to be there as witnesses, as the spectators of his shining presence 'graceful and abounding in truth':

> In the beginning was the logos[37] and the logos was with God and the logos was God … In the logos was life and the life was the light for human kind … He was the true light that gives light to everything human. He was in the cosmos and the cosmos had come into being because of him ... He gave the power to be children of God to those who accepted him, to those who put their trust in his name ... The logos became human and put up his tent among us.[38]

How to cope with such words is a problem not for the evangelist but for the reader. Theologies have been constructed around them. Sceptics have noted them. Debate, dogma and denial have circled around them, as indeed around every episode and every speech in the text. But however extensive the clash of interpretations there remains a general and abiding sense of the fourth gospel as a profoundly resonant presentation of the man from Nazareth.

NOTES

1 Boris Pasternak, *Dr. Zhivago* (London, 1958), p 427.

2 Nadezhda Mandelstam, *Hope against hope* (London, 1971), p 70.

3 Arthur Koestler, *The Invisible Writing* (London, 1954), pp 26–27.

4 *Ibid*, p. 33

5 Y. Courtonne, *Saint Basile: Lettres 1* (Paris, 1957).

6 Migne, *Patrologia Graeca* 27, Col. 24.

7 Czeslaw Milosz, *The Witness of Poetry* (Cambridge, Mass., 1983), p 25.

8 Osip Mandelstam, *The Collected Critical Prose and Letters* (London, 1991), p 117.

9 Andre Malraux, *Anti-Memoirs* (New York, 1968), p 161.

10 *Ibid.*

11 Serge Bramly, *Leonardo: The Artist and the Man* (London, 1992), p 49.

12 From the poem 'Sous le pont Mirabeau ...' Translation mine.

13 Odysseus Elytis, *The Sovereign Sun* (Newcastle-upon-Tyne, 1990), p 77.

14 Citations from the commentary of Origen, of which eight books survive, are from Volumes 120 157 and 222 in the series *Sources Chretiennes*, edited by Cecile Blanc, and published in Paris in 1966, 1970 and 1975.

15 Citations are from the 124 sermons in which Augustine dealt with the gospel. The Latin text, updated by D. Willems, O.S.B. is in *Corpus Christainorum. Series Latina* No. XXXVI, (Turnhout) 1954.

16 The Latin text of Thomas Aquinas' commentary is to be found in Volume 10 of the *Opera Omnia*, 25 Volumes, Parma, 1862–1870, reproduced New York, Musurgia 1948–1950. The

commentary is in the form of lectures in which a few verses are considered in sequence from the prologue to the end. Citations are therefore from these lectures and may be located by reference to the particular verse number commented upon by Thomas rather than upon the pages of the Latin text.

17 *Summa Theologica*, Part 1, Question 1, Article 10.

18 Colin Morris, *The Papal Monarchy* (Oxford, 1989).

19 Adrienne Rich, *Time's Power* (New York, 1989), p 28.

20 The text of Calvin's commentary on John is included in the series *loannis Calvini opera quae Supersunt*. 59 Volumes, (Braunchweig, 1863–1900).

21 Citations are from Rudolph Bultmann, *The Gospel of John: A Commentary*. Translated from the German by G.R. Beasley-Murray (Oxford, 1971).

22 John Ashton, *Understanding the Fourth Gospel* (Oxford, 1991)

23 Diarmaid McGann, *Journeying within transcendence* (London, 1989). Cf. Ravi Ravindra *The Yoga of the Christ*, (Dorset, 1990) 'Here I am interested in the spiritual heart of the Gospel rather than the details of any facts about it', p 8. Works such as these provide confirmation, if such is needed, of the sheer multiplicity of readings evoked by the text.

24 Such readers do not merely bring to their task the complex effects of their personalities, ambitions and aspirations. They also carry with them the outcome of their reading of other texts, and this is inevitably available as an influence in deciding how to construe the meaning of what is on any page of the fourth gospel.

25 A striking example of this is provided by Thomas Aquinas. A notable characteristic of his commentary is that he almost completely effaces himself behind a continuous series of quotations from the works of predecessors such as Basil, John Chrysostom, Hilary of Poitiers and Augustine, men who, themselves, had articulated their views on the meaning of the fourth gospel in works of varying kind. These quotations assembled by Aquinas are stitched together so as to create the immediate impression of an ongoing text, one which can be

read without reference to any of the authors involved and one which, furthermore, generates the clear implication that there is an authoritative mainstream of interpretation to which all these illustrious men have made their own substantial and harmonious contribution and by which all are meant to abide.

This image of a mainstream is not inappropriate, for what the quotations in Aquinas show clearly is that all these writers were concerned not so much with the critical evaluation of the fourth gospel as with an increasingly sophisticated elaboration of what they were certain was the meaning of the evangelist at any given point. But this concern with meaning was quite different from that of a historian who diagnoses the ingredients creating that specific context in which a particular meaning is formed and established. Something much more fundamental was clearly at work, a sense of the text as a final authority determining for all time the truth of that with which it dealt and, in consequence, precluding any new, any original, any innovative explanations of its own master themes. The writers quoted by Aquinas felt an obligation to derive from this ultimate authority the answers to questions posed long after the evangelist himself was dead and gone, questions, moreover, which were themselves regularly couched in terms deriving from understandings unavailable to the common discourse of the first Christian century. But to proceed in this way could only be possible on the assumption that every word in the gospel was set down in anticipation of every question which could ever arise regarding the subject matter of the text. Which is why Basil, for instance, conscious of the issues centred upon Arianism and believing, also, the divinely inspired character of scripture, would write the following words reproduced by Aquinas: 'The holy spirit foresaw that men would arise who would envy the glory of the only-begotten, subverting their hearers by sophistry, as if because being begotten he was not before he was begotten. That none might presume to babble such nonsense the holy spirit said "In the beginning was the word"'.

What this quotation indicates – as do all those other assembled by Aquinas – is that the text of the fourth gospel functions on an entirely privileged basis, with its words being taken to have an expanding potential to be a continuing magisterial criterion of truth amid the posing of all present and future questions. That the evangelist had long preceded the publicly articulated concerns of, say, Arianism is, in this scenario, no hindrance to the conviction that what he wrote contains the corrective to any views deemed at any time and for whatever reason to be acceptable or otherwise to those regarding themselves as the custodians of orthodoxy. In fact the fourth gospel is there for special use, with those who so use it reading into it meaning by which to explicate current preoccupations and also finding there the justification for whatever they proclaim. They assert the authority of the text and, as it were, the text supplies the authority for what they assert. It is as though inspiration of scripture is implicitly extended to themselves.

26 There is a point at which the otherness of someone preserves the mystery of its being, so that what it is truly like to be that other evades meaningful description. The reader of the gospel will know soon enough the moment when that other can only be acknowledged as such, when it becomes impossible to say the real Jesus. Which means that any glimpse of him becomes all the more precious. Therefore one reason why the Temple incident is so valuable is that the 'Jesus, meek and mild' of ongoing piety is nowhere in view. Instead, an awesome ravening fury is unloosed. Lashing around him, kicking over the tables, he is an intimidating figure. And all this to clear a space for prayer.

27 For a powerful image of the Temple and its crowds see Paula Fredrickson *Jesus of Nazareth* (London, 1999), pp 12–17.

28 The role of the imagination in giving body to an episode, such as the clearing of the Temple, is both central and very difficult to describe. But it raises the issue of creativity, one of the powers most closely associated with imagination. The workings of creativity show up not only in the techniques of composition employed by the writer but also in the deployment by the reader of personal talent, insight, attentiveness and much else besides. The actualisation of meaning is a drama which unfolds each time a reader construes the words on the page. See Mark S. Muldoon 'Readings, Imagination and Interpretation: A Ricoeurean Response' *International Philosophical Quarterly* 40 (2000), pp 69–83.

29 In the effort to get closer to a sense of the Jesus emerging in the pages of the gospel it is worth remembering that responsiveness to him takes the form not just of the anointing of his feet but of the stones picked up to be thrown at him.

30 'Mary's actions contributed an anointing of Jesus' body for burial, and thus, unconsciously, she performed a prophetic action', Raymond Brown *The Gospel according to John* (New York, 1966), p 454. Like so many commentators, Brown clearly takes his cue from the evangelist. But as an example of the many routes taken by interpreters cf. 'Mary's intent to court Jesus' love with a view to matrimony ... The choice of feet should signify to the reader who is apprised of ancient custom Mary's intent to demonstrate to possess Jesus' feet as her own, that is, her desire to enter into matrimony with Jesus'. Alternatively, 'perhaps the emphasis on the feet should also be related to the theological idea that everything, including death, is to be put under Jesus' feet (Eph. 1:22, 1 Cor. 15: 24–26)' Thomas L. Brodie *The Gospel according to John* (New York, Oxford, 1993), p 406. Jo-Ann A. Brant 'Husband Hunting: characterization and narrative art in the gospel of John', *Biblical Interpretation* 4 (1996), pp 205–223. Quotations p 217; p 218.

31 Thomas Nagle, *The Last Word* (Oxford, 1997), p 130.

32 Zbigniew Herbert, *Selected Poems* (Manchester, 1985), p 120.

33 Who is the source of this private conversation? Jesus? Nicodemus? Nobody can now say. On what basis, therefore, does the reader take this story aboard? The way in which a decision is made in regard to this issue has obvious implications for the reading of any other episode.

34 Zbigniew Herbert *op cit.*, p. 38.

35 Antoine de Saint Exupéry, *Wind, Sand and Stars* (London, 1987), p 1987.

36 Isaiah Berlin, *Personal Impressions* (Oxford, 1982), p 174.

37 To describe Jesus by way of words such as *Logos* is to emphasise not simply a unity of purpose uniting God and Jesus but to imply that Jesus is somehow God present and active in the world. The actions and the words of Jesus may, consequently, be understood as embodying the character and presence of God in the world. See Marianne Maye Thompson 'Thinking about God' *Critical Readings of John 6* (ed.), R. Alan Culpepper (Leiden, 1997), pp 221–246.

38 How the first readers of this preface would have reacted to the word *logos*, as used here, can only be a matter for speculation. But the question touches on an important issue, namely, that of the intended readership of the gospel. There appears to be no serious doubt that the fourth gospel was written in Greek, which means, presumably, that it was put together primarily for an audience reared in the cultural infra-structure surrounding the language. This fact deserves to be emphasised since it could offer a solution to a number of difficulties experienced by scholars who have considered the text in some detail.

There is, for instance, the question of how to deal with the references to Jews or to Jewish custom. There has been extensive discussion of what the term 'Jews' must actually signify in the gospel. One scholar claims that the word is 'almost a technical title for the religious authorities, particularly those in Jerusalem, who are hostile to Jesus' (Raymond E. Brown, *The Gospel according to John* (New York, 1966), p Lxxi). More recently, another scholar has remarked that 'in chapter 7 ... the Jews of verse 11 are just anyone; the Jews of verse 13 are the rulers; and the Jews of verse 15 are those who marvel that an untaught man is learned' (J. C. O'Neill 'The Jews in the Fourth Gospel', *Irish Biblical Studies* (1996), pp 58–74. Quotation p 63). The usage has been felt to be somehow problematic, and requiring considerable explanation. If in fact the text is written by a Jew for his co-religionists why speak at all of 'the Jews' or why for instance explain that the Pasch was a 'Jewish feast'?

If, however, a Greek or Hellenistic readership is envisaged by the writer, then, many of the reasons among scholars for wondering about 'the Jews' in the text will fade. So too will some of the grounds for the frequently expressed view that the gospel is a series of episodes cobbled together more or less on the hoof.

A further consequence of emphasising an intended Greek readership will be to focus on the versatility of the word *logos*, a versatility which is not naturally available to the translations of it, such as *verbum* and *word*. For when Jesus speaks of 'keeping my *logos*' and when he himself is described as the *logos* what is conveyed is firstly that he *is* what gives sense, point and purpose to the world and secondly that what he *says* reflects that fact. A Greek or Hellenistic reader, unlike someone from a different linguistic *milieu*, will require no theological or philosophical briefing to have some natural inkling of what is being said here. Words, after all, are not wholly independent of the environment in which they are uttered. This is one reason why the same reader may not feel the need to regard the preface as an extraneous document or hymn stuck on to the body of a roughly made text. *Logos*, the term once described as a heart-word of Greek, offers a unifying motif and a continuing comment on the episodes and speeches selected from the life of Jesus by an evangelist who is moved to remark that if everything accomplished by Jesus were to be written down 'the world itself would not hold all the books which would have to be written (21.25). If one leaves aside the cluster of meanings attached to the term *Logos* there is perhaps a more profound moment to be reckoned with here. At beginning of 21st century there is among many an increasing consciousness of words as debased coinage and the manifest shift to image has not yet done much to restore the full impact of the word. This, in turn, must inevitably interfere with the virtually automatic sense of the central importance of the infinitely disclosing capacity of words in that Greek-shaped culture out of which the fourth gospel emerges. Which means that it is necessary to try to recover some awareness of how bold, exciting and liberating must have been the decision of the fourth evangelist to begin his work with the proclamation that 'in the beginning was the *logos*'. That others before him, Philo, for example, had felt the power of the term *Logos* to encapsulate what they believed is of course interesting and to be explored. But this ought not to obscure an event, so full of consequence, namely, that as the evangelist sought to convey his sense of the significance of the passage of Jesus through the world the word seemingly best able to set the frame of reference for these events was, in fact, *Logos*.

reader's notes

reader's notes

reader's notes

reader's notes

reader's notes

reader's notes

reader's notes